BURN
THE
ORPHANAGE

SINA GRACE
CO-WRITER / ARTIST

DANIEL FREEDMAN
CO-WRITER

JOHN RAUCH
COLORIST

RUS WOOTON
LETTERER

BURN THE ORPHANAGE CREATED BY
DANIEL FREEDMAN & SINA GRACE

LOGO DESIGNED BY
TIM DANIEL

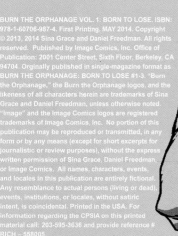

IMAGE COMICS, INC.
Robert Kirkman – Chief Operating Officer
Erik Larsen – Chief Financial Officer
Todd McFarlane – President
Marc Silvestri – Chief Executive Officer
Jim Valentino – Vice-President

Eric Stephenson – Publisher
Ron Richards – Director of Business Development
Jennifer de Guzman – Director of Trade Book Sales
Kat Salazar – Director of PR & Marketing
Jeremy Sullivan – Director of Digital Sales
Emilio Bautista – Sales Assistant
Branwyn Bigglestone – Senior Accounts Manager
Emily Miller – Accounts Manager
Jessica Ambriz – Administrative Assistant
Tyler Shainline – Events Coordinator
David Brothers – Content Manager
Jonathan Chan – Production Manager
Drew Gill – Art Director
Meredith Wallace – Print Manager
Monica Garcia – Senior Production Artist
Jenna Savage – Production Artist
Addison Duke – Production Artist
Tricia Ramos – Production Assistant
IMAGECOMICS.COM

BURN THE ORPHANAGE VOL. 1: BORN TO LOSE. ISBN: 978-1-60706-987-4. First Printing. MAY 2014.

Published by Image Comics, Inc. Office of Publication: 2001 Center Street, Sixth Floor, Berkeley, CA 94704. Orginally published in single-magazine format as BURN THE ORPHANAGE: BORN TO LOSE #1-3.

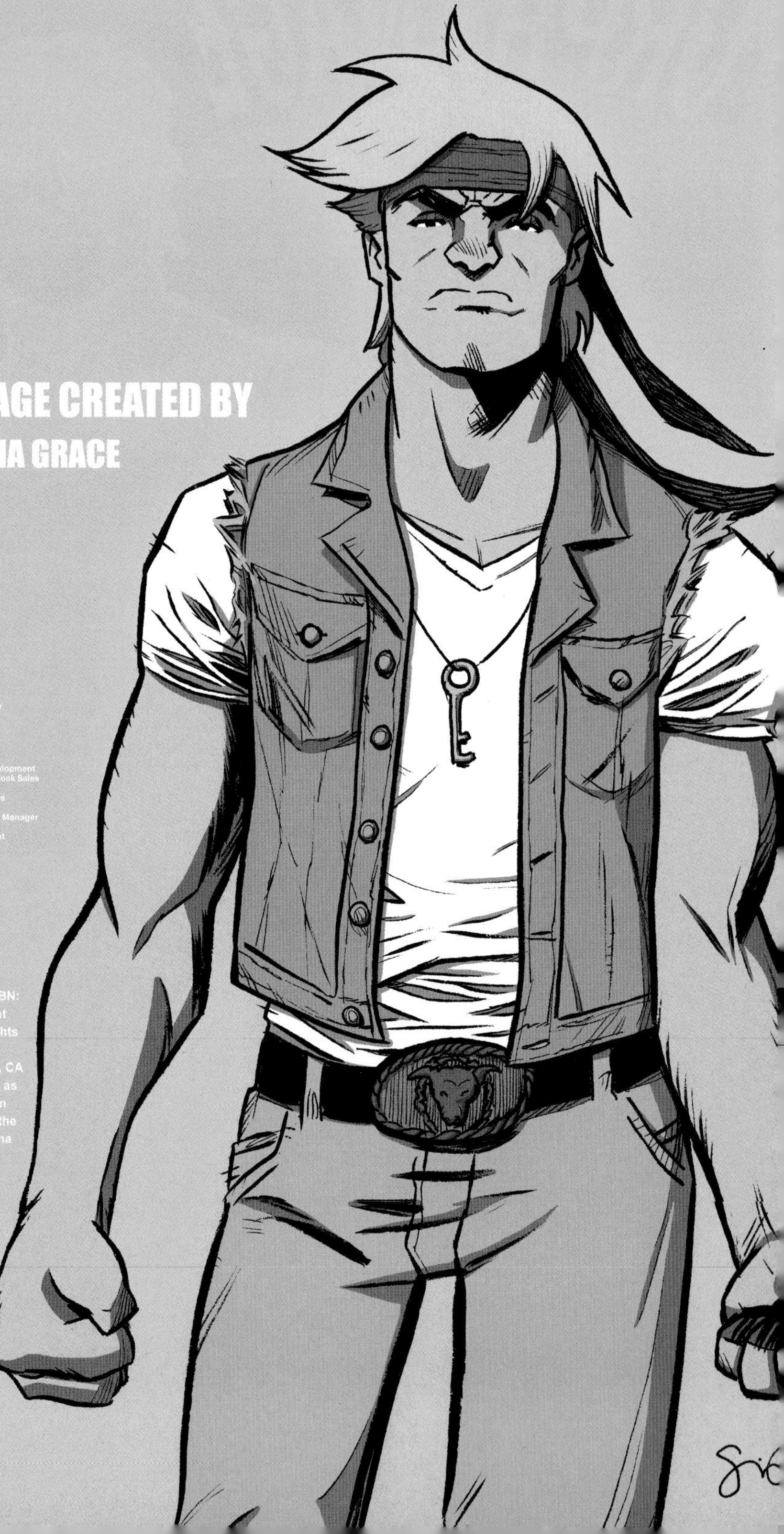

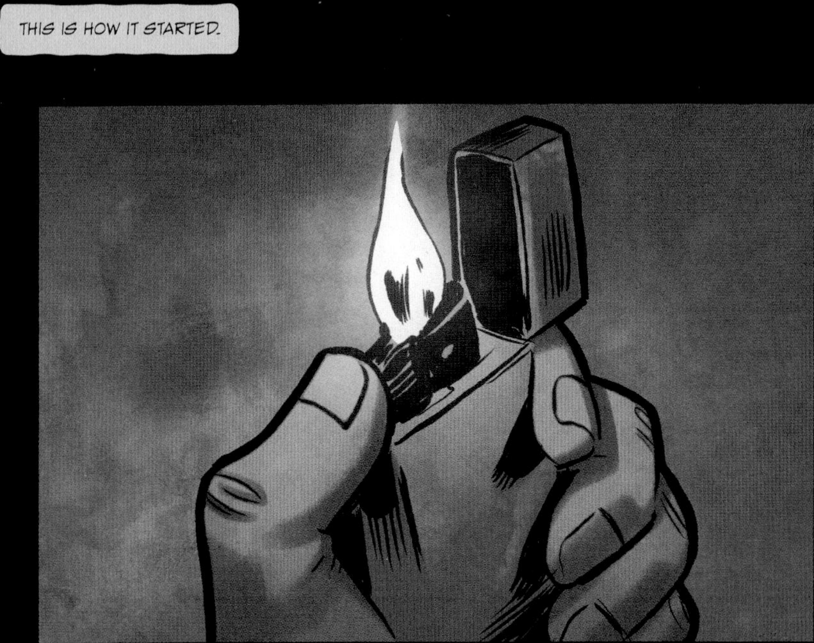
THIS IS HOW IT STARTED.

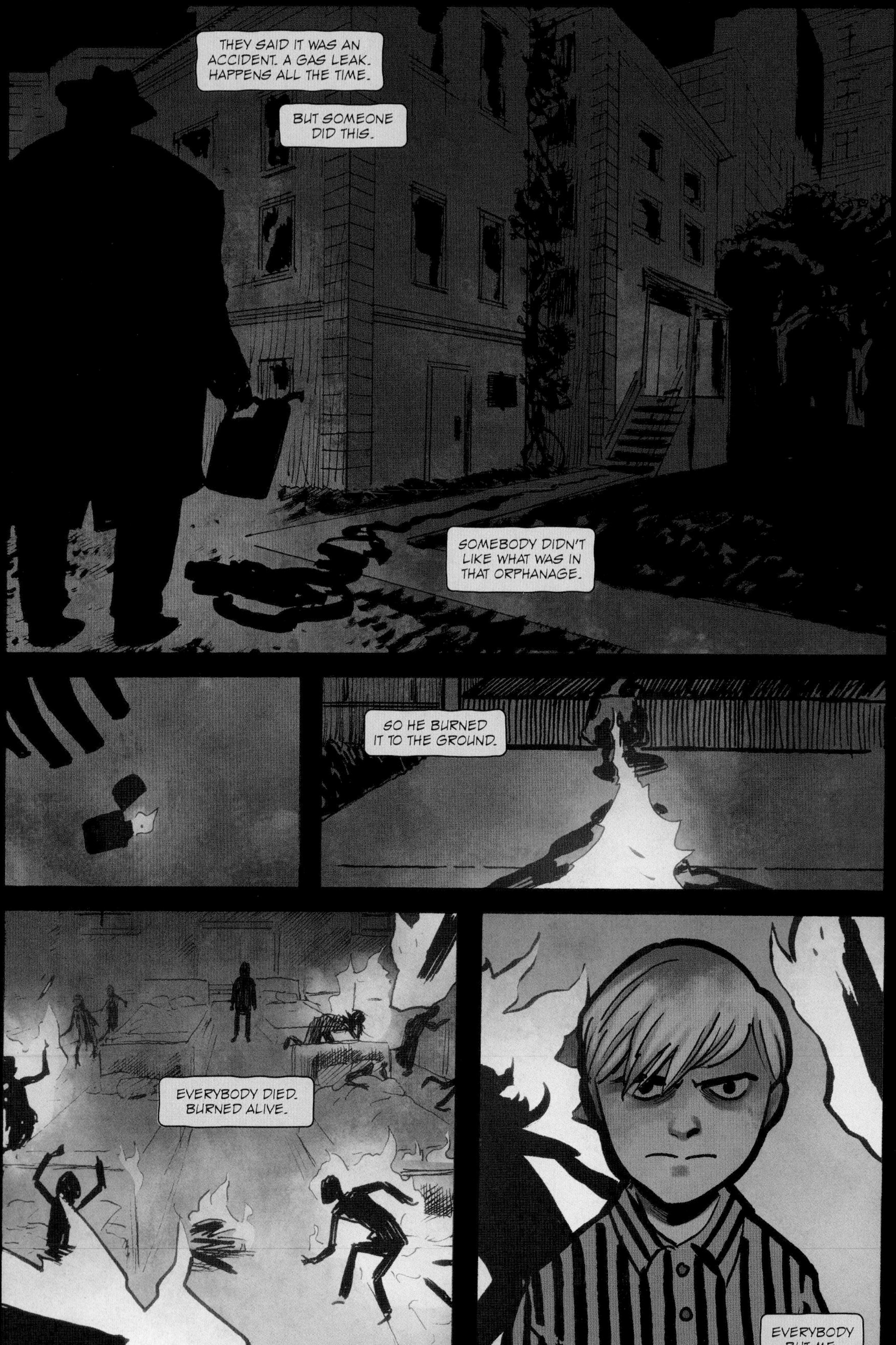
THEY SAID IT WAS AN ACCIDENT. A GAS LEAK. HAPPENS ALL THE TIME.
BUT SOMEONE DID THIS.
SOMEBODY DIDN'T LIKE WHAT WAS IN THAT ORPHANAGE.
SO HE BURNED IT TO THE GROUND.
EVERYBODY DIED. BURNED ALIVE.
EVERYBODY BUT ME.

IMAGE COMICS PRESENTS

A Story By
DANIEL FREEDMAN

& SINA GRACE

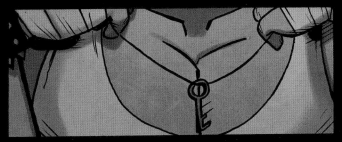

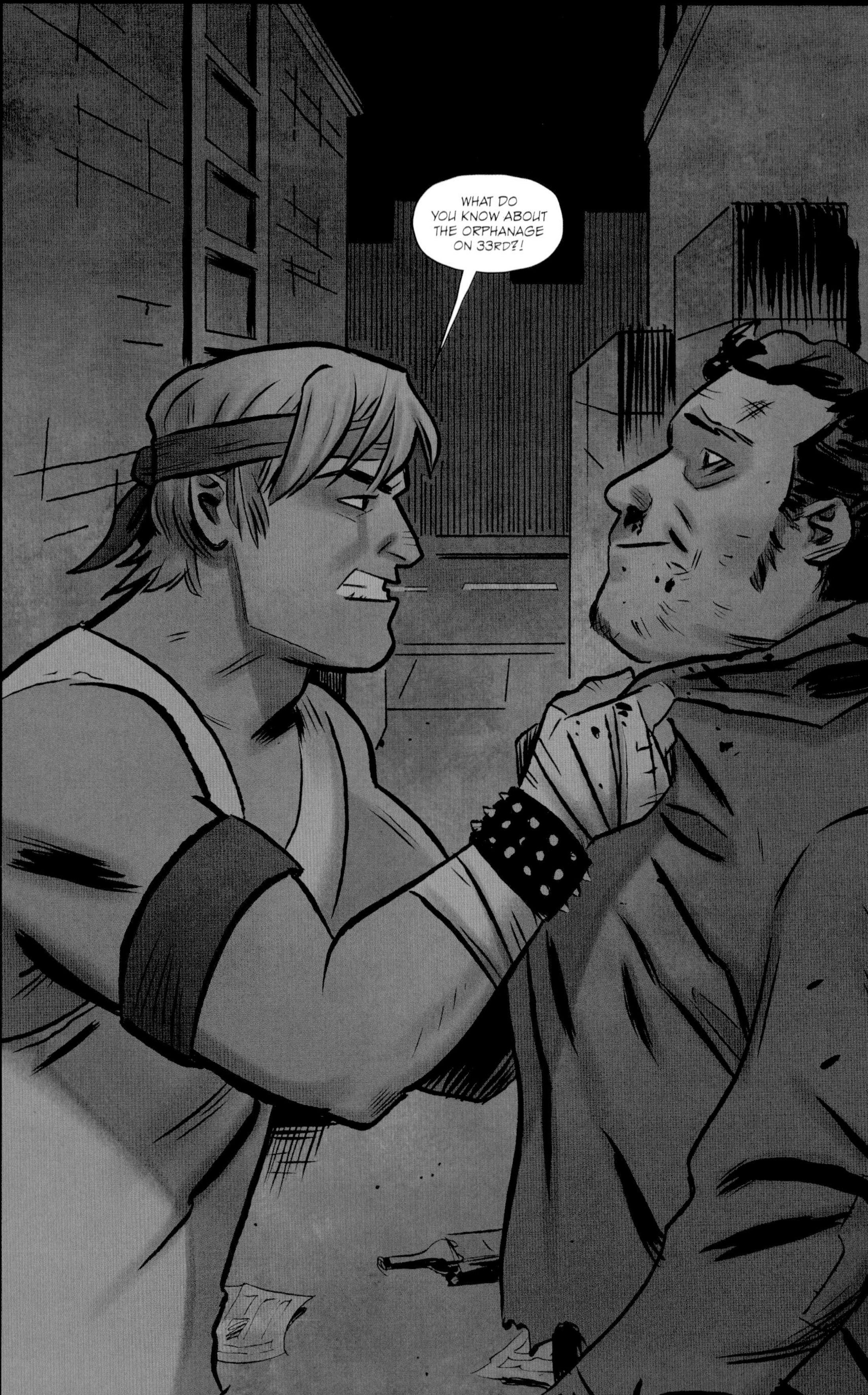
WHAT DO YOU KNOW ABOUT THE ORPHANAGE ON 33RD?!

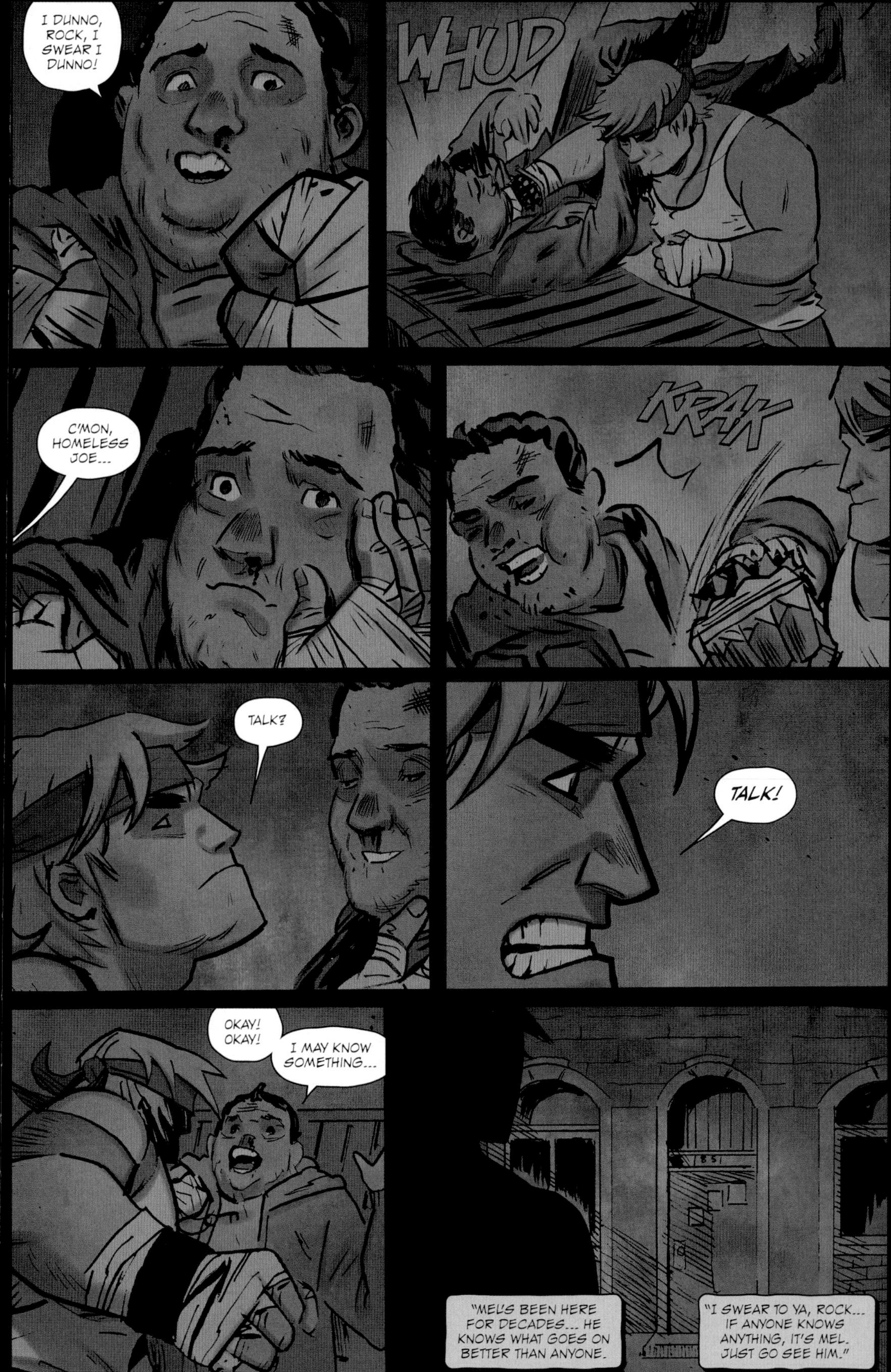
I DUNNO, ROCK, I SWEAR I DUNNO!
WHUD
C'MON, HOMELESS JOE...
KRAK
TALK?
TALK!
OKAY! OKAY!
I MAY KNOW SOMETHING...
"MEL'S BEEN HERE FOR DECADES... HE KNOWS WHAT GOES ON BETTER THAN ANYONE.
"I SWEAR TO YA, ROCK... IF ANYONE KNOWS ANYTHING, IT'S MEL. JUST GO SEE HIM."

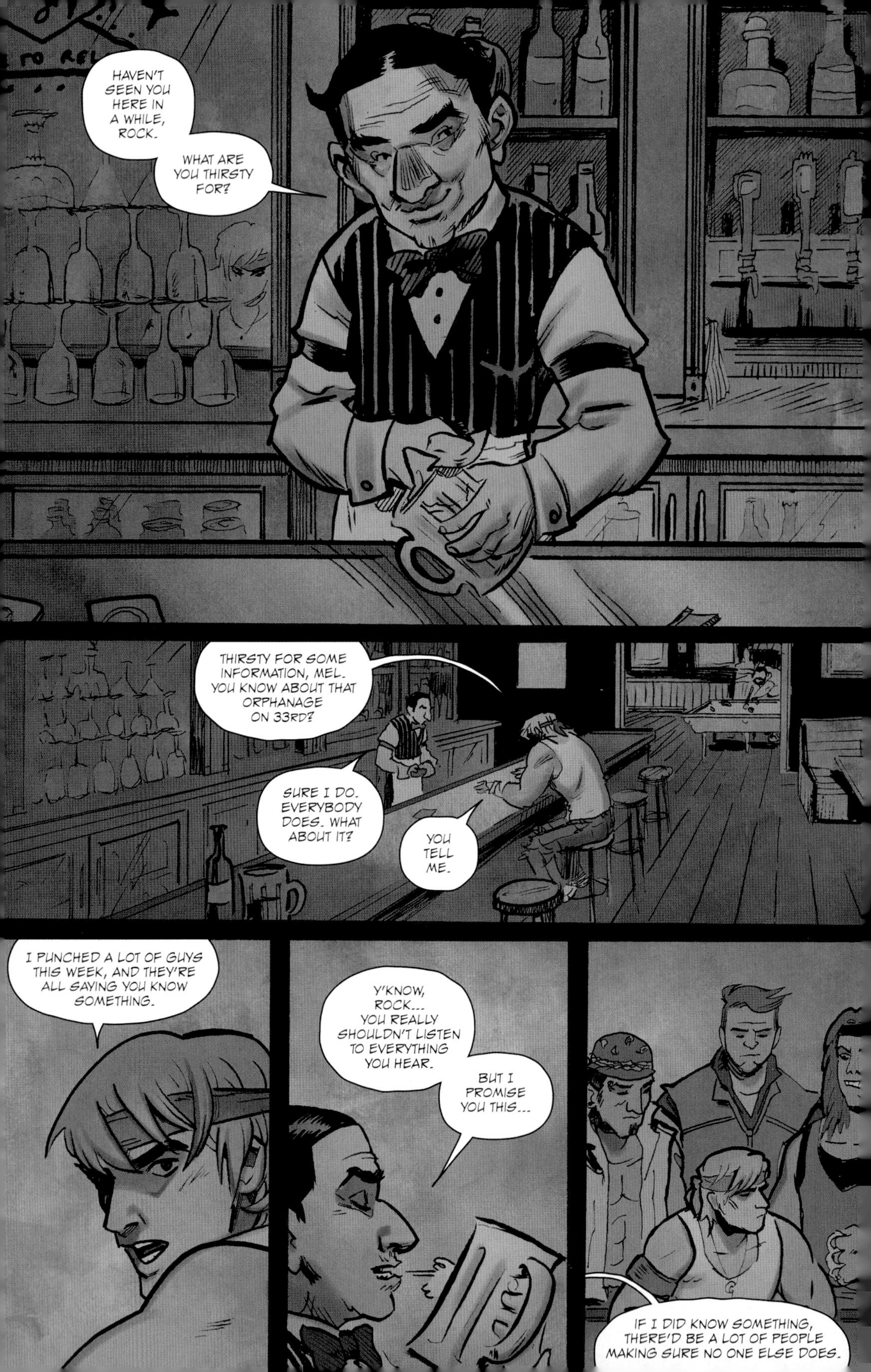
HAVEN'T SEEN YOU HERE IN A WHILE, ROCK.
WHAT ARE YOU THIRSTY FOR?
THIRSTY FOR SOME INFORMATION, MEL. YOU KNOW ABOUT THAT ORPHANAGE ON 33RD?
SURE I DO. EVERYBODY DOES. WHAT ABOUT IT?
YOU TELL ME.
I PUNCHED A LOT OF GUYS THIS WEEK, AND THEY'RE ALL SAYING YOU KNOW SOMETHING.
Y'KNOW, ROCK... YOU REALLY SHOULDN'T LISTEN TO EVERYTHING YOU HEAR.
BUT I PROMISE YOU THIS...
IF I DID KNOW SOMETHING, THERE'D BE A LOT OF PEOPLE MAKING SURE NO ONE ELSE DOES.

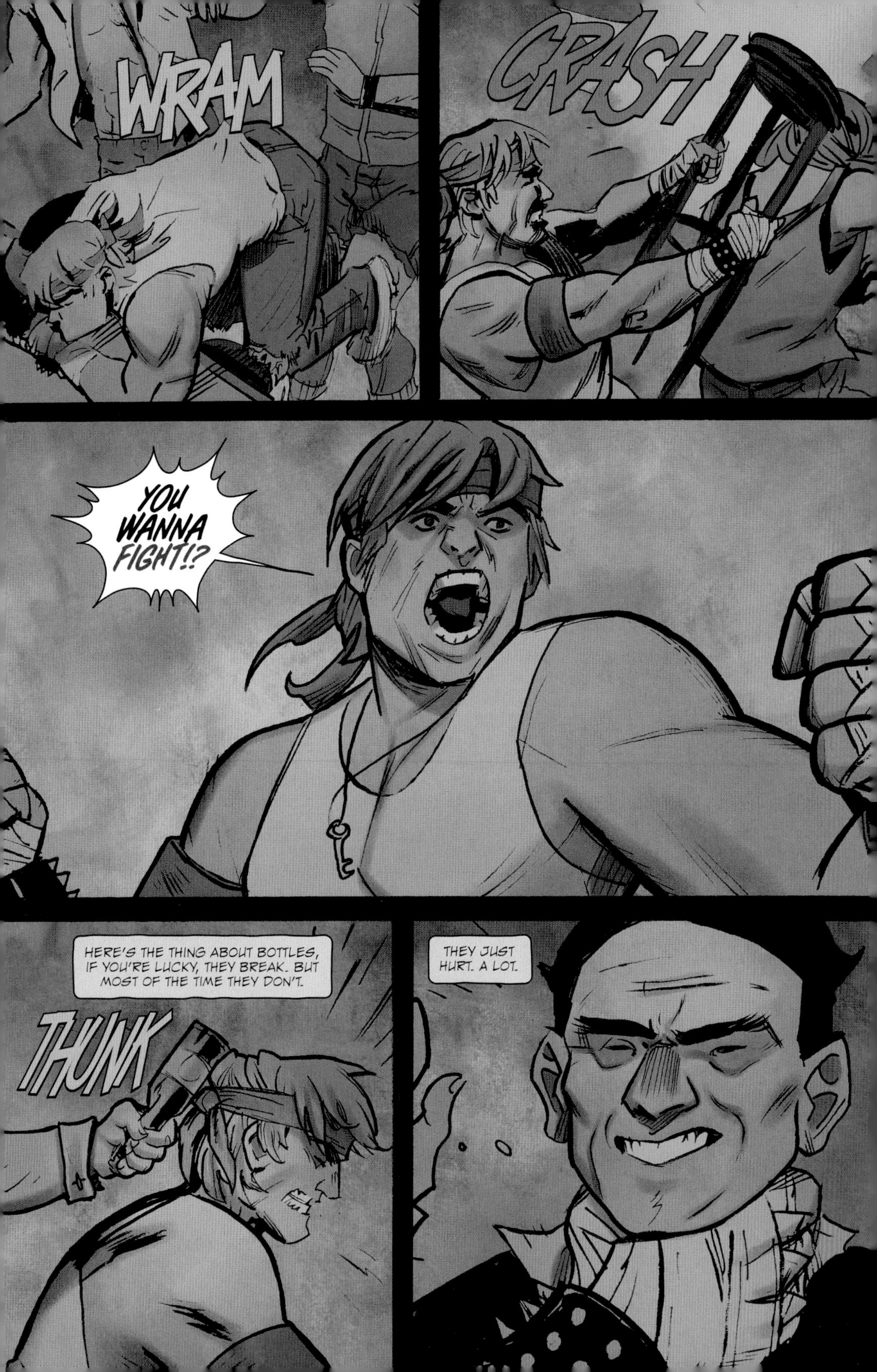
WRAM
CRASH
YOU WANNA FIGHT!?
HERE'S THE THING ABOUT BOTTLES, IF YOU'RE LUCKY, THEY BREAK. BUT MOST OF THE TIME THEY DON'T.
THUNK
THEY JUST HURT. A LOT.

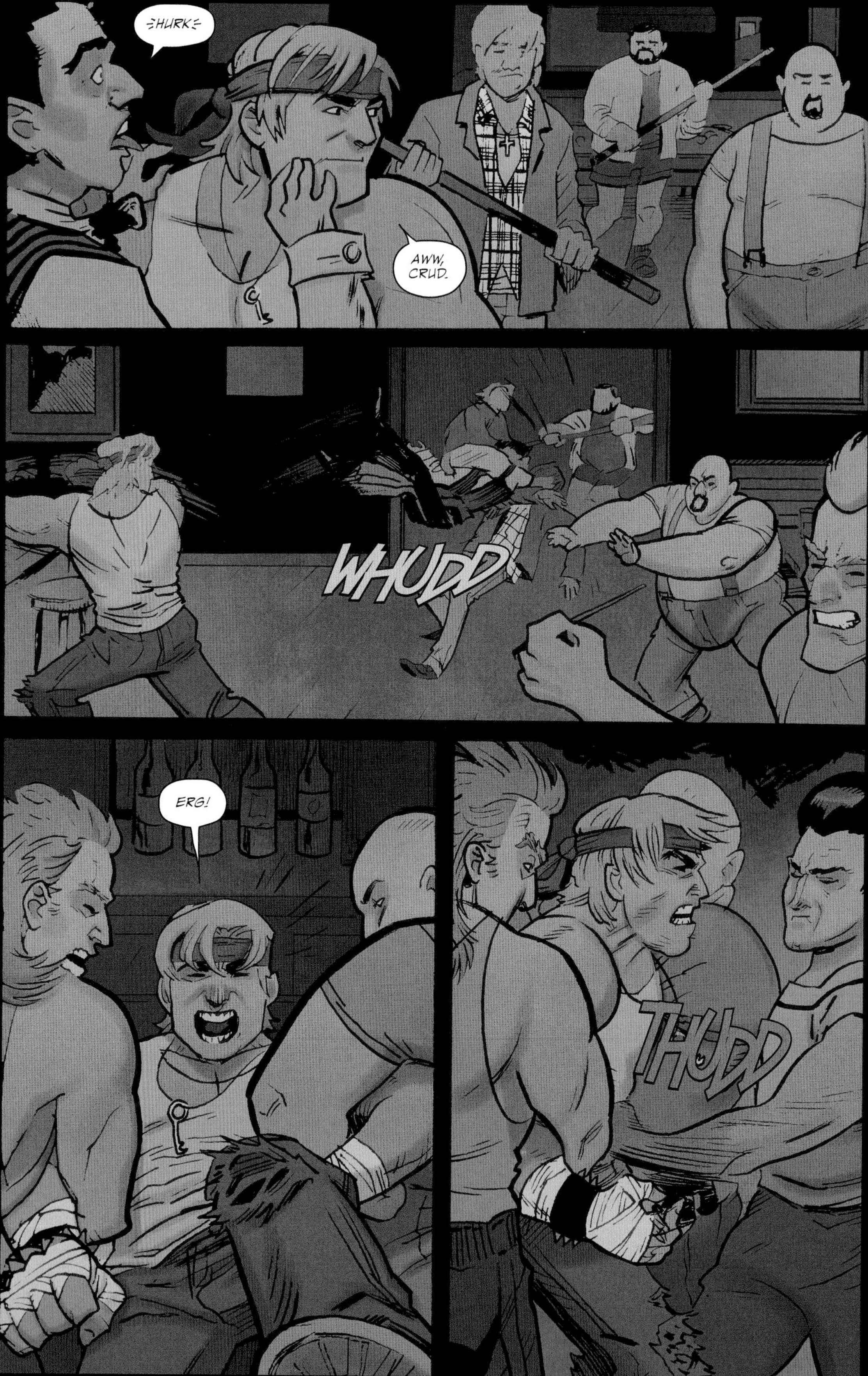
HURK
AWW, CRUD.
WHUDD
ERG!
THUDD

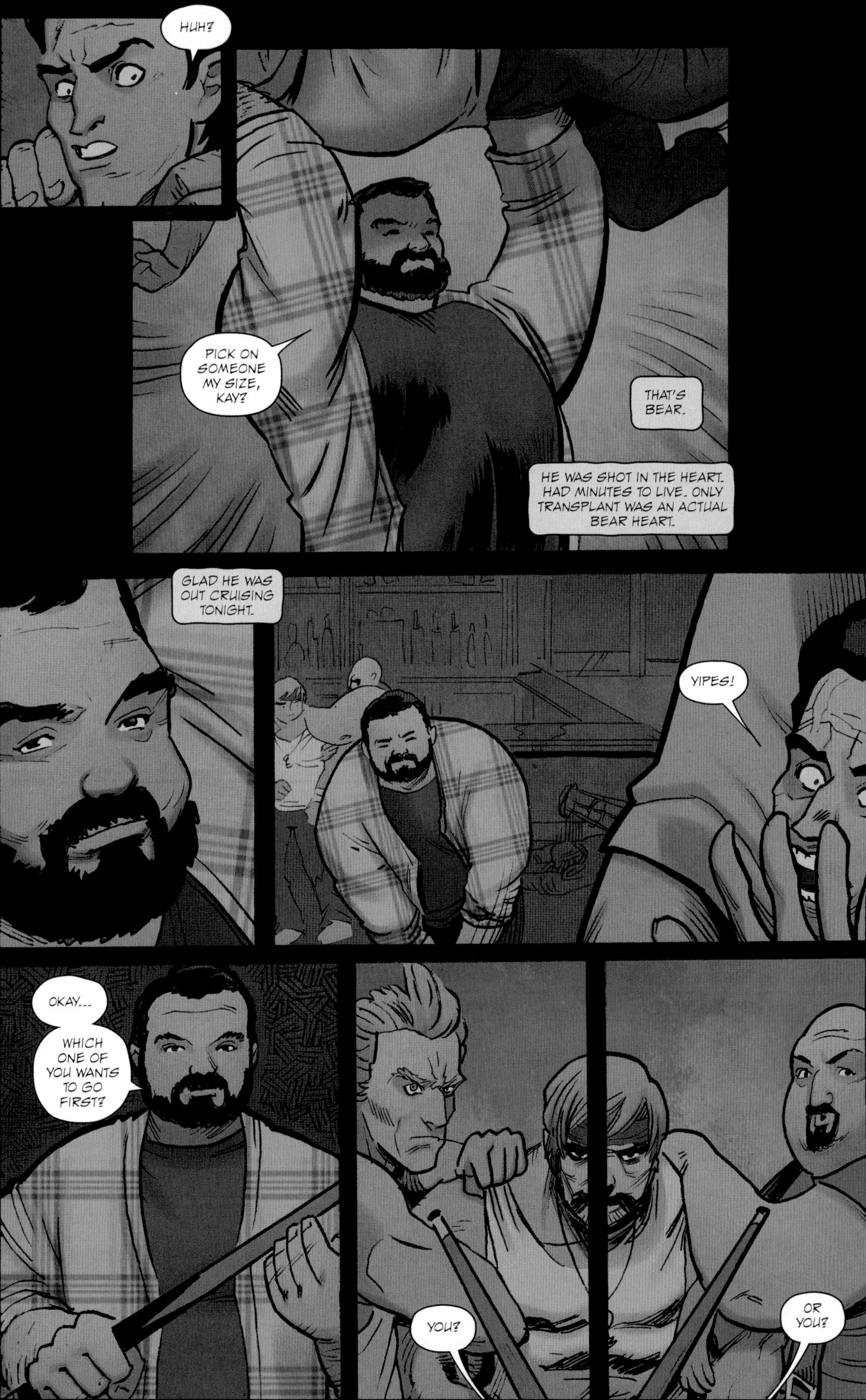
HUH?
PICK ON SOMEONE MY SIZE, KAY?
THAT'S BEAR.
HE WAS SHOT IN THE HEART. HAD MINUTES TO LIVE. ONLY TRANSPLANT WAS AN ACTUAL BEAR HEART.
GLAD HE WAS OUT CRUISING TONIGHT.
YIPES!
OKAY...
WHICH ONE OF YOU WANTS TO GO FIRST?
YOU?
OR YOU?

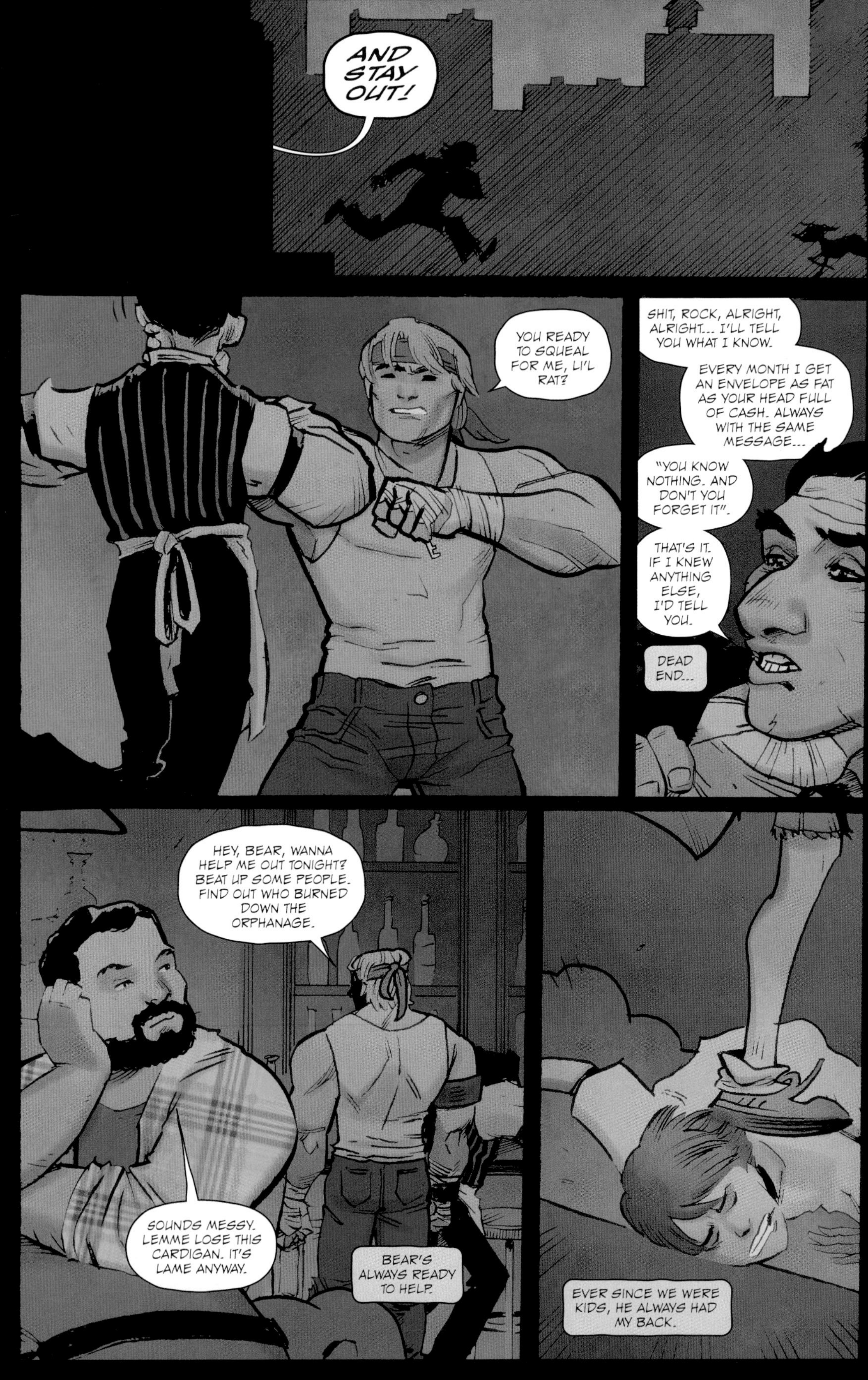
AND STAY OUT!
YOU READY TO SQUEAL FOR ME, LI'L RAT?
SHIT, ROCK, ALRIGHT, ALRIGHT... I'LL TELL YOU WHAT I KNOW.
EVERY MONTH I GET AN ENVELOPE AS FAT AS YOUR HEAD FULL OF CASH. ALWAYS WITH THE SAME MESSAGE...
"YOU KNOW NOTHING. AND DON'T YOU FORGET IT".
THAT'S IT. IF I KNEW ANYTHING ELSE, I'D TELL YOU.
DEAD END...
HEY, BEAR, WANNA HELP ME OUT TONIGHT? BEAT UP SOME PEOPLE. FIND OUT WHO BURNED DOWN THE ORPHANAGE.
SOUNDS MESSY. LEMME LOSE THIS CARDIGAN. IT'S LAME ANYWAY.
BEAR'S ALWAYS READY TO HELP.
EVER SINCE WE WERE KIDS, HE ALWAYS HAD MY BACK.

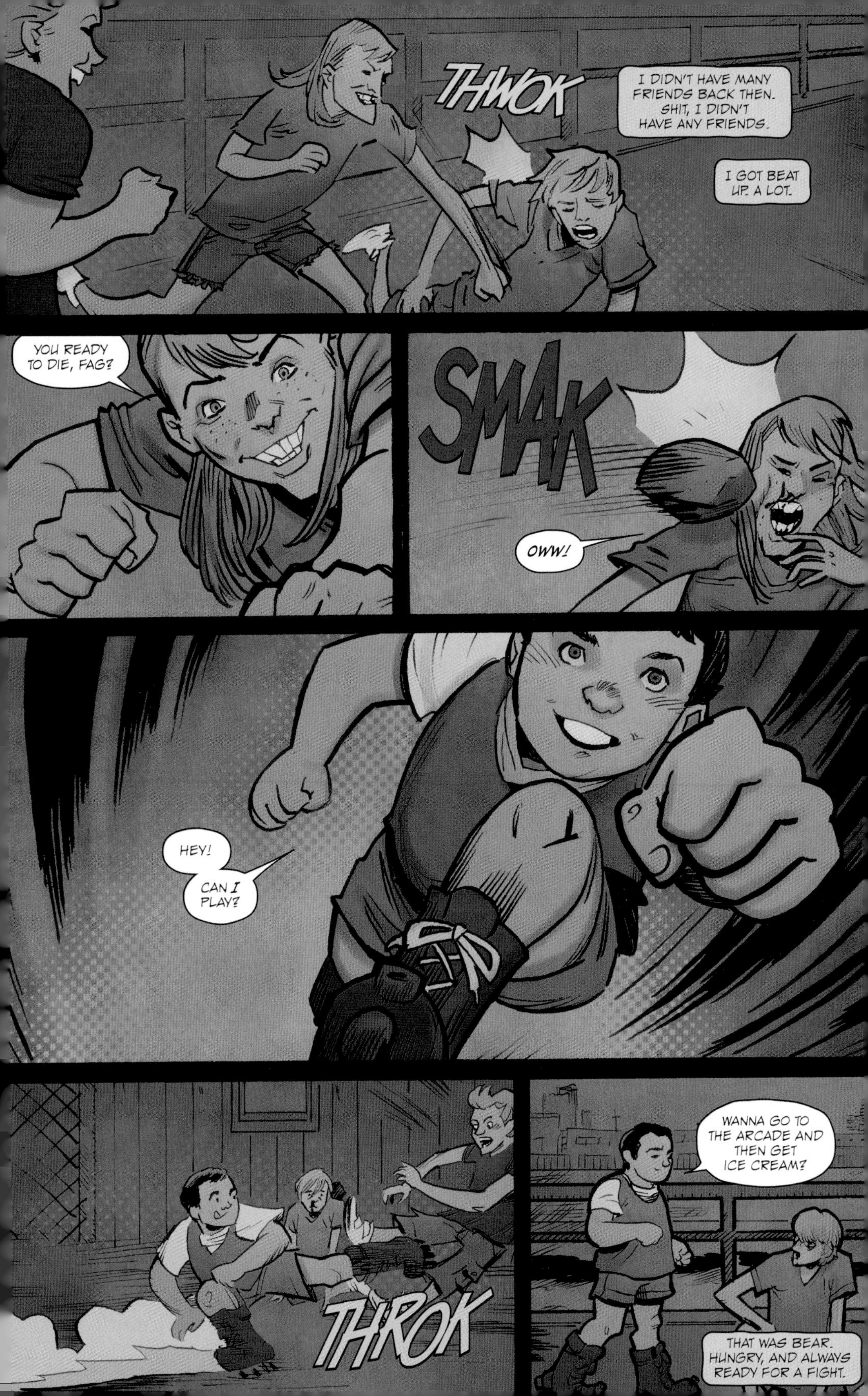
THWOK
I DIDN'T HAVE MANY FRIENDS BACK THEN. SHIT, I DIDN'T HAVE ANY FRIENDS.
I GOT BEAT UP. A LOT.
YOU READY TO DIE, FAG?
SMAK
OWW!
HEY!
CAN I PLAY?
THROK
WANNA GO TO THE ARCADE AND THEN GET ICE CREAM?
THAT WAS BEAR. HUNGRY, AND ALWAYS READY FOR A FIGHT.

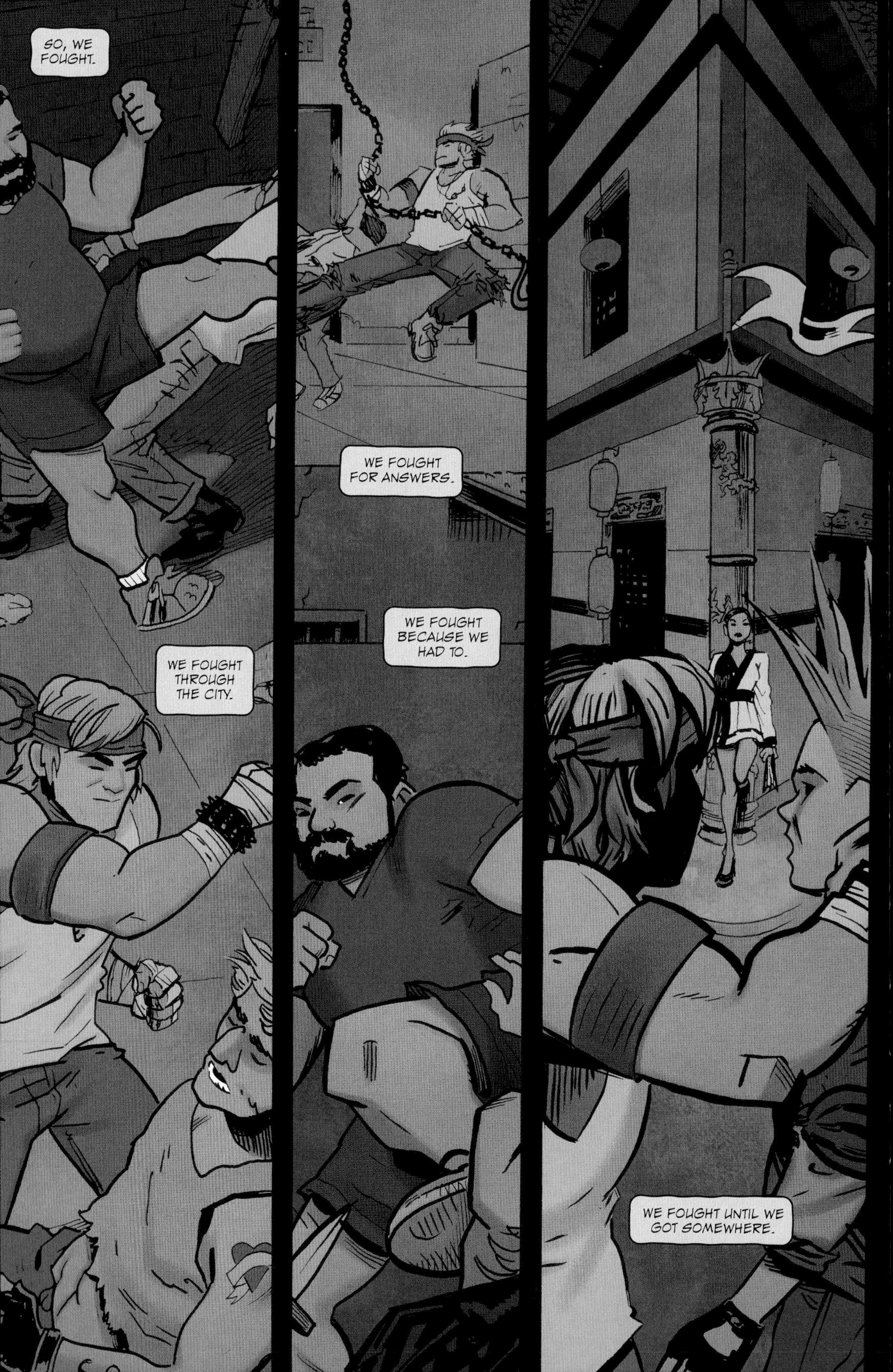
SO, WE FOUGHT.
WE FOUGHT THROUGH THE CITY.
WE FOUGHT FOR ANSWERS.
WE FOUGHT BECAUSE WE HAD TO.
WE FOUGHT UNTIL WE GOT SOMEWHERE.

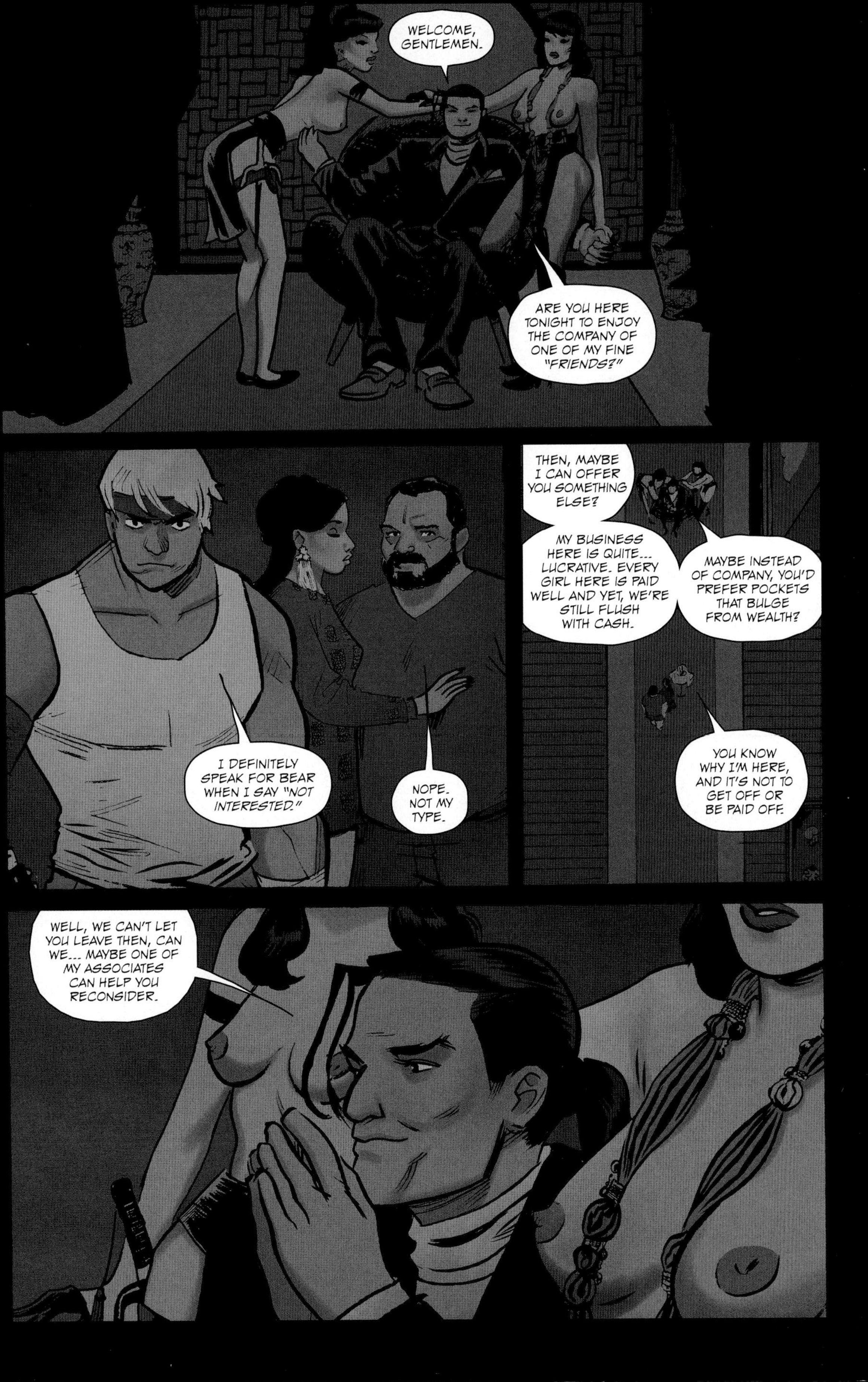
WELCOME, GENTLEMEN.
ARE YOU HERE TONIGHT TO ENJOY THE COMPANY OF ONE OF MY FINE "FRIENDS?"
I DEFINITELY SPEAK FOR BEAR WHEN I SAY "NOT INTERESTED."
NOPE. NOT MY TYPE.
THEN, MAYBE I CAN OFFER YOU SOMETHING ELSE?
MY BUSINESS HERE IS QUITE... LUCRATIVE. EVERY GIRL HERE IS PAID WELL AND YET, WE'RE STILL FLUSH WITH CASH.
MAYBE INSTEAD OF COMPANY, YOU'D PREFER POCKETS THAT BULGE FROM WEALTH?
YOU KNOW WHY I'M HERE, AND IT'S NOT TO GET OFF OR BE PAID OFF.
WELL, WE CAN'T LET YOU LEAVE THEN, CAN WE... MAYBE ONE OF MY ASSOCIATES CAN HELP YOU RECONSIDER.

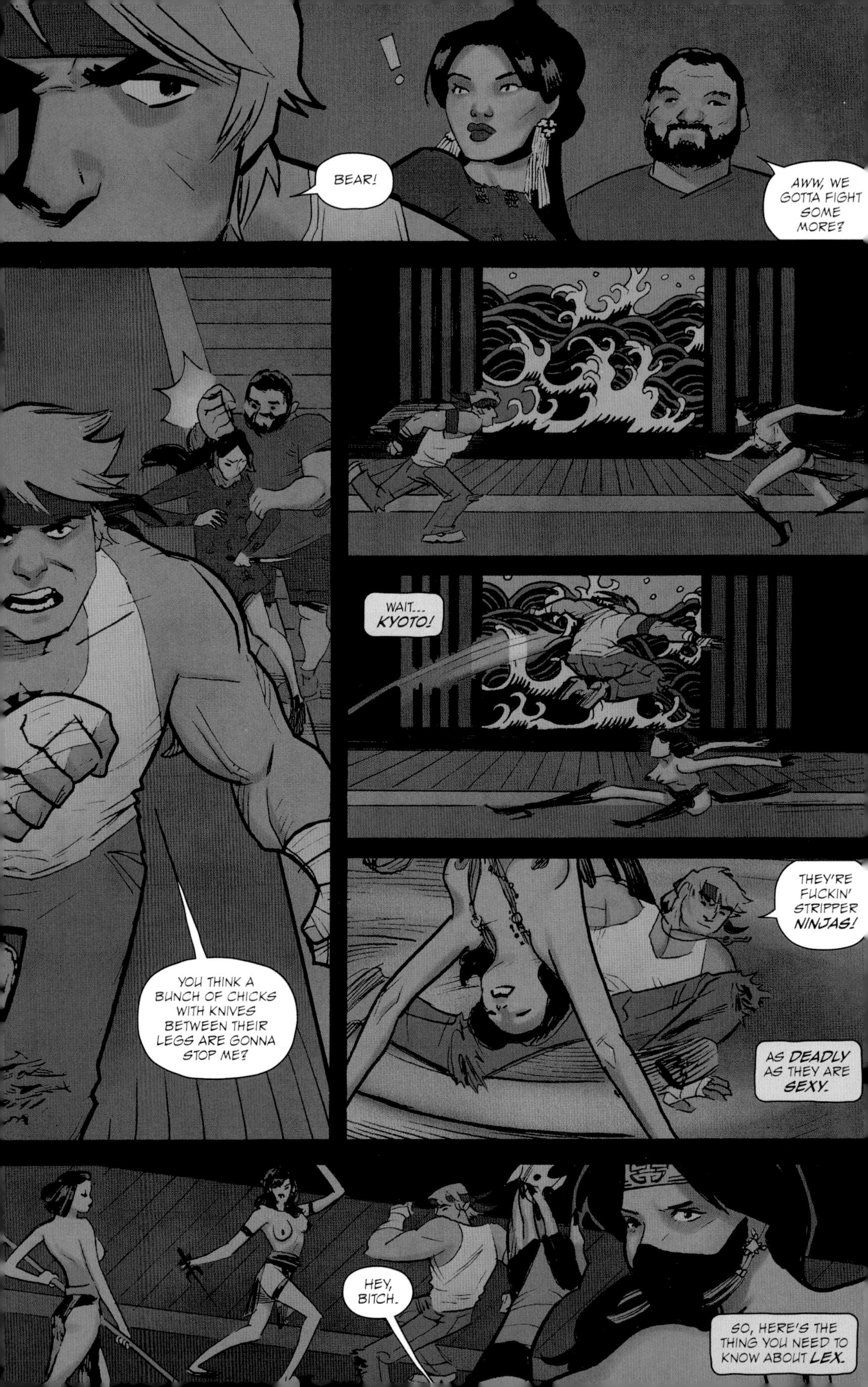
BEAR!
AWW, WE GOTTA FIGHT SOME MORE?
YOU THINK A BUNCH OF CHICKS WITH KNIVES BETWEEN THEIR LEGS ARE GONNA STOP ME?
WAIT... KYOTO!
THEY'RE FUCKIN' STRIPPER NINJAS!
AS DEADLY AS THEY ARE SEXY.
HEY, BITCH.
SO, HERE'S THE THING YOU NEED TO KNOW ABOUT LEX.

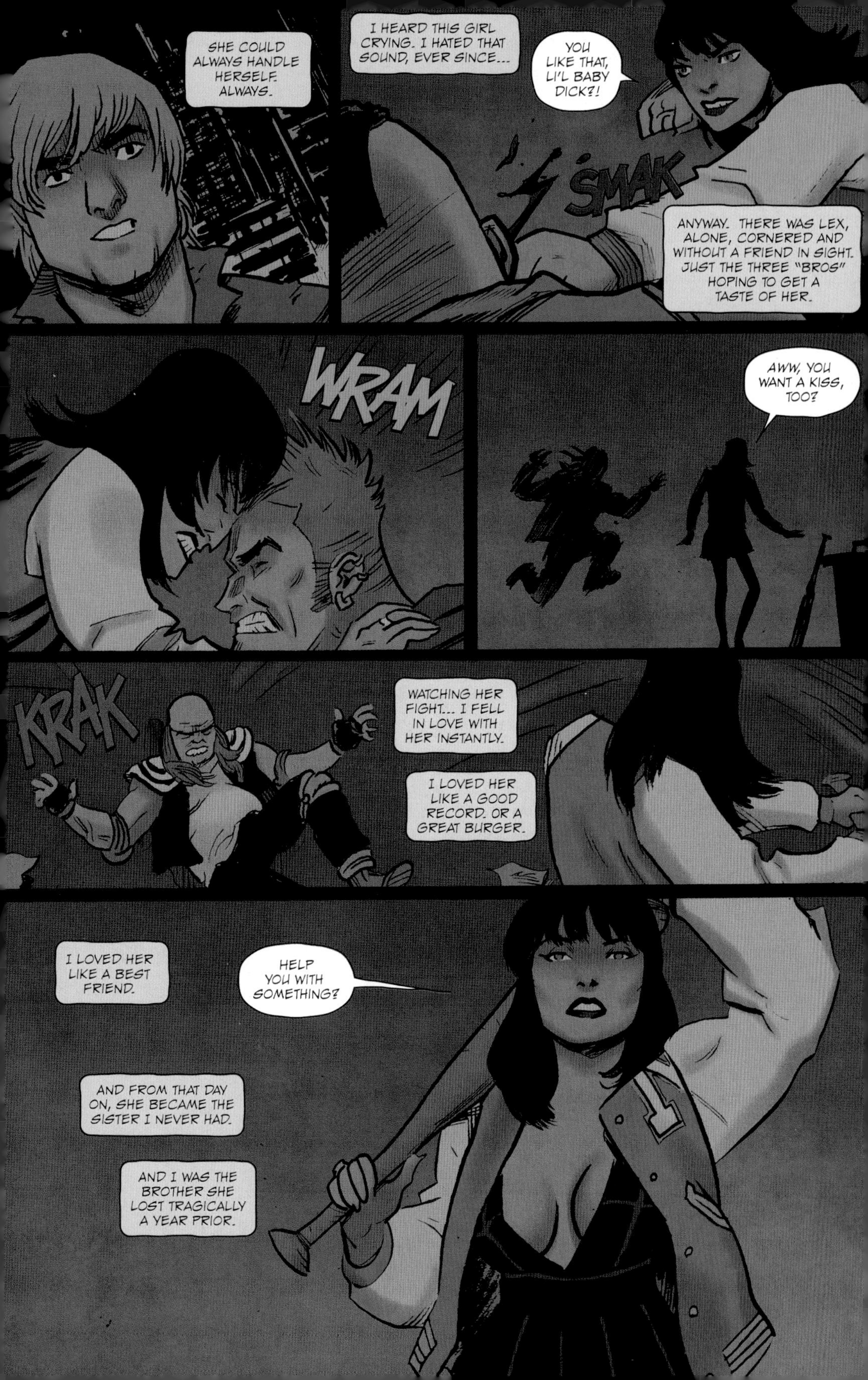
SHE COULD ALWAYS HANDLE HERSELF. ALWAYS.
I HEARD THIS GIRL CRYING. I HATED THAT SOUND, EVER SINCE...
YOU LIKE THAT, LI'L BABY DICK?!
SMAK
ANYWAY. THERE WAS LEX, ALONE, CORNERED AND WITHOUT A FRIEND IN SIGHT. JUST THE THREE "BROS" HOPING TO GET A TASTE OF HER.
WRAM
AWW, YOU WANT A KISS, TOO?
KRAK
WATCHING HER FIGHT... I FELL IN LOVE WITH HER INSTANTLY.
I LOVED HER LIKE A GOOD RECORD. OR A GREAT BURGER.
I LOVED HER LIKE A BEST FRIEND.
HELP YOU WITH SOMETHING?
AND FROM THAT DAY ON, SHE BECAME THE SISTER I NEVER HAD.
AND I WAS THE BROTHER SHE LOST TRAGICALLY A YEAR PRIOR.

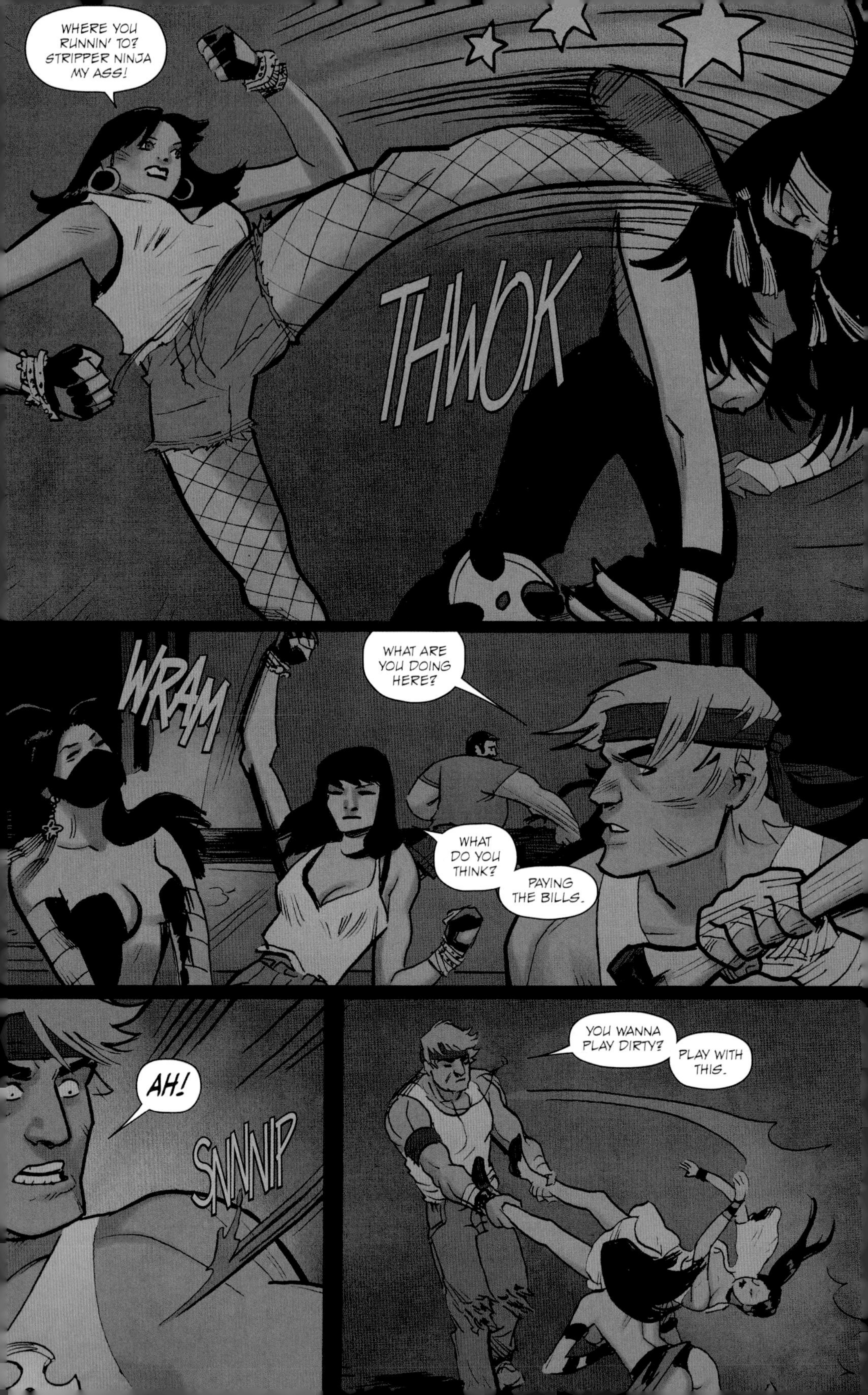
WHERE YOU RUNNIN' TO? STRIPPER NINJA MY ASS!
THWOK
WRAM
WHAT ARE YOU DOING HERE?
WHAT DO YOU THINK?
PAYING THE BILLS.
AH!
SNNNIP
YOU WANNA PLAY DIRTY?
PLAY WITH THIS.

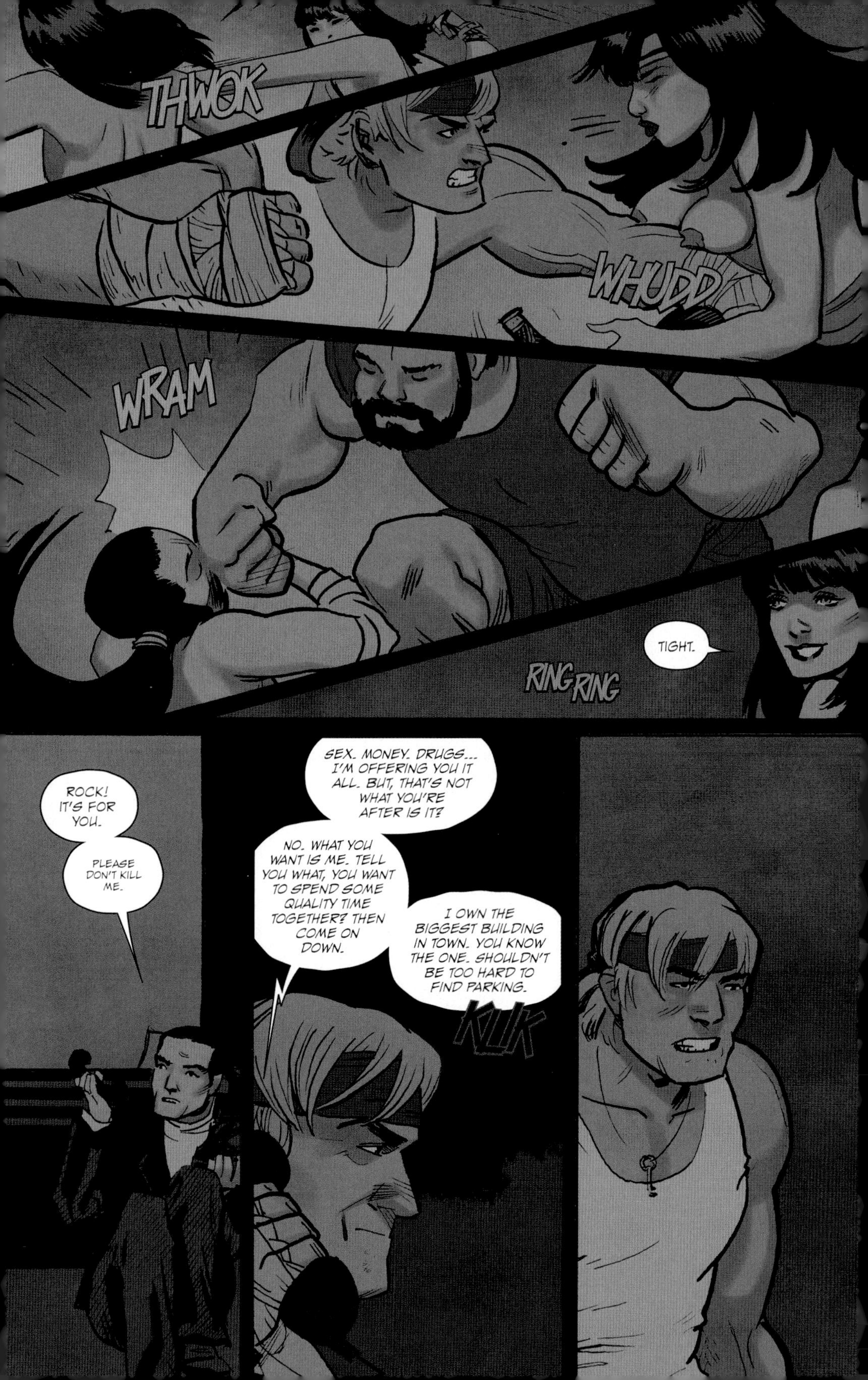
THWOK
WHUDD
WRAM
RING RING
TIGHT.
ROCK! IT'S FOR YOU.
PLEASE DON'T KILL ME.
SEX. MONEY. DRUGS... I'M OFFERING YOU IT ALL. BUT, THAT'S NOT WHAT YOU'RE AFTER IS IT?
NO. WHAT YOU WANT IS ME. TELL YOU WHAT, YOU WANT TO SPEND SOME QUALITY TIME TOGETHER? THEN COME ON DOWN.
I OWN THE BIGGEST BUILDING IN TOWN. YOU KNOW THE ONE. SHOULDN'T BE TOO HARD TO FIND PARKING.
KLIK

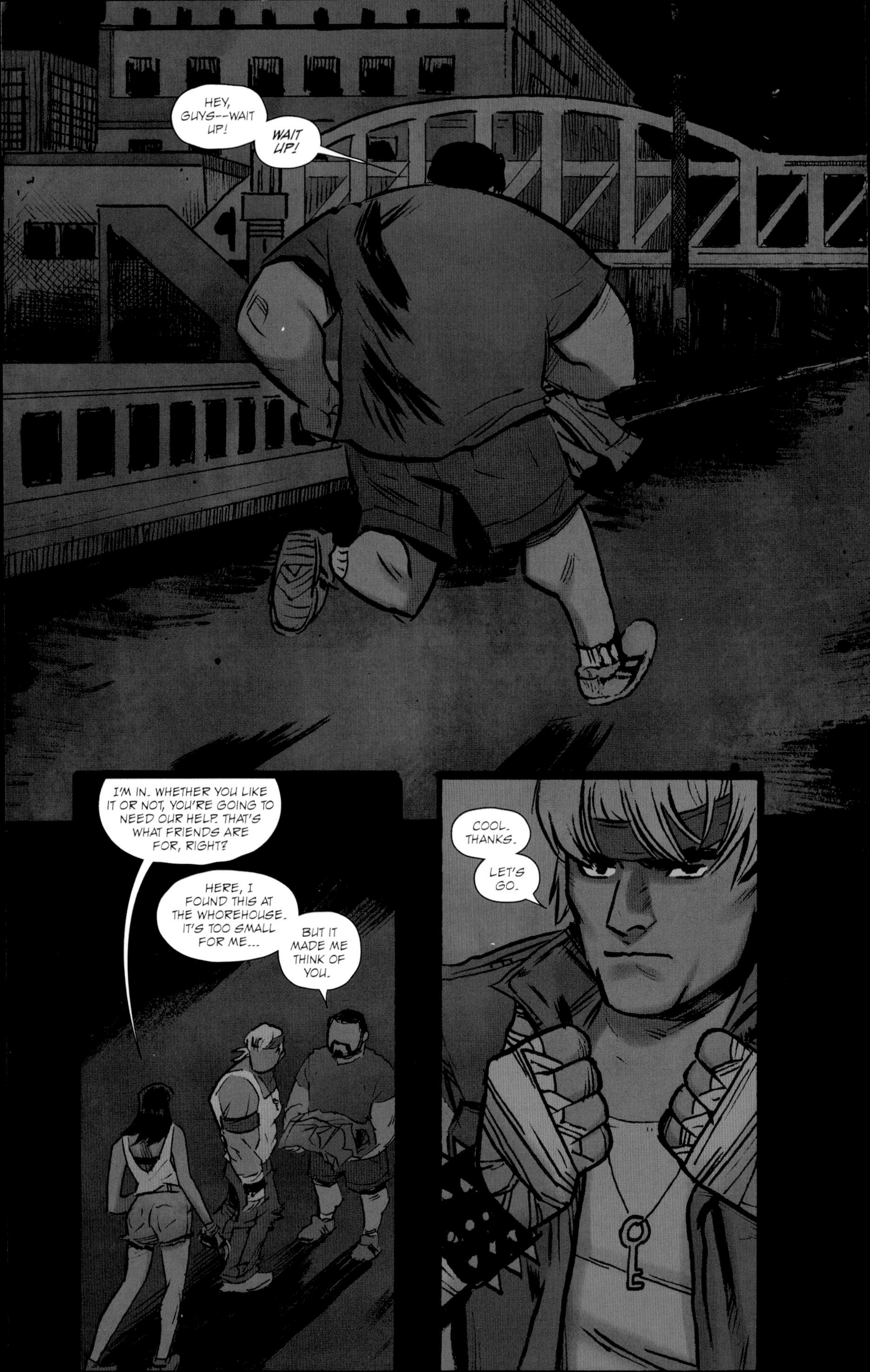
HEY, GUYS--WAIT UP!
WAIT UP!
I'M IN. WHETHER YOU LIKE IT OR NOT, YOU'RE GOING TO NEED OUR HELP. THAT'S WHAT FRIENDS ARE FOR, RIGHT?
HERE, I FOUND THIS AT THE WHOREHOUSE. IT'S TOO SMALL FOR ME...
BUT IT MADE ME THINK OF YOU.
COOL. THANKS.
LET'S GO.

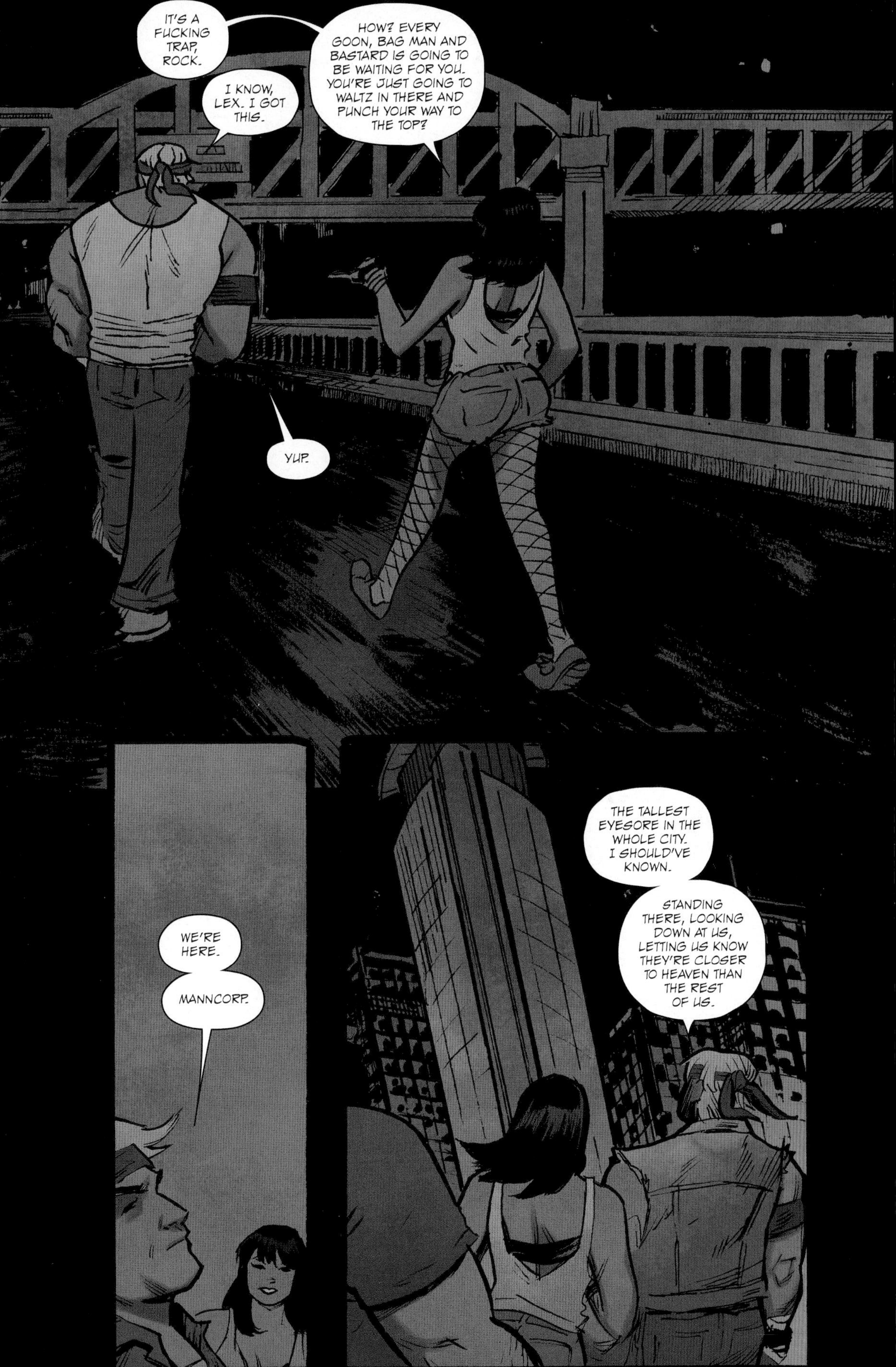
IT'S A FUCKING TRAP, ROCK.
HOW? EVERY GOON, BAG MAN AND BASTARD IS GOING TO BE WAITING FOR YOU. YOU'RE JUST GOING TO WALTZ IN THERE AND PUNCH YOUR WAY TO THE TOP?
I KNOW, LEX. I GOT THIS.
YUP.
WE'RE HERE.
MANNCORP.
THE TALLEST EYESORE IN THE WHOLE CITY. I SHOULD'VE KNOWN.
STANDING THERE, LOOKING DOWN AT US, LETTING US KNOW THEY'RE CLOSER TO HEAVEN THAN THE REST OF US.

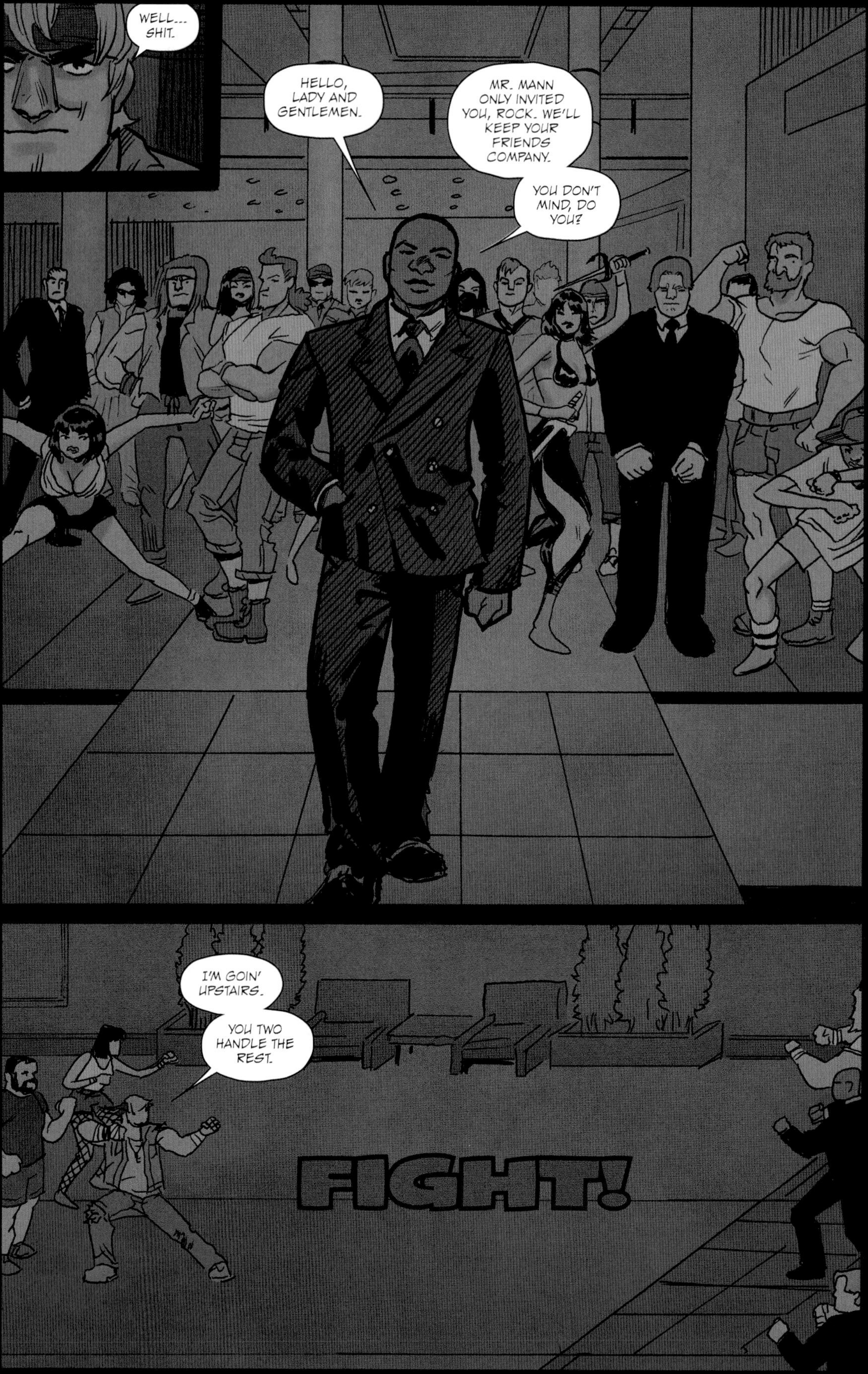
WELL... SHIT.
HELLO, LADY AND GENTLEMEN.
MR. MANN ONLY INVITED YOU, ROCK. WE'LL KEEP YOUR FRIENDS COMPANY.
YOU DON'T MIND, DO YOU?
I'M GOIN' UPSTAIRS.
YOU TWO HANDLE THE REST.
FIGHT!

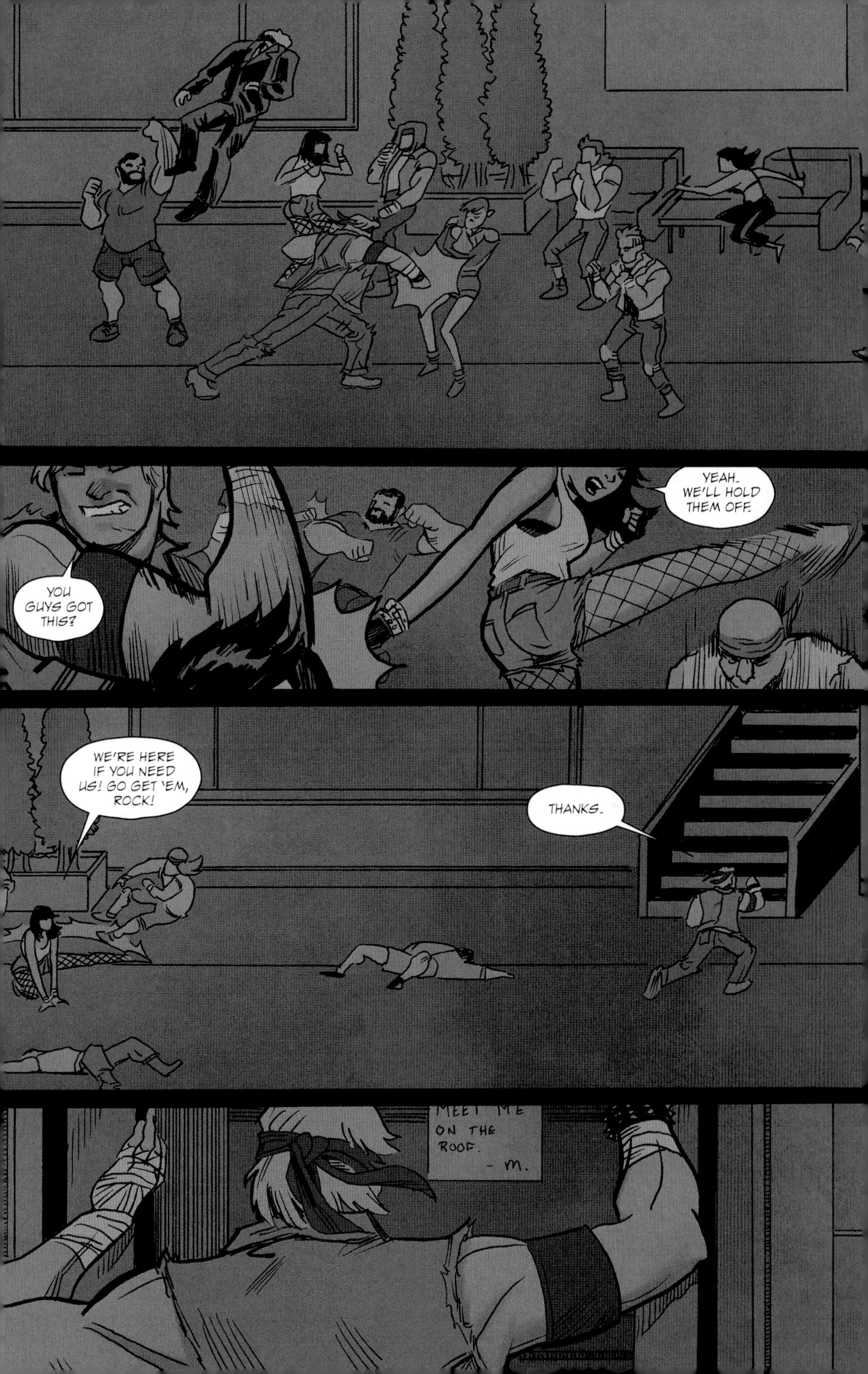
YOU GUYS GOT THIS?
YEAH. WE'LL HOLD THEM OFF.
WE'RE HERE IF YOU NEED US! GO GET 'EM, ROCK!
THANKS.
MEET ME ON THE ROOF. - m.

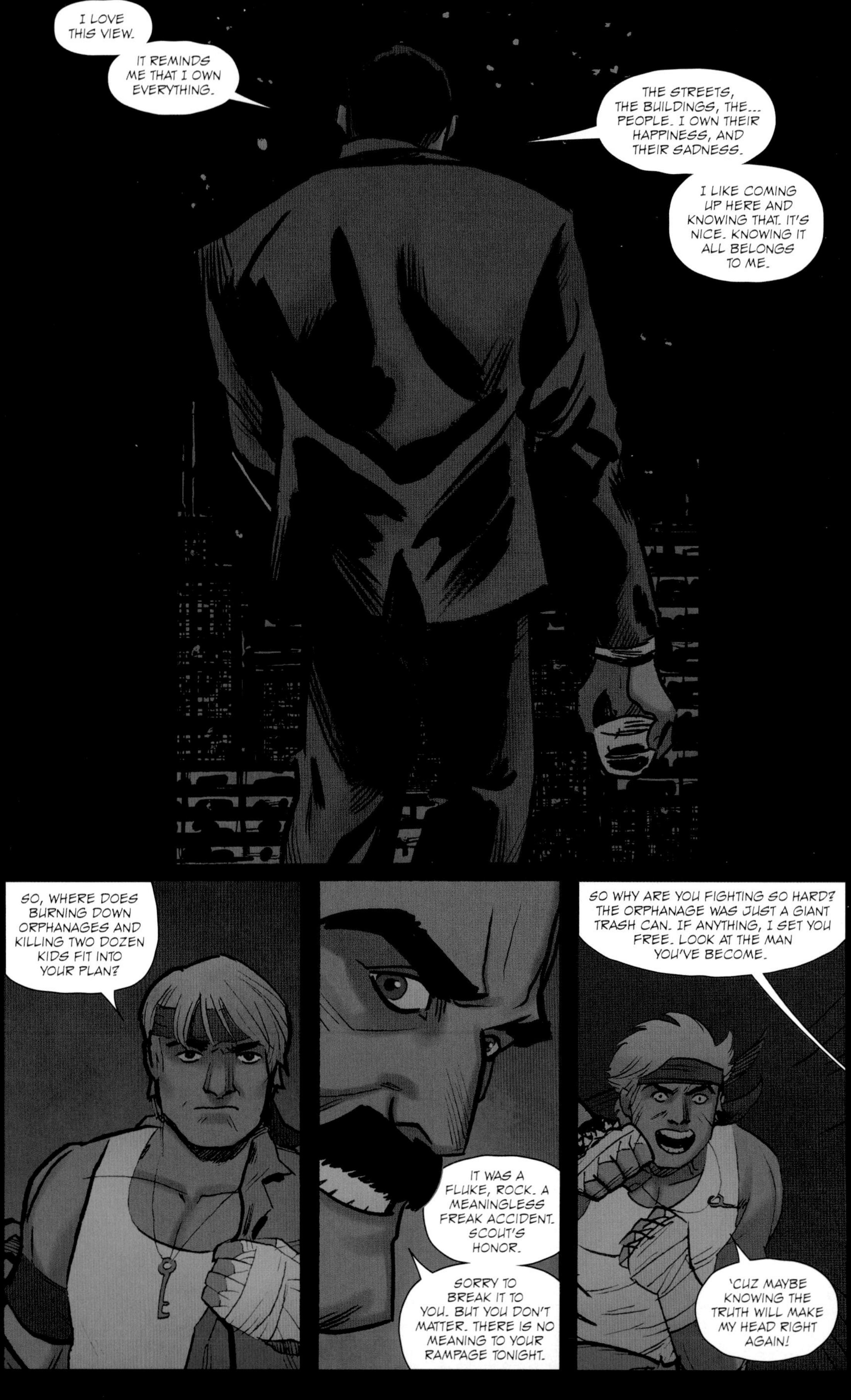
I LOVE THIS VIEW.
IT REMINDS ME THAT I OWN EVERYTHING.
THE STREETS, THE BUILDINGS, THE... PEOPLE. I OWN THEIR HAPPINESS, AND THEIR SADNESS.
I LIKE COMING UP HERE AND KNOWING THAT. IT'S NICE. KNOWING IT ALL BELONGS TO ME.
SO, WHERE DOES BURNING DOWN ORPHANAGES AND KILLING TWO DOZEN KIDS FIT INTO YOUR PLAN?
IT WAS A FLUKE, ROCK. A MEANINGLESS FREAK ACCIDENT. SCOUT'S HONOR.
SORRY TO BREAK IT TO YOU. BUT YOU DON'T MATTER. THERE IS NO MEANING TO YOUR RAMPAGE TONIGHT.
SO WHY ARE YOU FIGHTING SO HARD? THE ORPHANAGE WAS JUST A GIANT TRASH CAN. IF ANYTHING, I SET YOU FREE. LOOK AT THE MAN YOU'VE BECOME.
'CUZ MAYBE KNOWING THE TRUTH WILL MAKE MY HEAD RIGHT AGAIN!

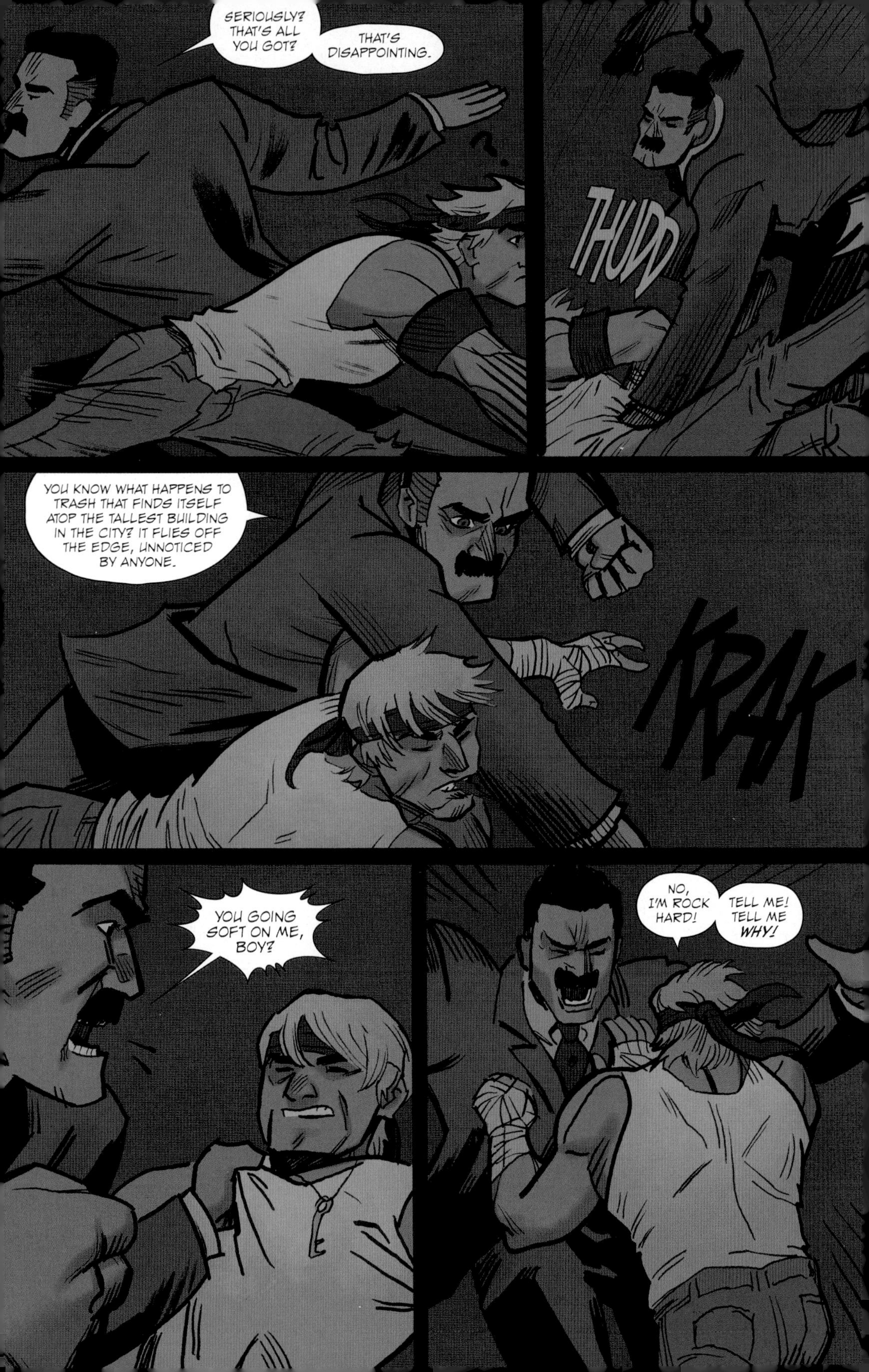
SERIOUSLY? THAT'S ALL YOU GOT?
THAT'S DISAPPOINTING.
?
THUDD
YOU KNOW WHAT HAPPENS TO TRASH THAT FINDS ITSELF ATOP THE TALLEST BUILDING IN THE CITY? IT FLIES OFF THE EDGE, UNNOTICED BY ANYONE.
KRAK
YOU GOING SOFT ON ME, BOY?
NO, I'M ROCK HARD!
TELL ME! TELL ME *WHY!*

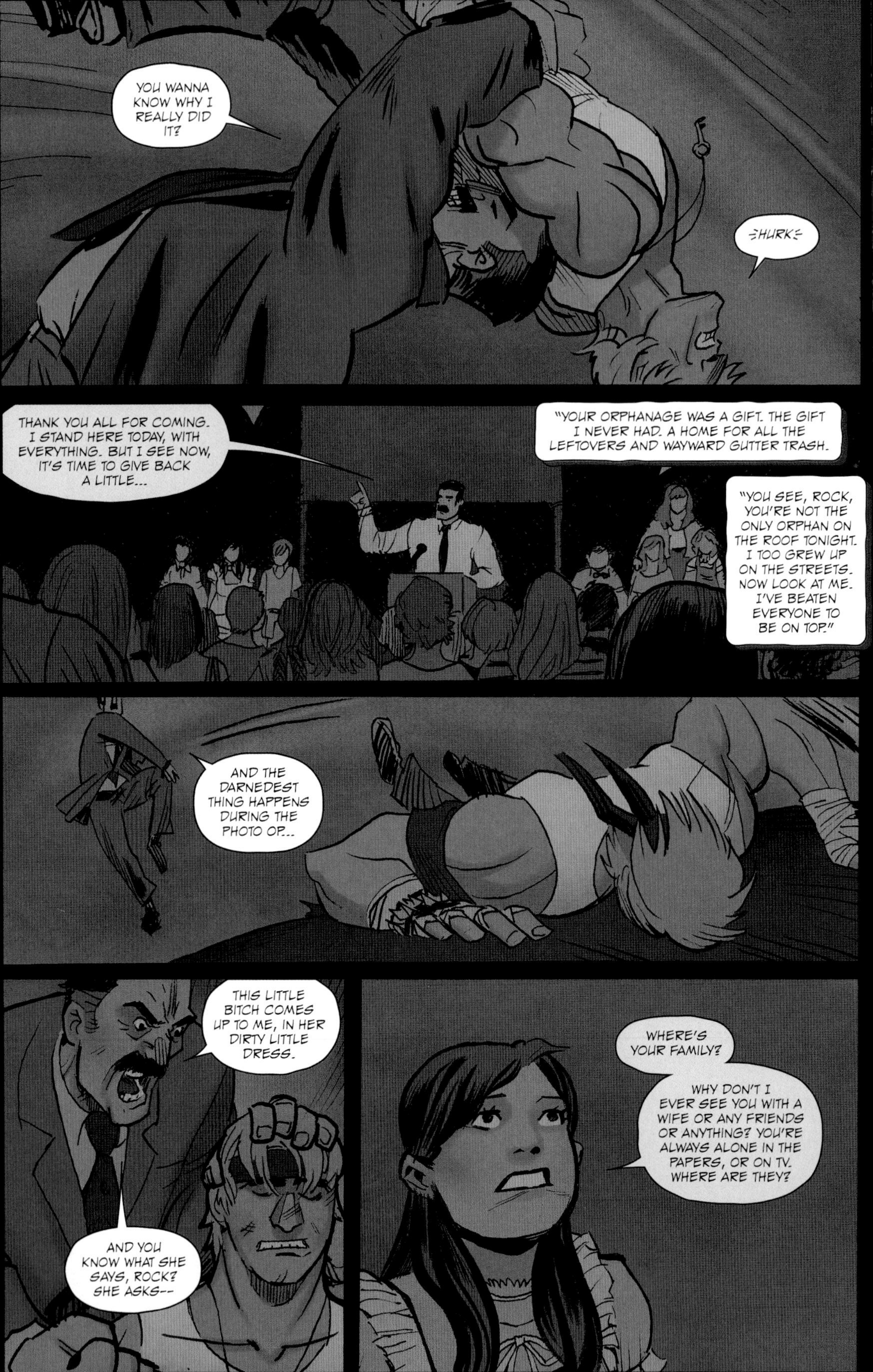
YOU WANNA KNOW WHY I REALLY DID IT?
HURK
THANK YOU ALL FOR COMING. I STAND HERE TODAY, WITH EVERYTHING. BUT I SEE NOW, IT'S TIME TO GIVE BACK A LITTLE...
"YOUR ORPHANAGE WAS A GIFT. THE GIFT I NEVER HAD. A HOME FOR ALL THE LEFTOVERS AND WAYWARD GUTTER TRASH.
"YOU SEE, ROCK, YOU'RE NOT THE ONLY ORPHAN ON THE ROOF TONIGHT. I TOO GREW UP ON THE STREETS. NOW LOOK AT ME. I'VE BEATEN EVERYONE TO BE ON TOP."
AND THE DARNEDEST THING HAPPENS DURING THE PHOTO OP...
THIS LITTLE BITCH COMES UP TO ME, IN HER DIRTY LITTLE DRESS.
AND YOU KNOW WHAT SHE SAYS, ROCK? SHE ASKS--
WHERE'S YOUR FAMILY?
WHY DON'T I EVER SEE YOU WITH A WIFE OR ANY FRIENDS OR ANYTHING? YOU'RE ALWAYS ALONE IN THE PAPERS, OR ON TV. WHERE ARE THEY?

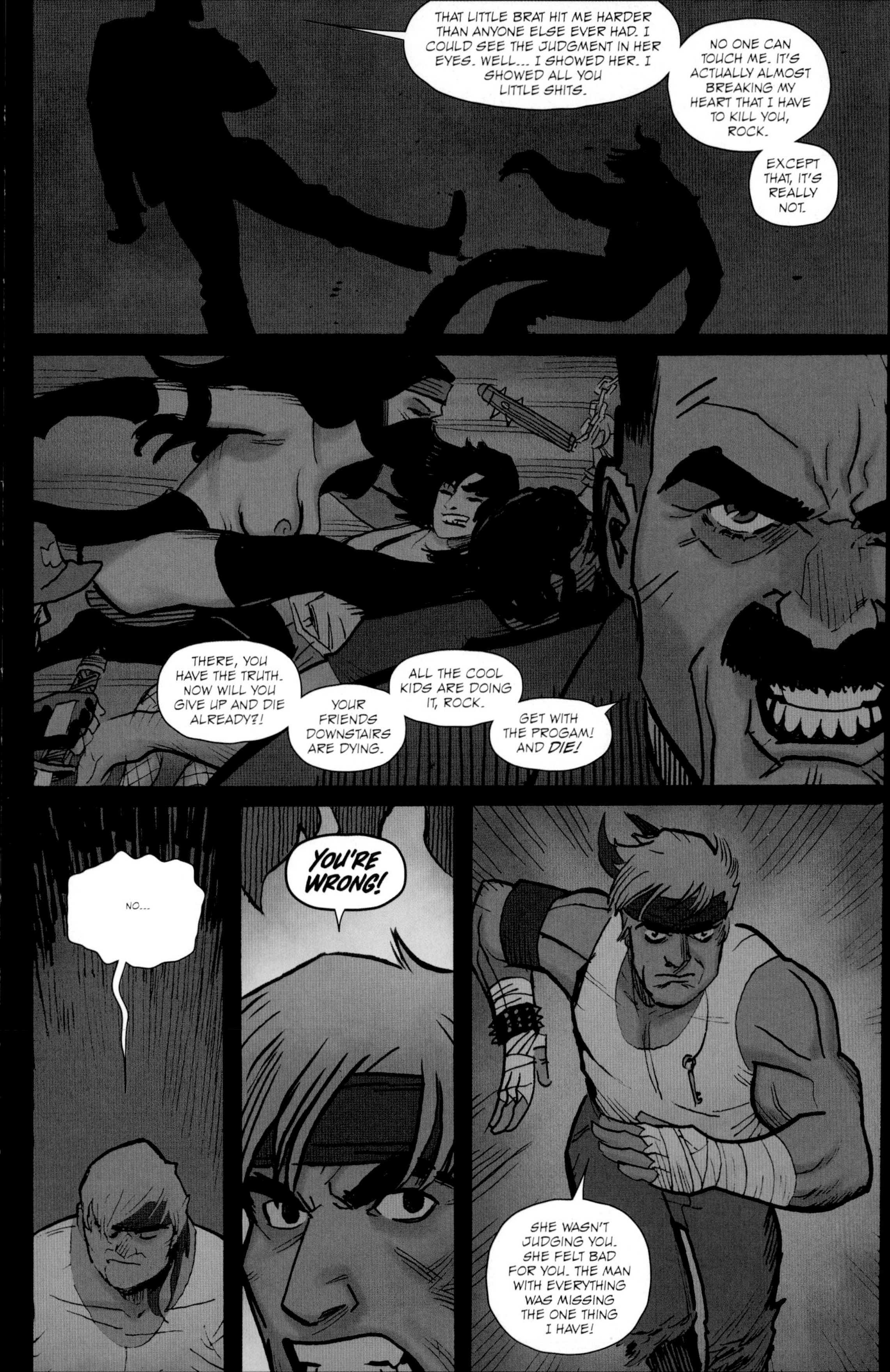
THAT LITTLE BRAT HIT ME HARDER THAN ANYONE ELSE EVER HAD. I COULD SEE THE JUDGMENT IN HER EYES. WELL... I SHOWED HER. I SHOWED ALL YOU LITTLE SHITS.
NO ONE CAN TOUCH ME. IT'S ACTUALLY ALMOST BREAKING MY HEART THAT I HAVE TO KILL YOU, ROCK.
EXCEPT THAT, IT'S REALLY NOT.
THERE, YOU HAVE THE TRUTH. NOW WILL YOU GIVE UP AND DIE ALREADY?!
YOUR FRIENDS DOWNSTAIRS ARE DYING.
ALL THE COOL KIDS ARE DOING IT, ROCK.
GET WITH THE PROGAM! AND DIE!
NO...
YOU'RE WRONG!
SHE WASN'T JUDGING YOU. SHE FELT BAD FOR YOU. THE MAN WITH EVERYTHING WAS MISSING THE ONE THING I HAVE!

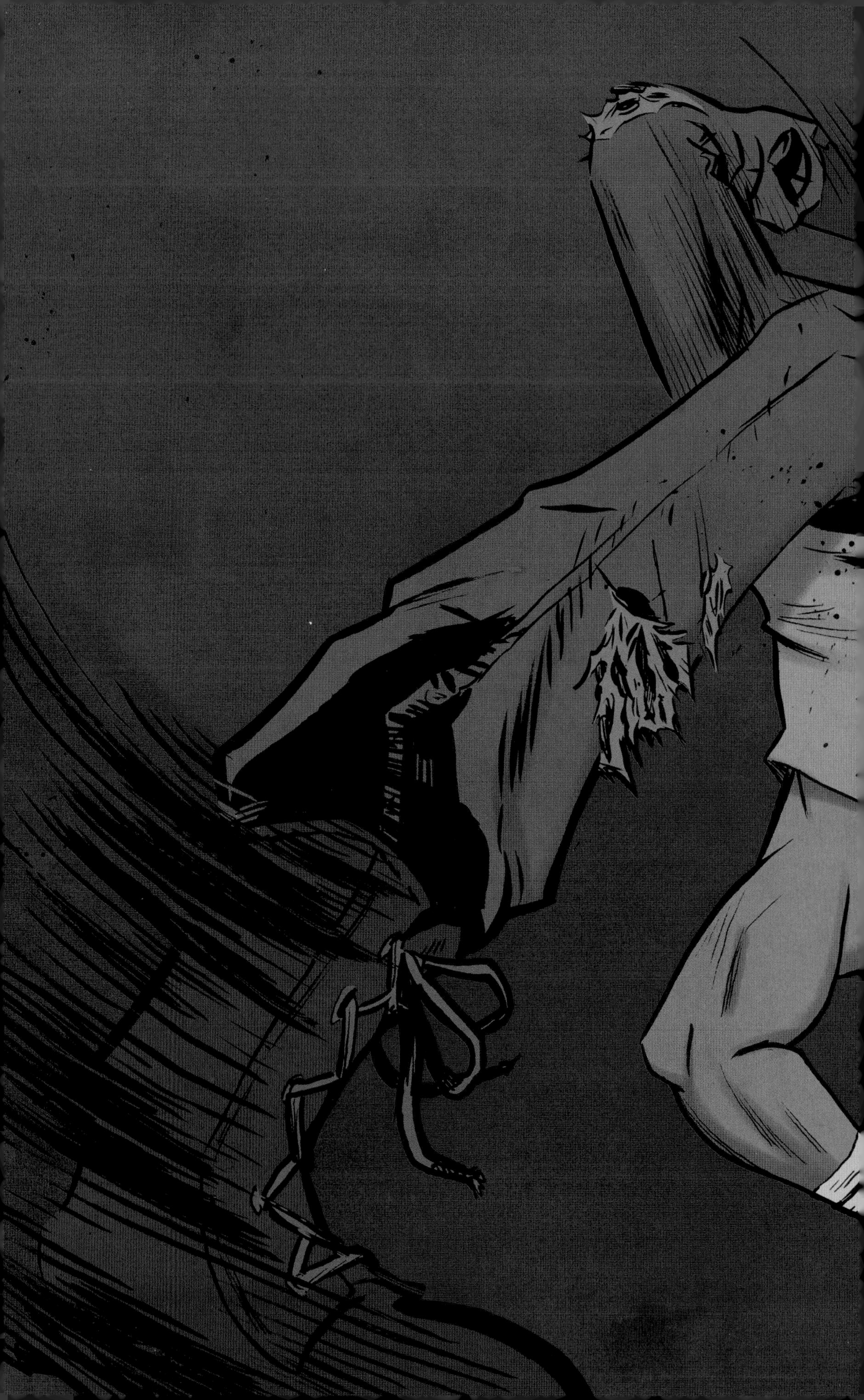

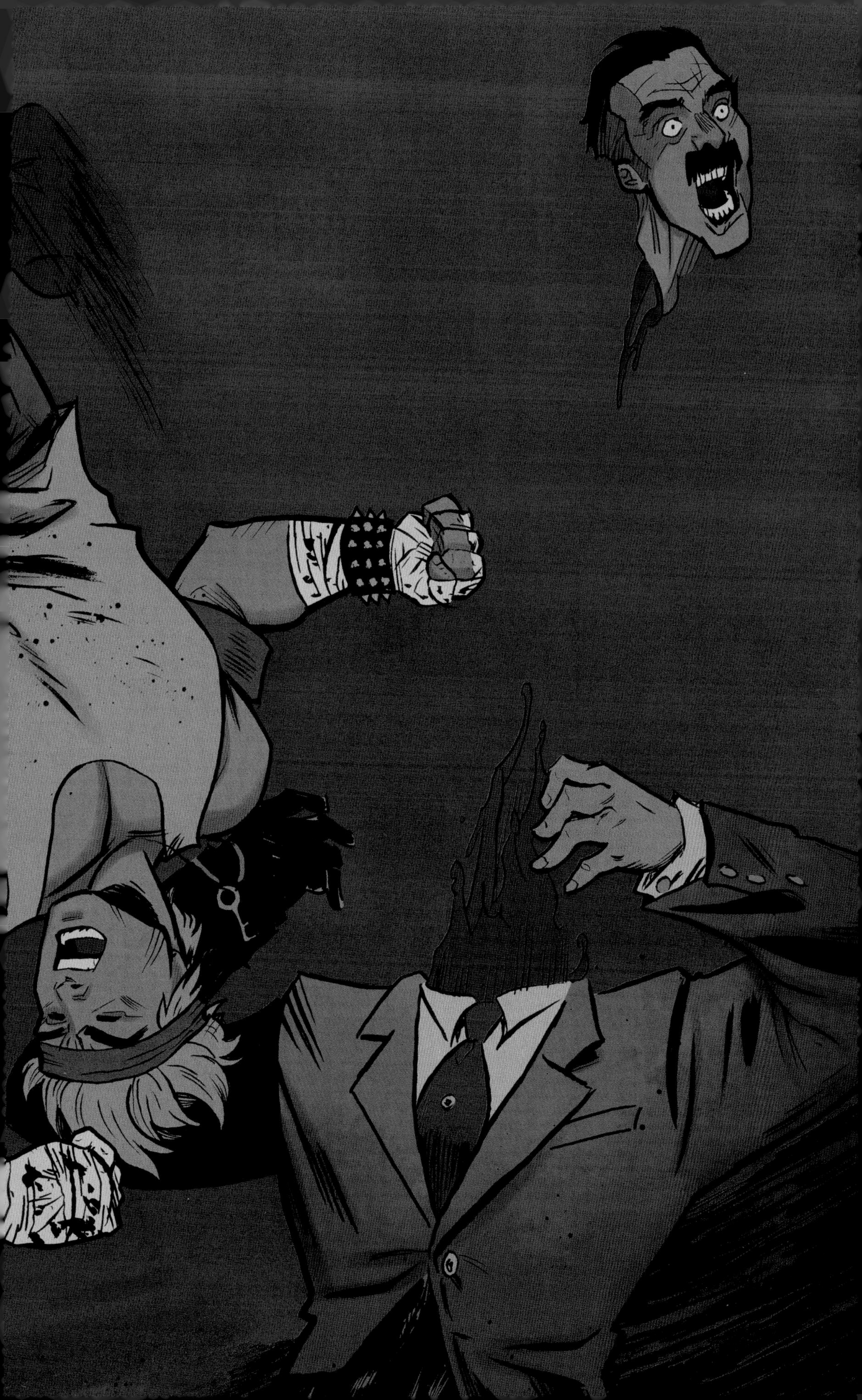

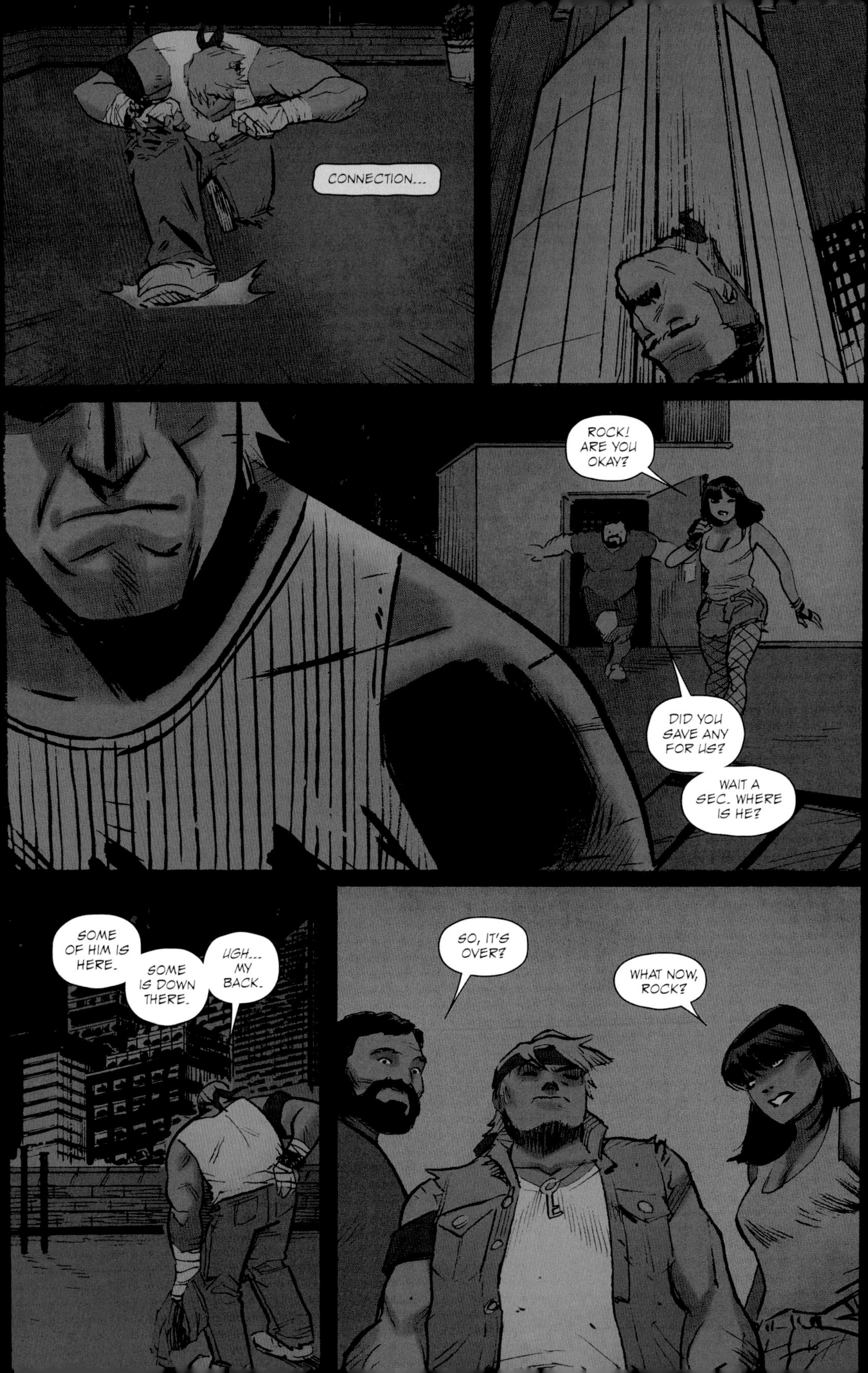
CONNECTION...
ROCK! ARE YOU OKAY?
DID YOU SAVE ANY FOR US?
WAIT A SEC. WHERE IS HE?
SOME OF HIM IS HERE.
SOME IS DOWN THERE.
UGH... MY BACK.
SO, IT'S OVER?
WHAT NOW, ROCK?

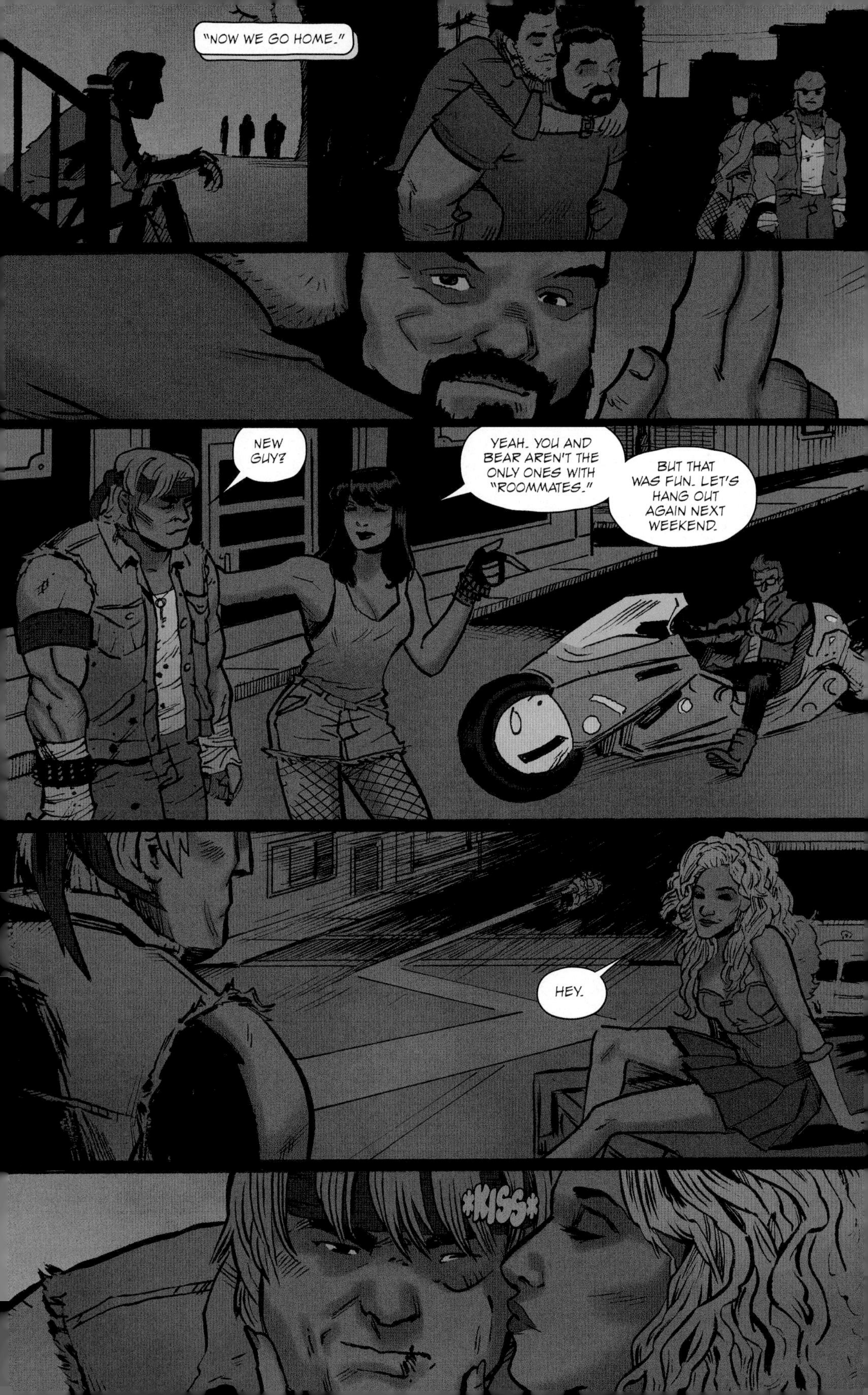
"NOW WE GO HOME."
NEW GUY?
YEAH. YOU AND BEAR AREN'T THE ONLY ONES WITH "ROOMMATES."
BUT THAT WAS FUN. LET'S HANG OUT AGAIN NEXT WEEKEND.
HEY.
KISS

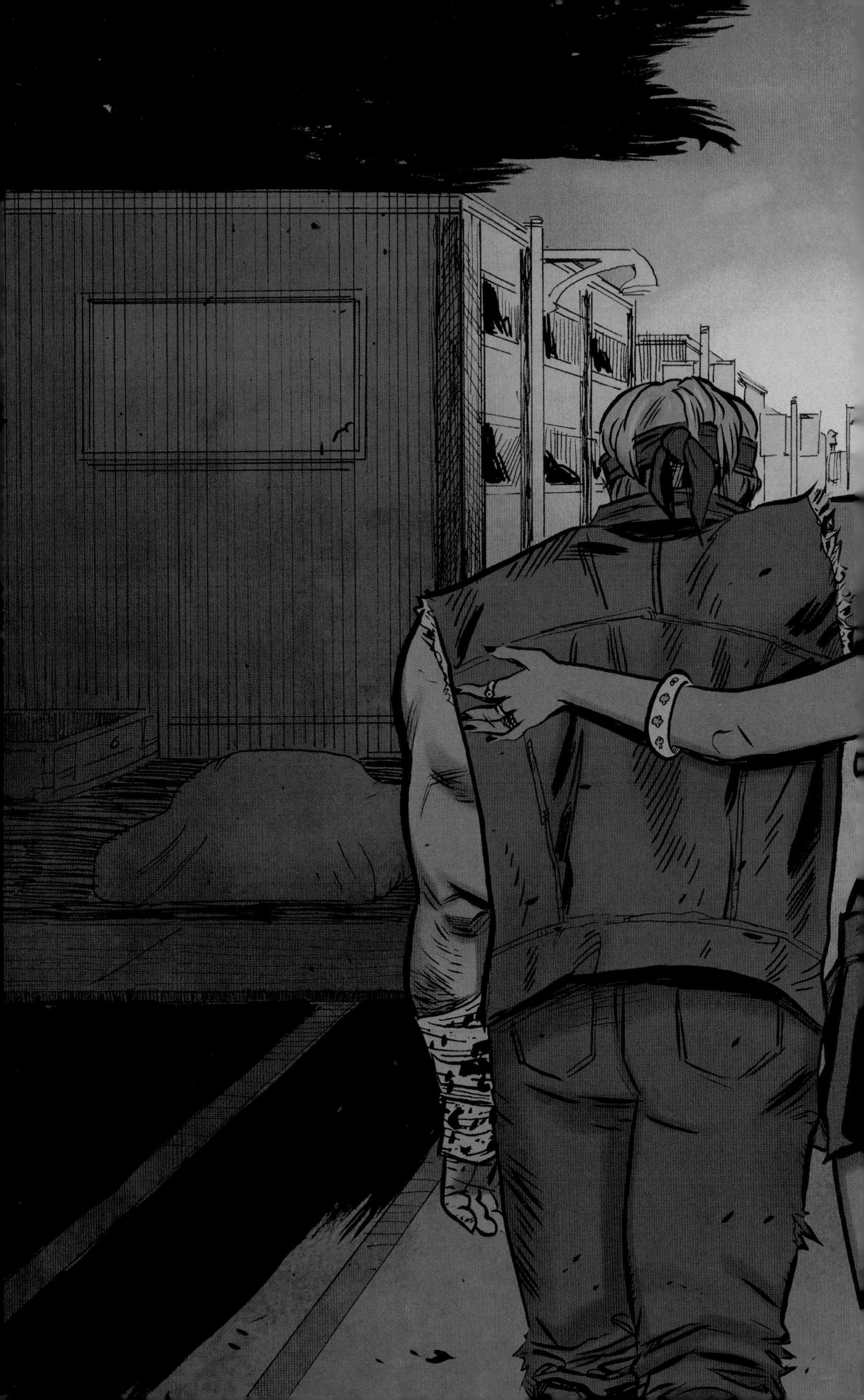

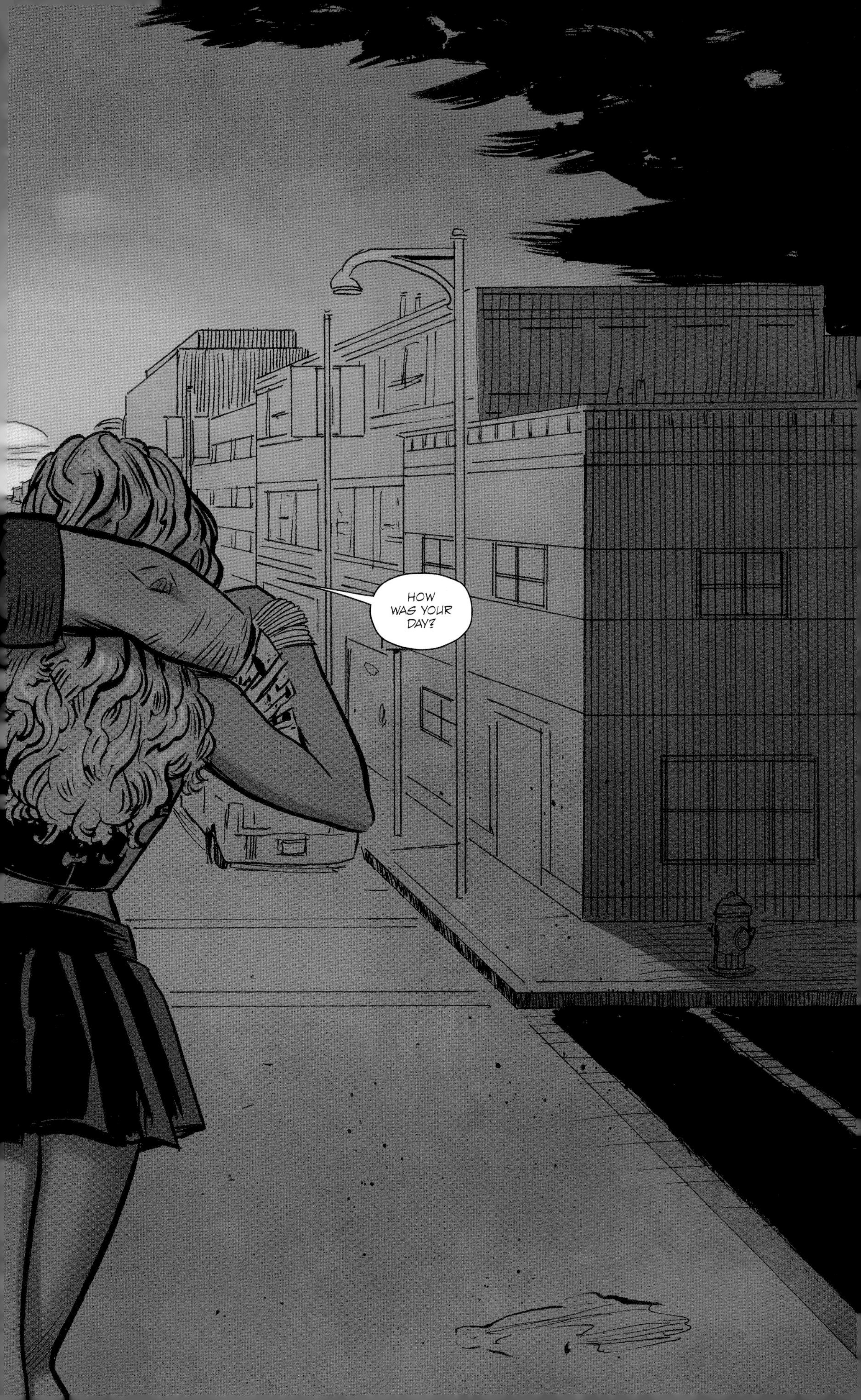
HOW WAS YOUR DAY?

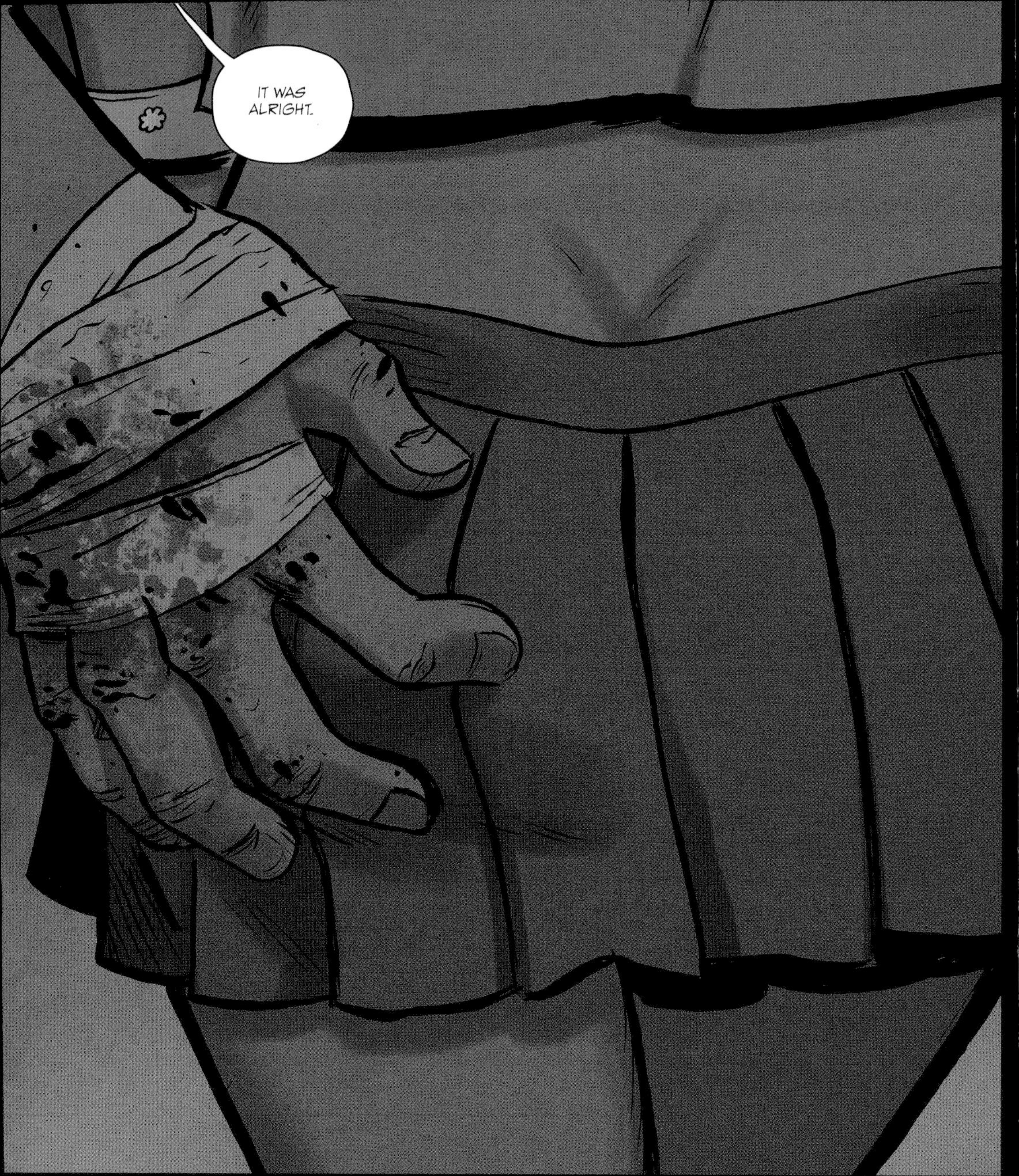
IT WAS ALRIGHT.

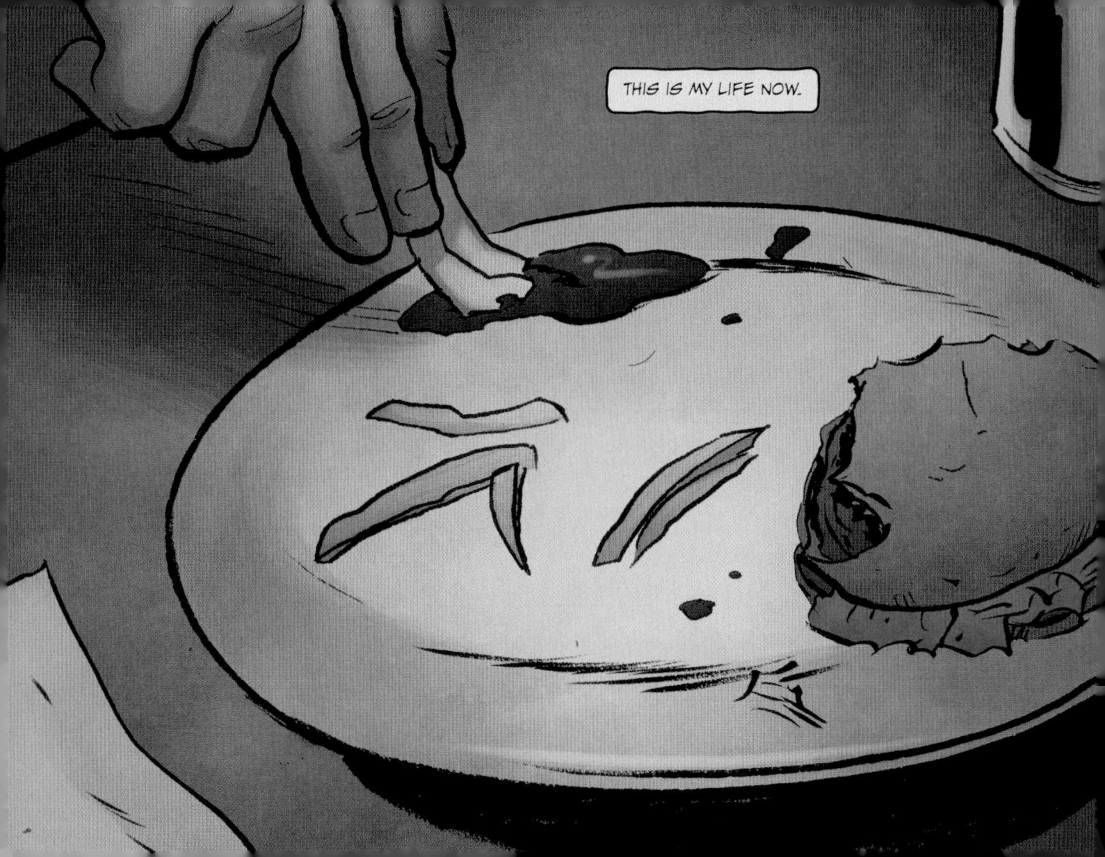
THIS IS MY LIFE NOW.

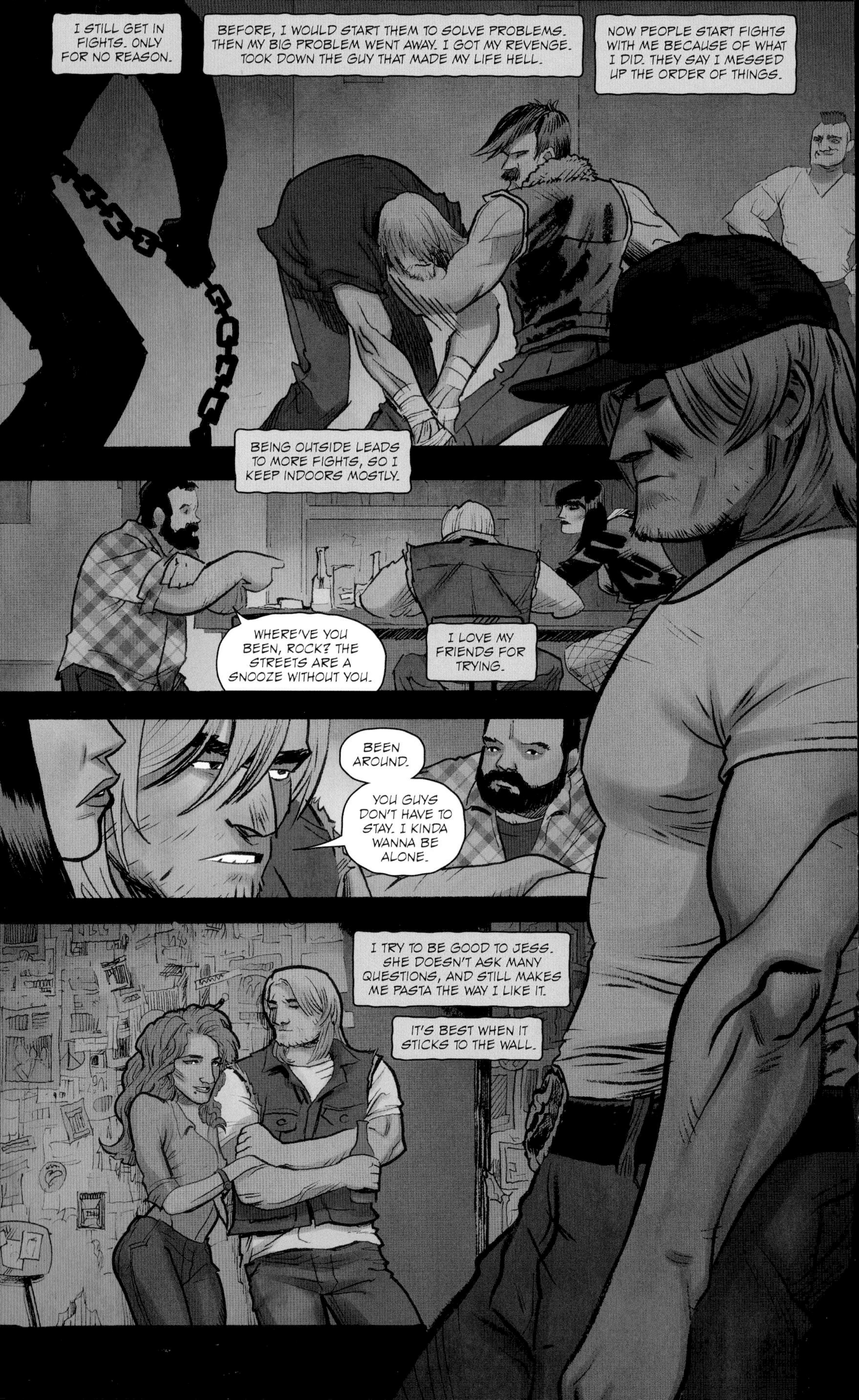
I STILL GET IN FIGHTS. ONLY FOR NO REASON.
BEFORE, I WOULD START THEM TO SOLVE PROBLEMS. THEN MY BIG PROBLEM WENT AWAY. I GOT MY REVENGE. TOOK DOWN THE GUY THAT MADE MY LIFE HELL.
NOW PEOPLE START FIGHTS WITH ME BECAUSE OF WHAT I DID. THEY SAY I MESSED UP THE ORDER OF THINGS.
BEING OUTSIDE LEADS TO MORE FIGHTS, SO I KEEP INDOORS MOSTLY.
WHERE'VE YOU BEEN, ROCK? THE STREETS ARE A SNOOZE WITHOUT YOU.
I LOVE MY FRIENDS FOR TRYING.
BEEN AROUND.
YOU GUYS DON'T HAVE TO STAY. I KINDA WANNA BE ALONE.
I TRY TO BE GOOD TO JESS. SHE DOESN'T ASK MANY QUESTIONS, AND STILL MAKES ME PASTA THE WAY I LIKE IT.
IT'S BEST WHEN IT STICKS TO THE WALL.

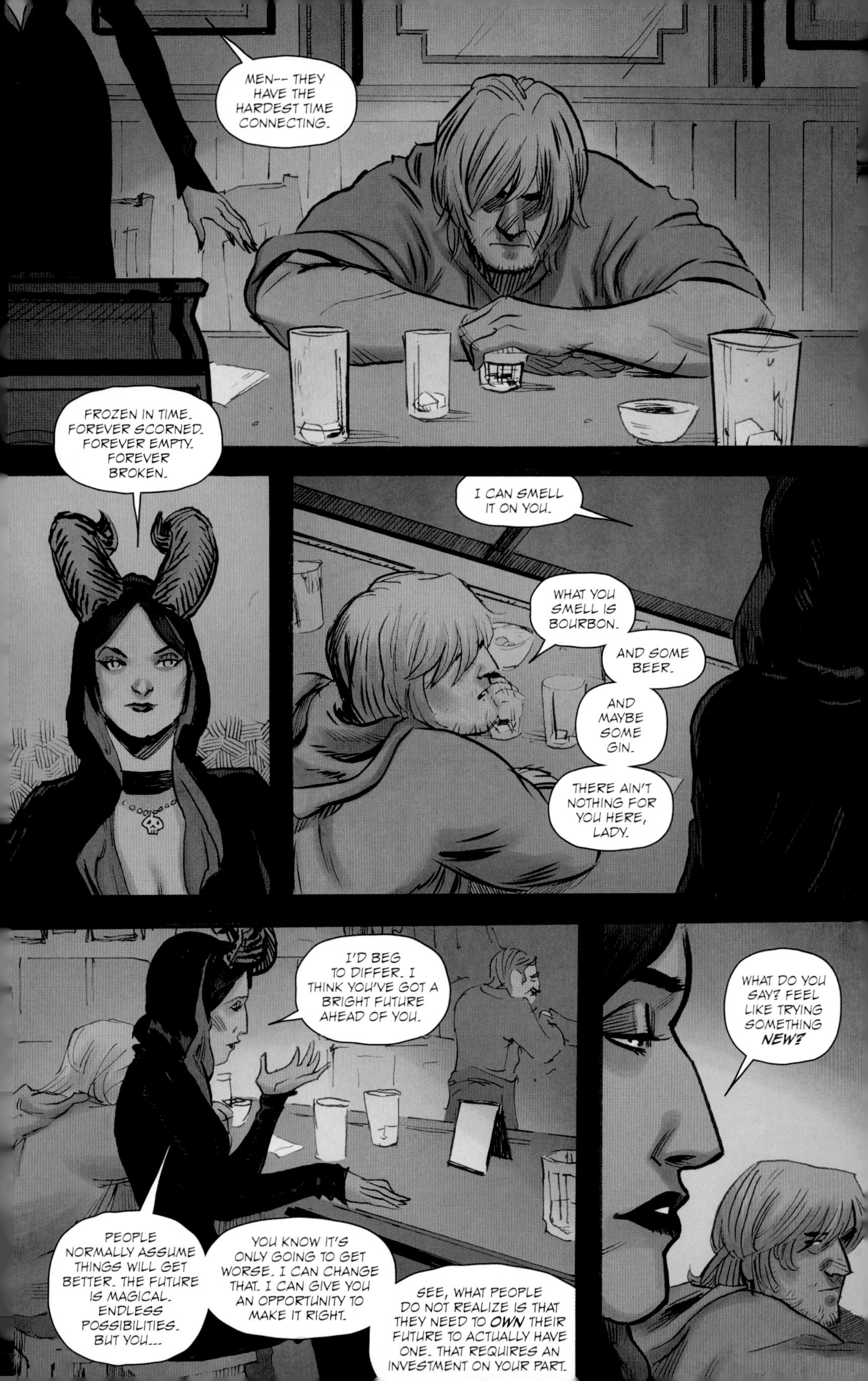
MEN-- THEY HAVE THE HARDEST TIME CONNECTING.
FROZEN IN TIME. FOREVER SCORNED. FOREVER EMPTY. FOREVER BROKEN.
I CAN SMELL IT ON YOU.
WHAT YOU SMELL IS BOURBON.
AND SOME BEER.
AND MAYBE SOME GIN.
THERE AIN'T NOTHING FOR YOU HERE, LADY.
I'D BEG TO DIFFER. I THINK YOU'VE GOT A BRIGHT FUTURE AHEAD OF YOU.
PEOPLE NORMALLY ASSUME THINGS WILL GET BETTER. THE FUTURE IS MAGICAL. ENDLESS POSSIBILITIES. BUT YOU...
YOU KNOW IT'S ONLY GOING TO GET WORSE. I CAN CHANGE THAT. I CAN GIVE YOU AN OPPORTUNITY TO MAKE IT RIGHT.
SEE, WHAT PEOPLE DO NOT REALIZE IS THAT THEY NEED TO ***OWN*** THEIR FUTURE TO ACTUALLY HAVE ONE. THAT REQUIRES AN INVESTMENT ON YOUR PART.
WHAT DO YOU SAY? FEEL LIKE TRYING SOMETHING ***NEW?***

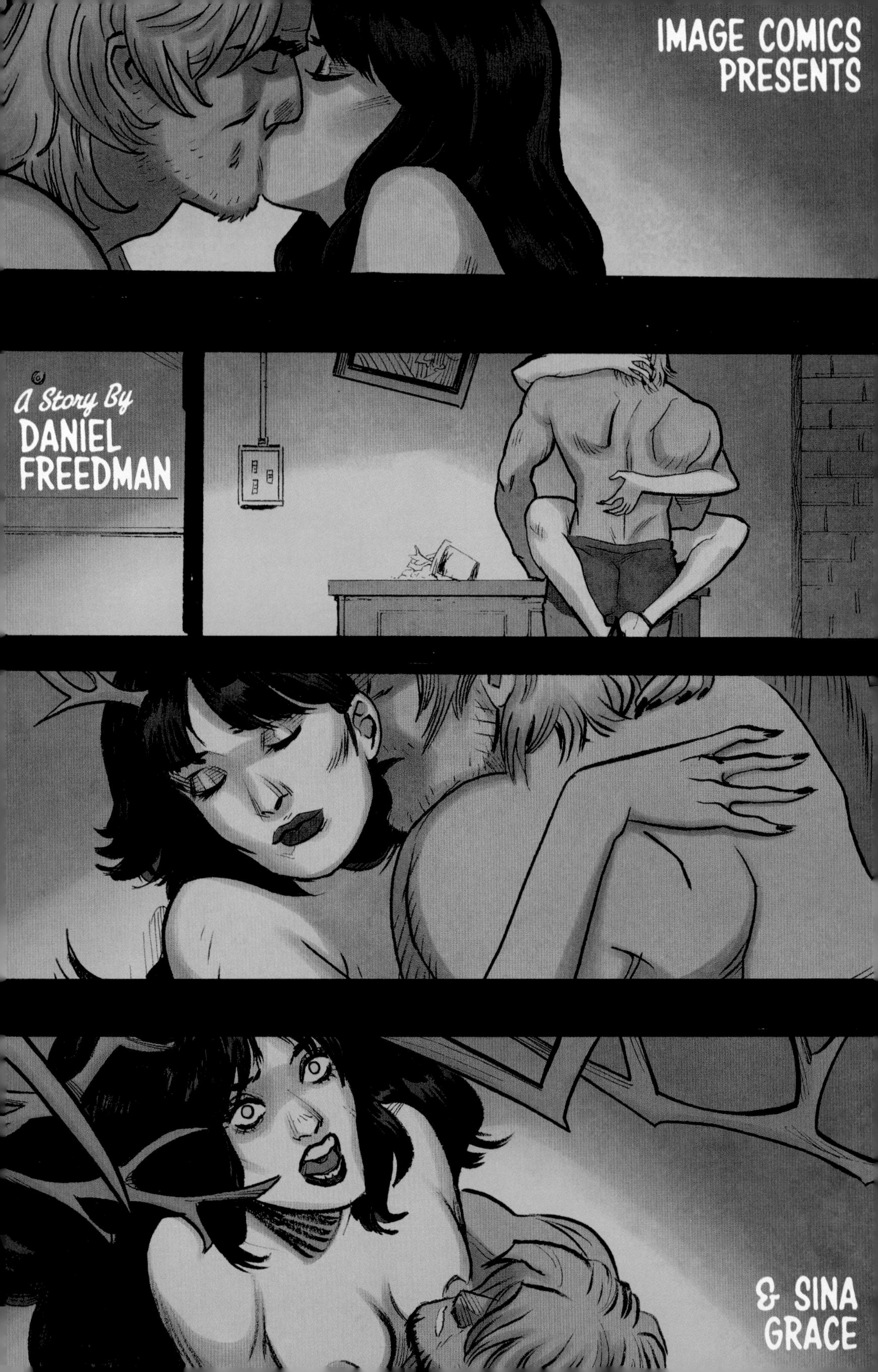
IMAGE COMICS
PRESENTS
A Story By
DANIEL
FREEDMAN
& SINA
GRACE

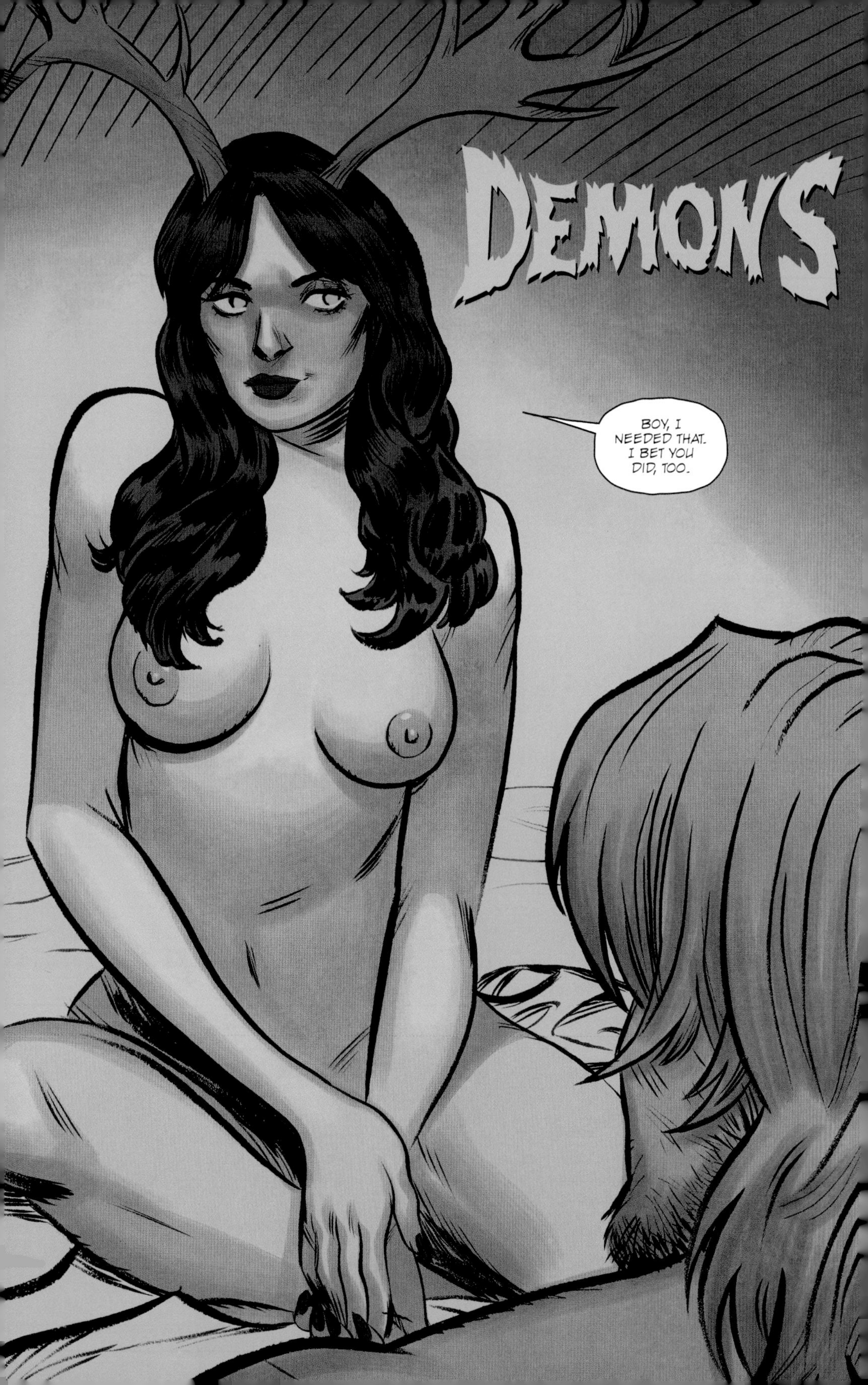
DEMONS
BOY, I NEEDED THAT. I BET YOU DID, TOO.

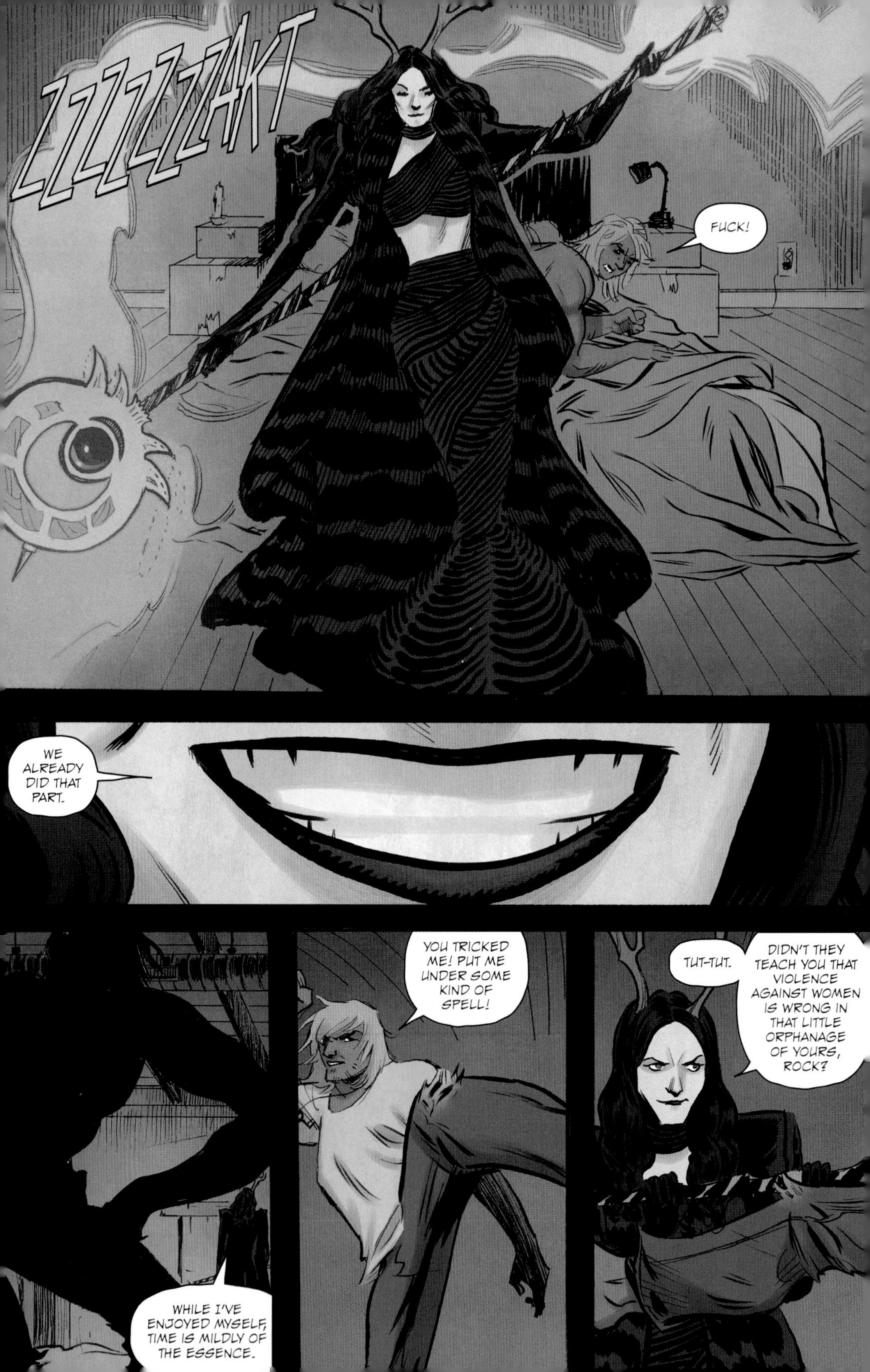
ZZZZZZZAKT
FUCK!
WE ALREADY DID THAT PART.
WHILE I'VE ENJOYED MYSELF, TIME IS MILDLY OF THE ESSENCE.
YOU TRICKED ME! PUT ME UNDER SOME KIND OF SPELL!
TUT-TUT.
DIDN'T THEY TEACH YOU THAT VIOLENCE AGAINST WOMEN IS WRONG IN THAT LITTLE ORPHANAGE OF YOURS, ROCK?

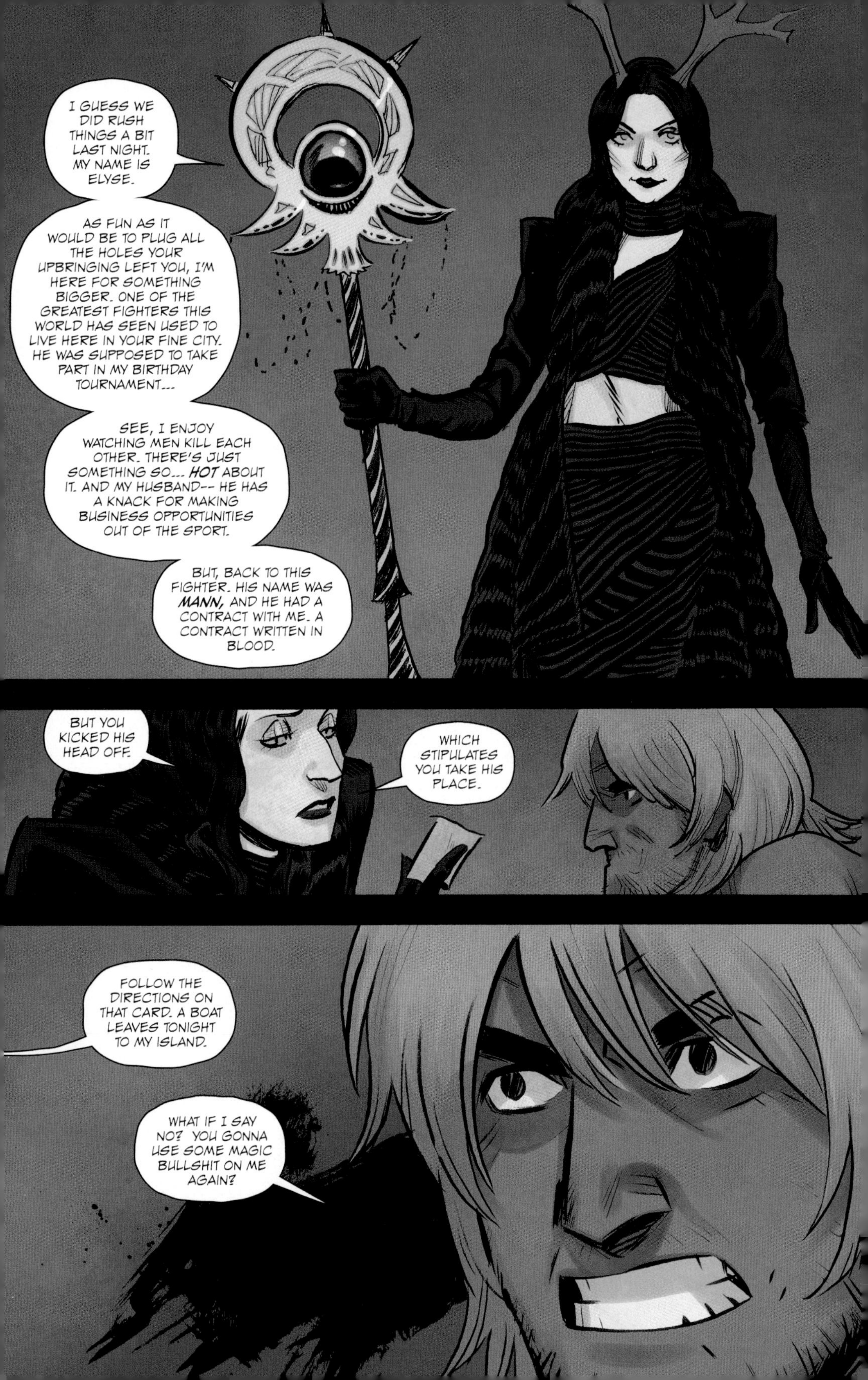
I GUESS WE DID RUSH THINGS A BIT LAST NIGHT. MY NAME IS ELYSE.
AS FUN AS IT WOULD BE TO PLUG ALL THE HOLES YOUR UPBRINGING LEFT YOU, I'M HERE FOR SOMETHING BIGGER. ONE OF THE GREATEST FIGHTERS THIS WORLD HAS SEEN USED TO LIVE HERE IN YOUR FINE CITY. HE WAS SUPPOSED TO TAKE PART IN MY BIRTHDAY TOURNAMENT...
SEE, I ENJOY WATCHING MEN KILL EACH OTHER. THERE'S JUST SOMETHING SO... HOT ABOUT IT. AND MY HUSBAND-- HE HAS A KNACK FOR MAKING BUSINESS OPPORTUNITIES OUT OF THE SPORT.
BUT, BACK TO THIS FIGHTER. HIS NAME WAS MANN, AND HE HAD A CONTRACT WITH ME. A CONTRACT WRITTEN IN BLOOD.
BUT YOU KICKED HIS HEAD OFF.
WHICH STIPULATES YOU TAKE HIS PLACE.
FOLLOW THE DIRECTIONS ON THAT CARD. A BOAT LEAVES TONIGHT TO MY ISLAND.
WHAT IF I SAY NO? YOU GONNA USE SOME MAGIC BULLSHIT ON ME AGAIN?

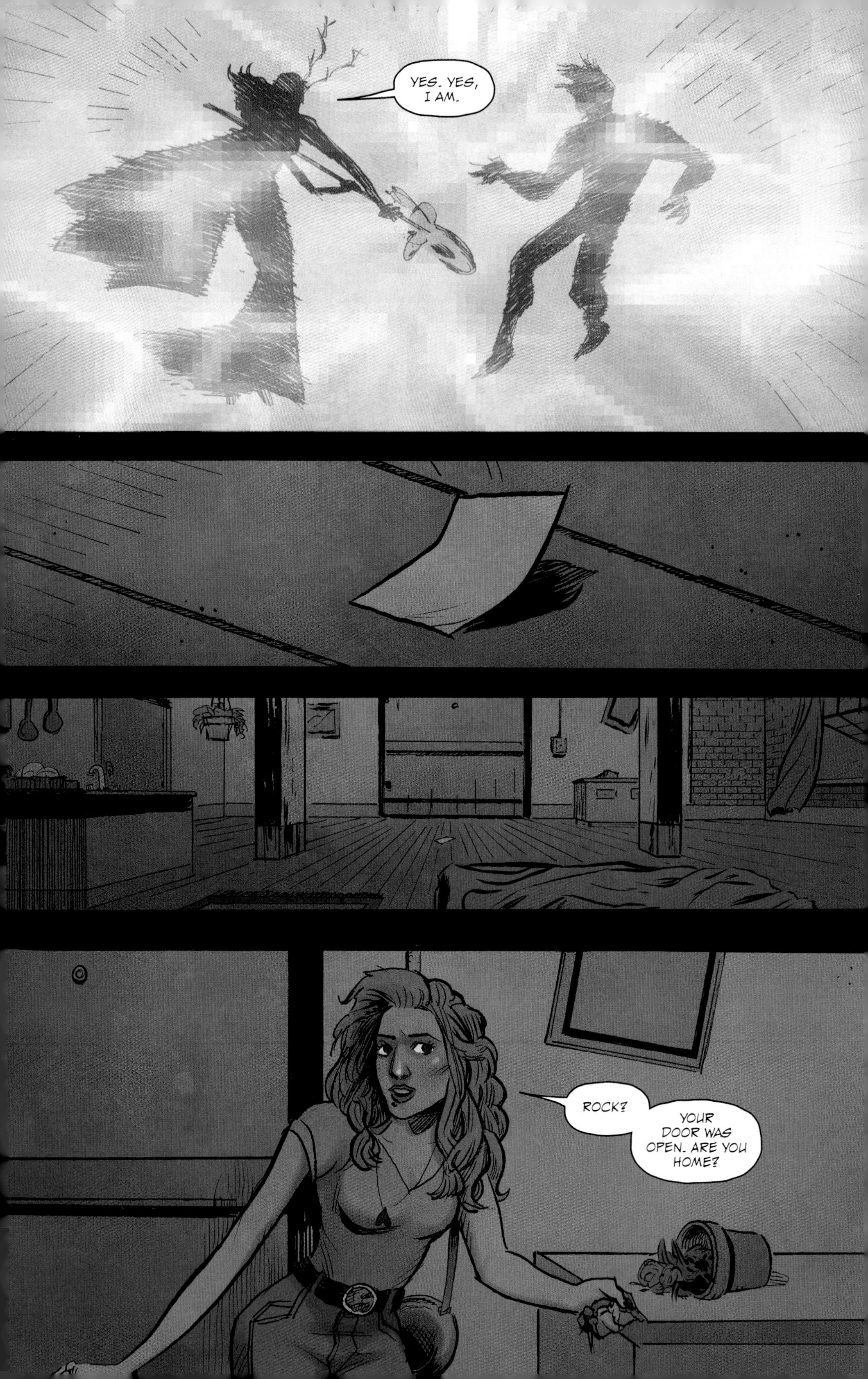
YES. YES, I AM.
ROCK?
YOUR DOOR WAS OPEN. ARE YOU HOME?

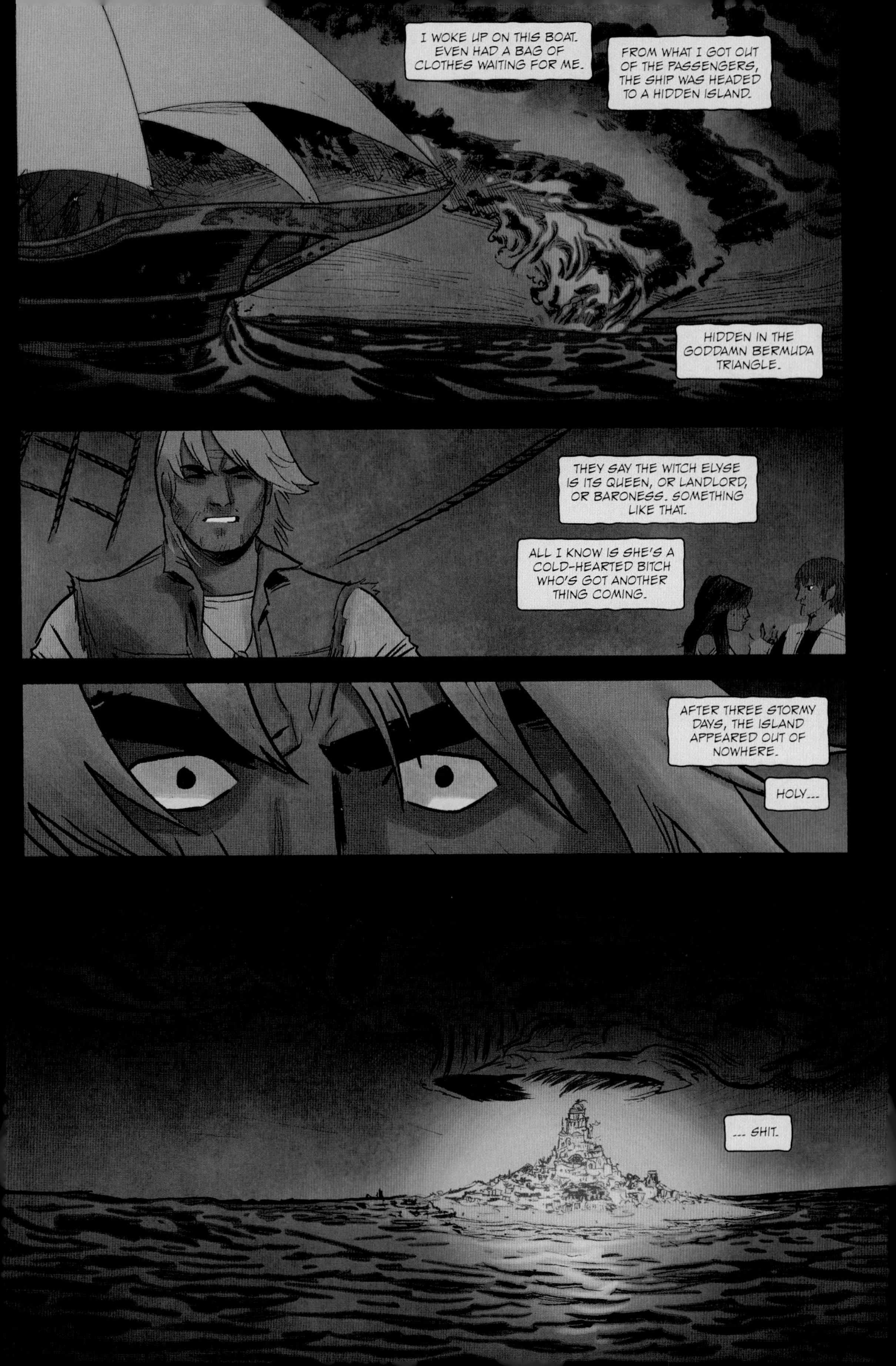
I WOKE UP ON THIS BOAT. EVEN HAD A BAG OF CLOTHES WAITING FOR ME.
FROM WHAT I GOT OUT OF THE PASSENGERS, THE SHIP WAS HEADED TO A HIDDEN ISLAND.
HIDDEN IN THE GODDAMN BERMUDA TRIANGLE.
THEY SAY THE WITCH ELYSE IS ITS QUEEN, OR LANDLORD, OR BARONESS. SOMETHING LIKE THAT.
ALL I KNOW IS SHE'S A COLD-HEARTED BITCH WHO'S GOT ANOTHER THING COMING.
AFTER THREE STORMY DAYS, THE ISLAND APPEARED OUT OF NOWHERE.
HOLY...
... SHIT.

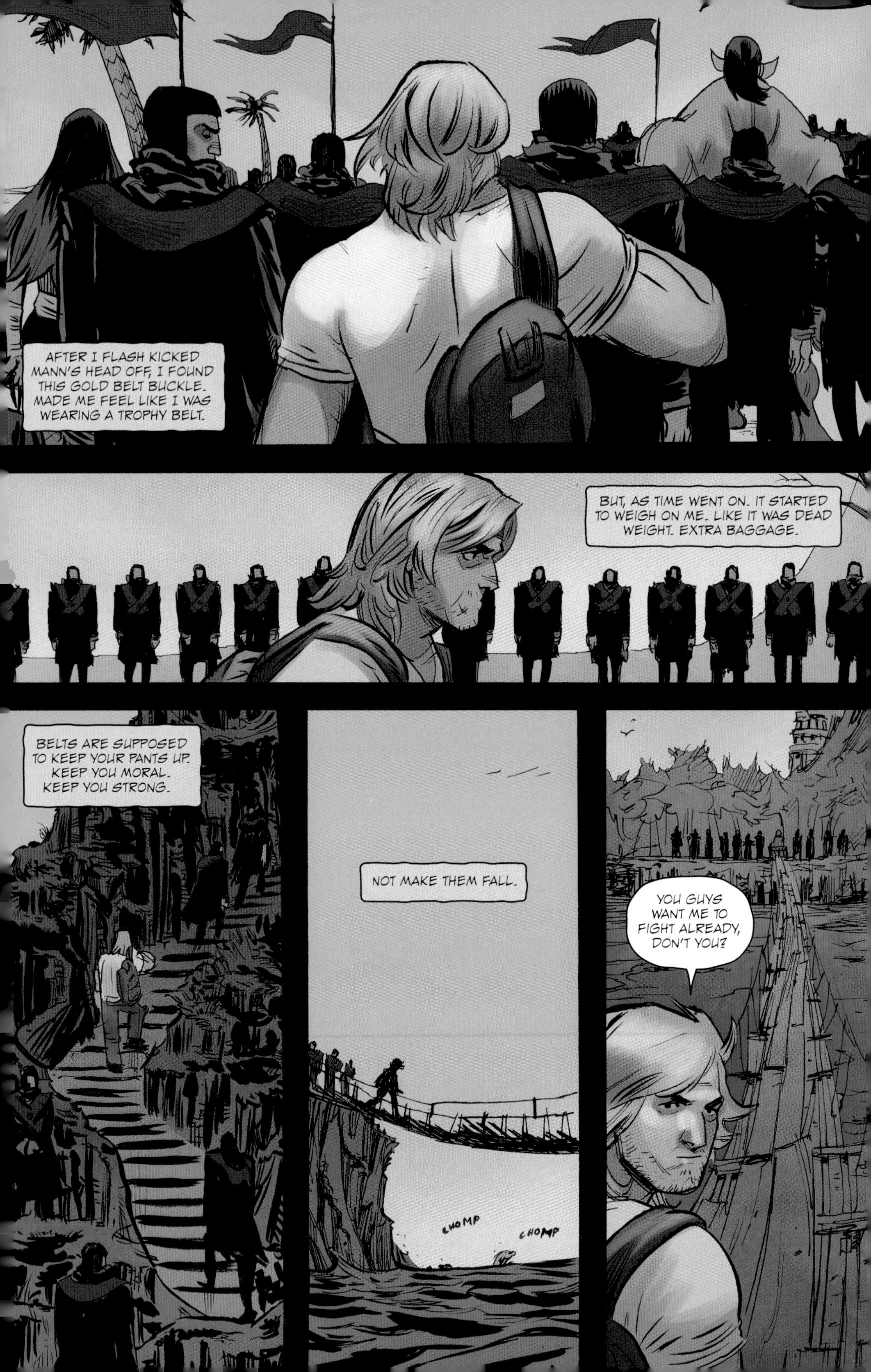
AFTER I FLASH KICKED MANN'S HEAD OFF, I FOUND THIS GOLD BELT BUCKLE. MADE ME FEEL LIKE I WAS WEARING A TROPHY BELT.
BUT, AS TIME WENT ON. IT STARTED TO WEIGH ON ME. LIKE IT WAS DEAD WEIGHT. EXTRA BAGGAGE.
BELTS ARE SUPPOSED TO KEEP YOUR PANTS UP. KEEP YOU MORAL. KEEP YOU STRONG.
NOT MAKE THEM FALL.
CHOMP
CHOMP
YOU GUYS WANT ME TO FIGHT ALREADY, DON'T YOU?

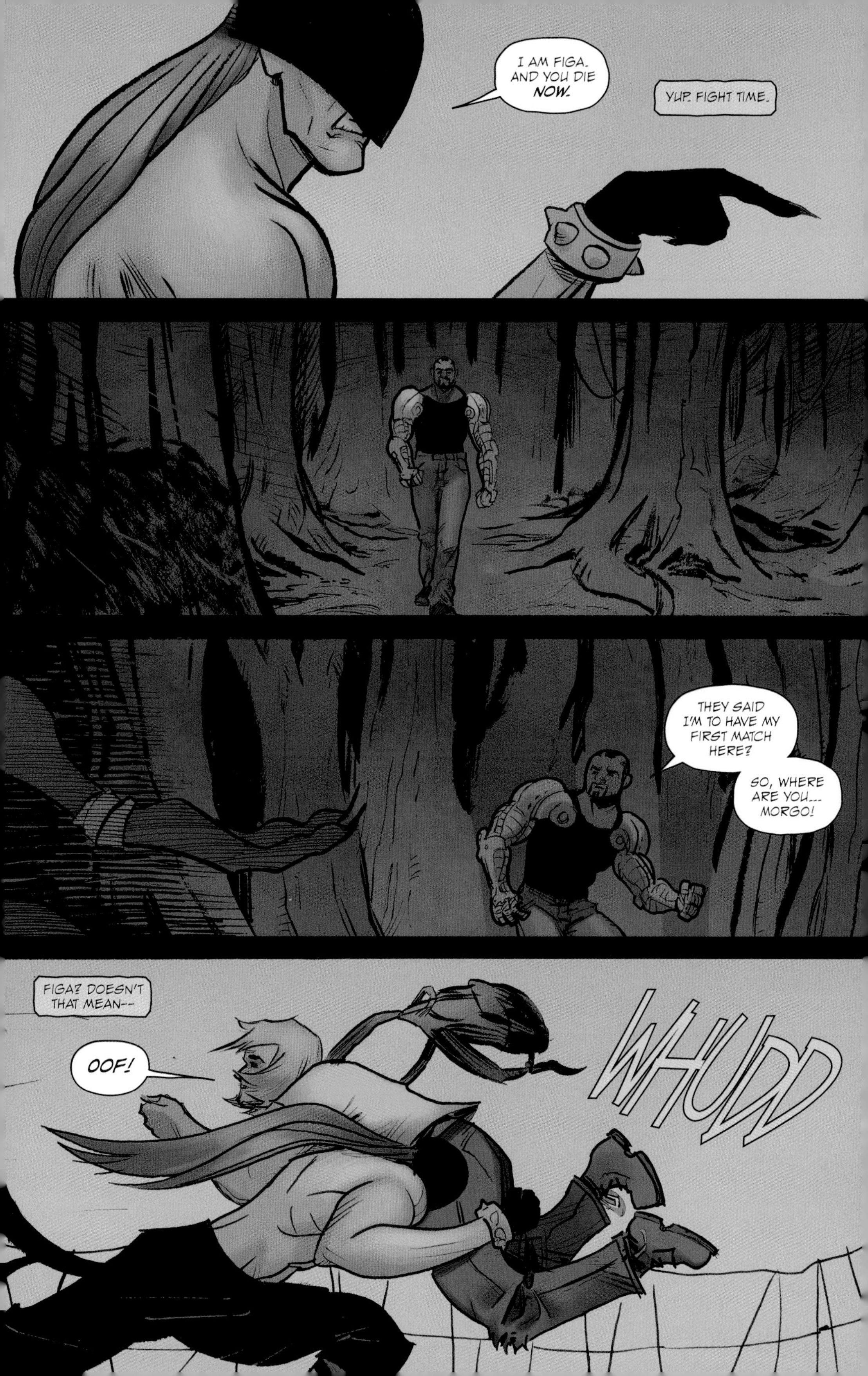
I AM FIGA. AND YOU DIE NOW.
YUP. FIGHT TIME.
THEY SAID I'M TO HAVE MY FIRST MATCH HERE?
SO, WHERE ARE YOU... MORGO!
FIGA? DOESN'T THAT MEAN--
OOF!
WHUDD

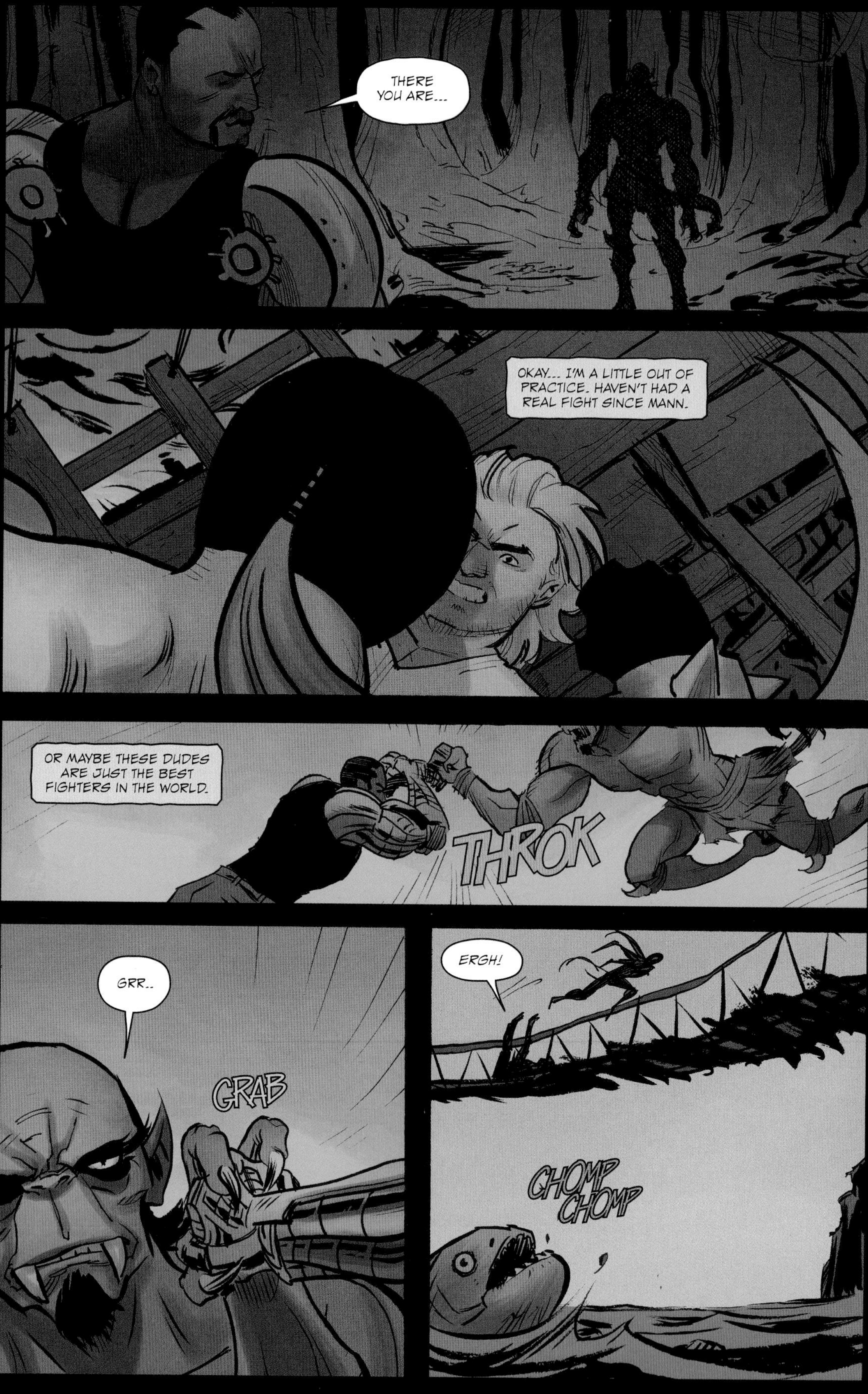
THERE YOU ARE...
OKAY... I'M A LITTLE OUT OF PRACTICE. HAVEN'T HAD A REAL FIGHT SINCE MANN.
OR MAYBE THESE DUDES ARE JUST THE BEST FIGHTERS IN THE WORLD.
THROK
GRR..
GRAB
ERGH!
CHOMP CHOMP

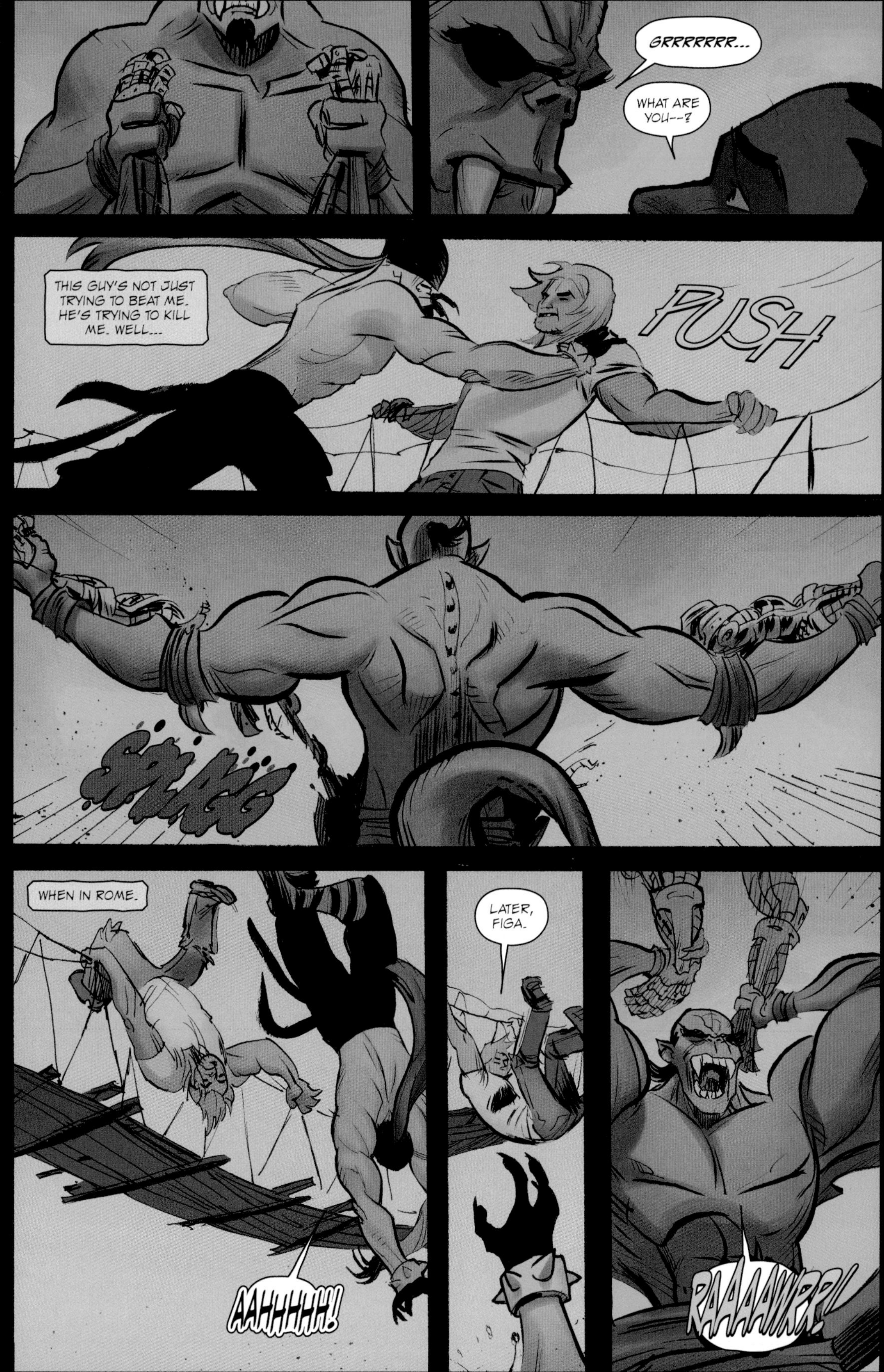
GRRRRRRR...
WHAT ARE YOU--?
THIS GUY'S NOT JUST TRYING TO BEAT ME. HE'S TRYING TO KILL ME. WELL...
PUSH
SPLAGG
WHEN IN ROME.
AAHHHHH!
LATER, FIGA.
RAAAAWRR!!

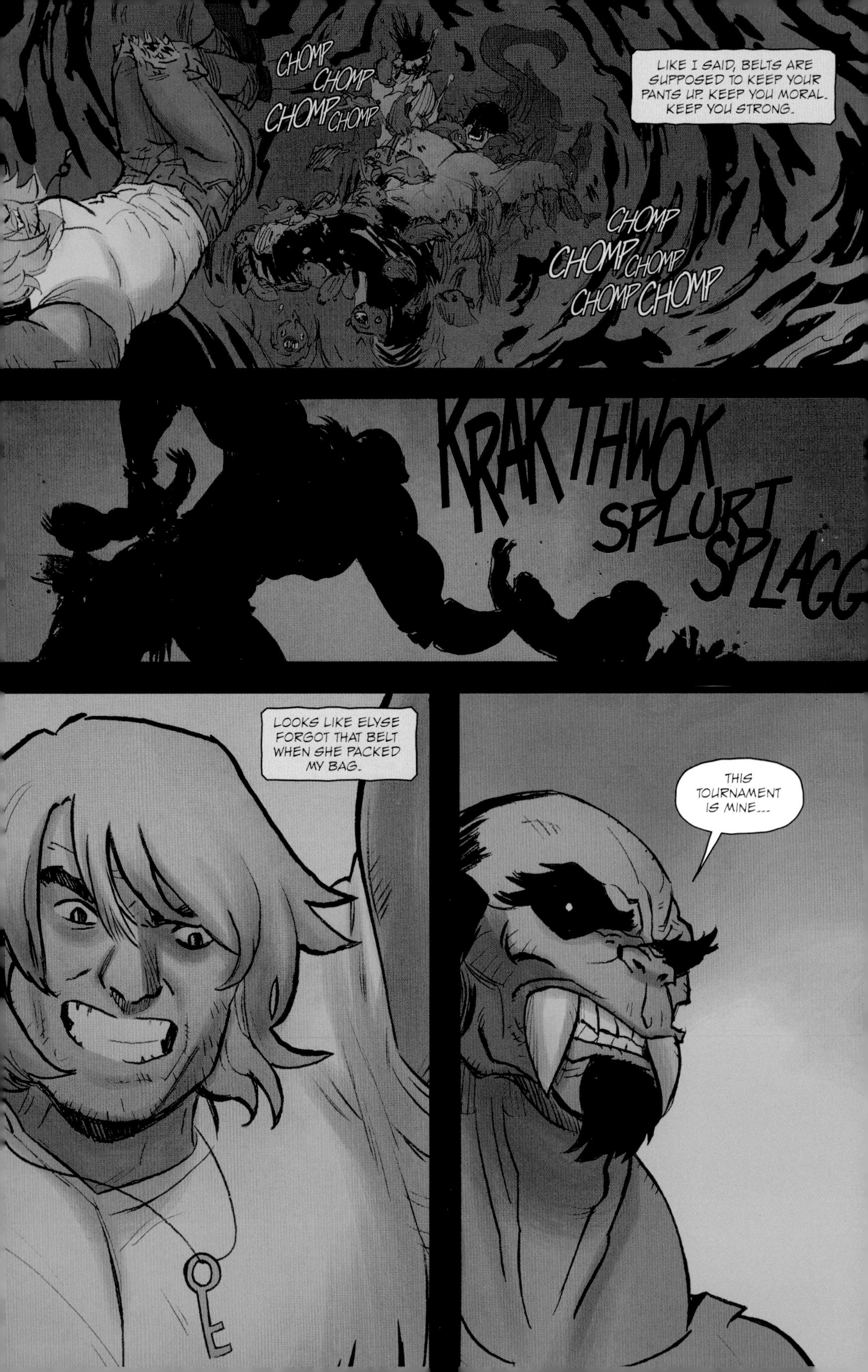
CHOMP CHOMP CHOMP CHOMP
LIKE I SAID, BELTS ARE SUPPOSED TO KEEP YOUR PANTS UP. KEEP YOU MORAL. KEEP YOU STRONG.
CHOMP CHOMP CHOMP CHOMP CHOMP
KRAK THWOK
SPLURT
SPLAGG
LOOKS LIKE ELYSE FORGOT THAT BELT WHEN SHE PACKED MY BAG.
THIS TOURNAMENT IS MINE...

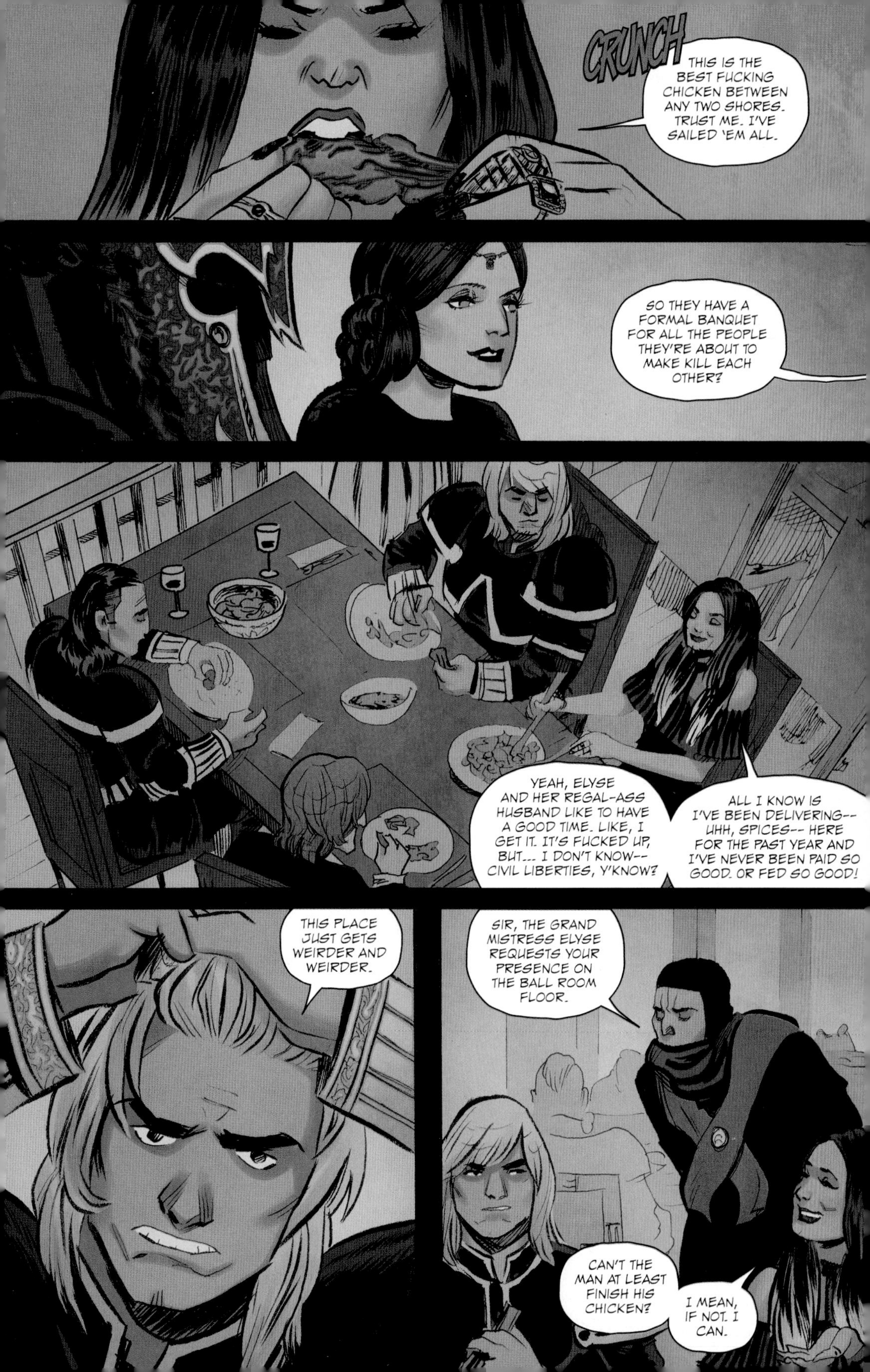
CRUNCH
THIS IS THE BEST FUCKING CHICKEN BETWEEN ANY TWO SHORES. TRUST ME. I'VE SAILED 'EM ALL.
SO THEY HAVE A FORMAL BANQUET FOR ALL THE PEOPLE THEY'RE ABOUT TO MAKE KILL EACH OTHER?
ALL I KNOW IS I'VE BEEN DELIVERING-- UHH, SPICES-- HERE FOR THE PAST YEAR AND I'VE NEVER BEEN PAID SO GOOD. OR FED SO GOOD!
YEAH, ELYSE AND HER REGAL-ASS HUSBAND LIKE TO HAVE A GOOD TIME. LIKE, I GET IT. IT'S FUCKED UP, BUT... I DON'T KNOW-- CIVIL LIBERTIES, Y'KNOW?
THIS PLACE JUST GETS WEIRDER AND WEIRDER.
SIR, THE GRAND MISTRESS ELYSE REQUESTS YOUR PRESENCE ON THE BALL ROOM FLOOR.
CAN'T THE MAN AT LEAST FINISH HIS CHICKEN?
I MEAN, IF NOT, I CAN.

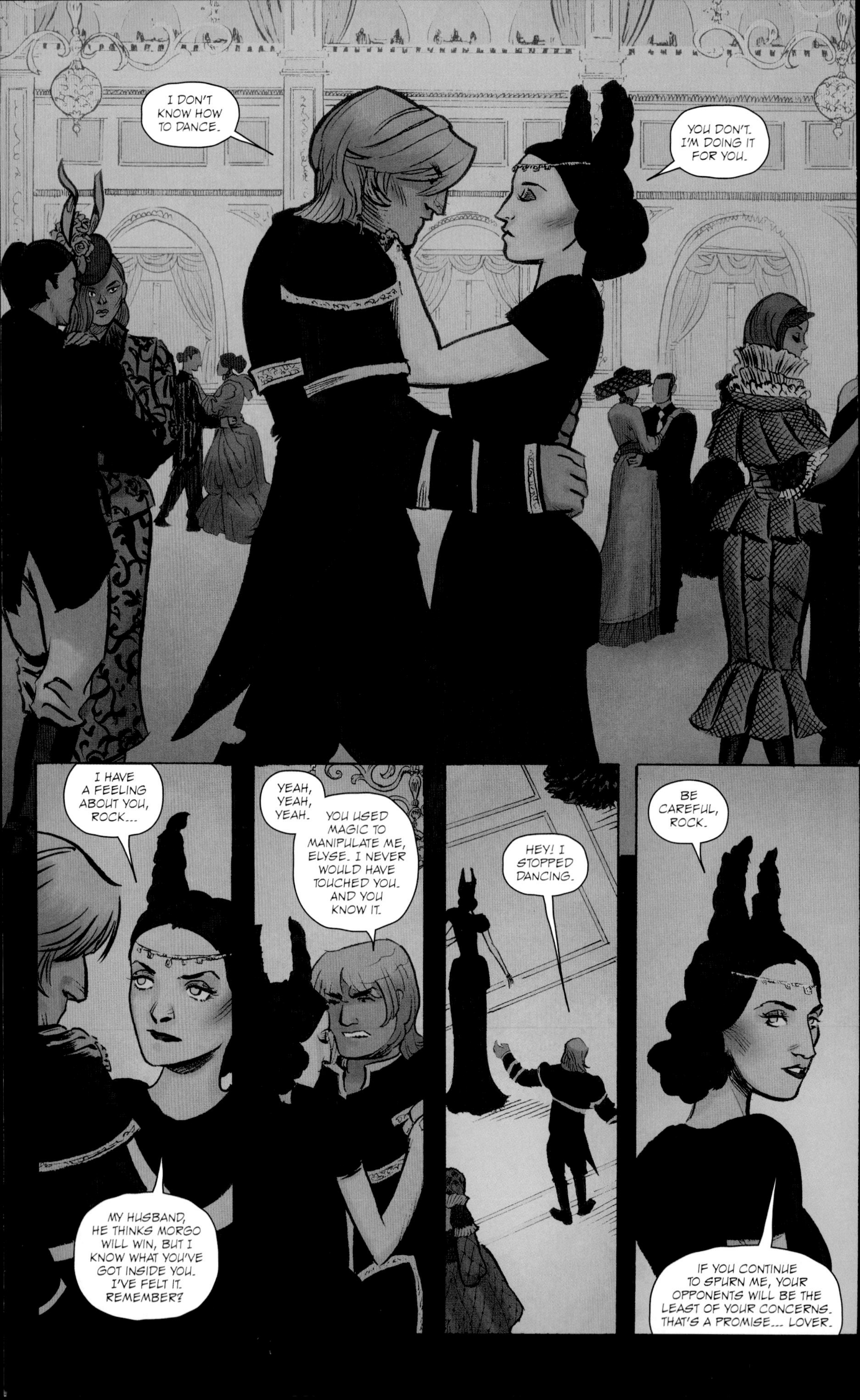
I DON'T KNOW HOW TO DANCE.
YOU DON'T. I'M DOING IT FOR YOU.
I HAVE A FEELING ABOUT YOU, ROCK...
MY HUSBAND, HE THINKS MORGO WILL WIN, BUT I KNOW WHAT YOU'VE GOT INSIDE YOU. I'VE FELT IT. REMEMBER?
YEAH, YEAH, YEAH.
YOU USED MAGIC TO MANIPULATE ME, ELYSE. I NEVER WOULD HAVE TOUCHED YOU. AND YOU KNOW IT.
HEY! I STOPPED DANCING.
BE CAREFUL, ROCK.
IF YOU CONTINUE TO SPURN ME, YOUR OPPONENTS WILL BE THE LEAST OF YOUR CONCERNS. THAT'S A PROMISE... LOVER.

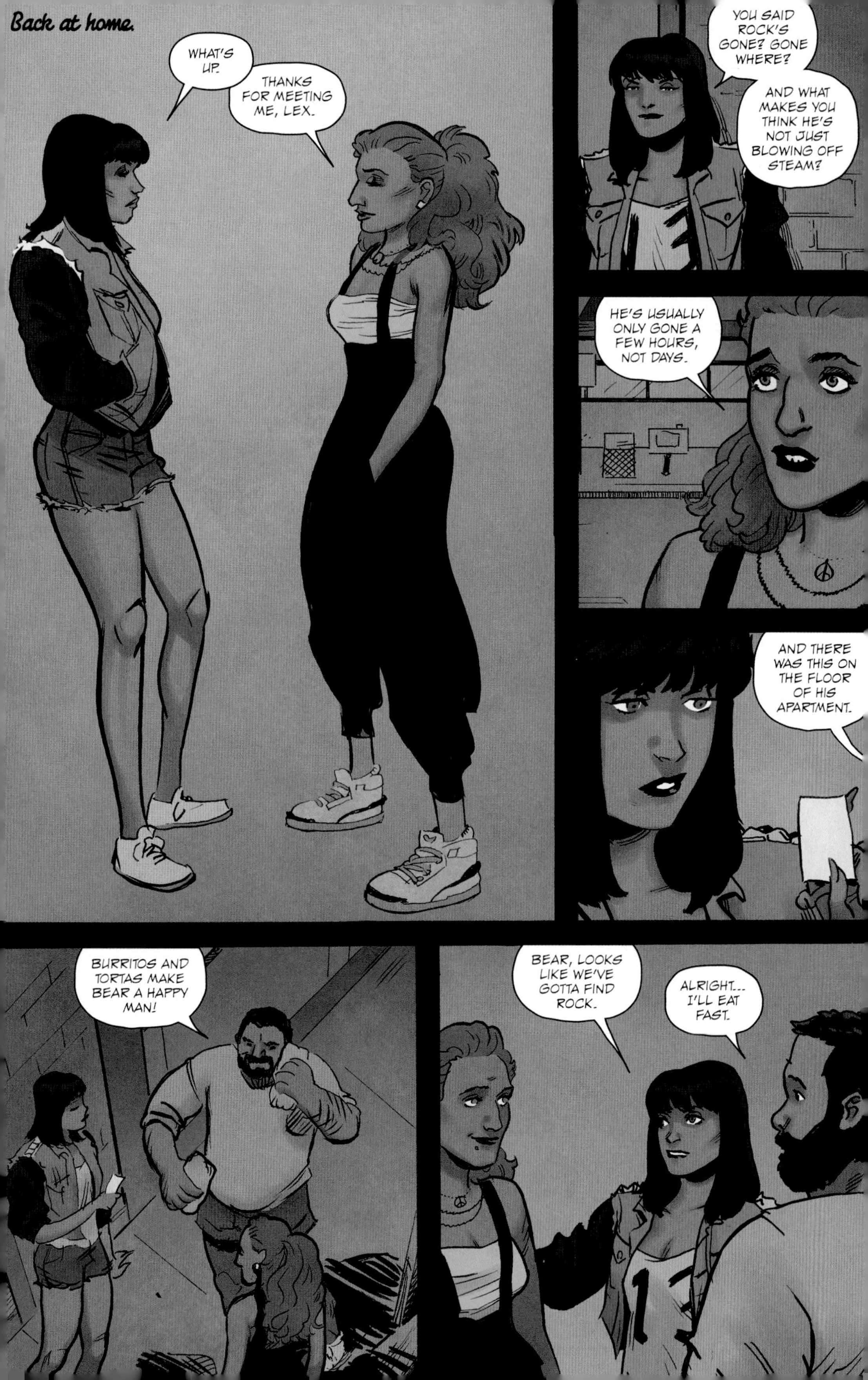
Back at home.
WHAT'S UP.
THANKS FOR MEETING ME, LEX.
YOU SAID ROCK'S GONE? GONE WHERE?
AND WHAT MAKES YOU THINK HE'S NOT JUST BLOWING OFF STEAM?
HE'S USUALLY ONLY GONE A FEW HOURS, NOT DAYS.
AND THERE WAS THIS ON THE FLOOR OF HIS APARTMENT.
BURRITOS AND TORTAS MAKE BEAR A HAPPY MAN!
BEAR, LOOKS LIKE WE'VE GOTTA FIND ROCK.
ALRIGHT... I'LL EAT FAST.

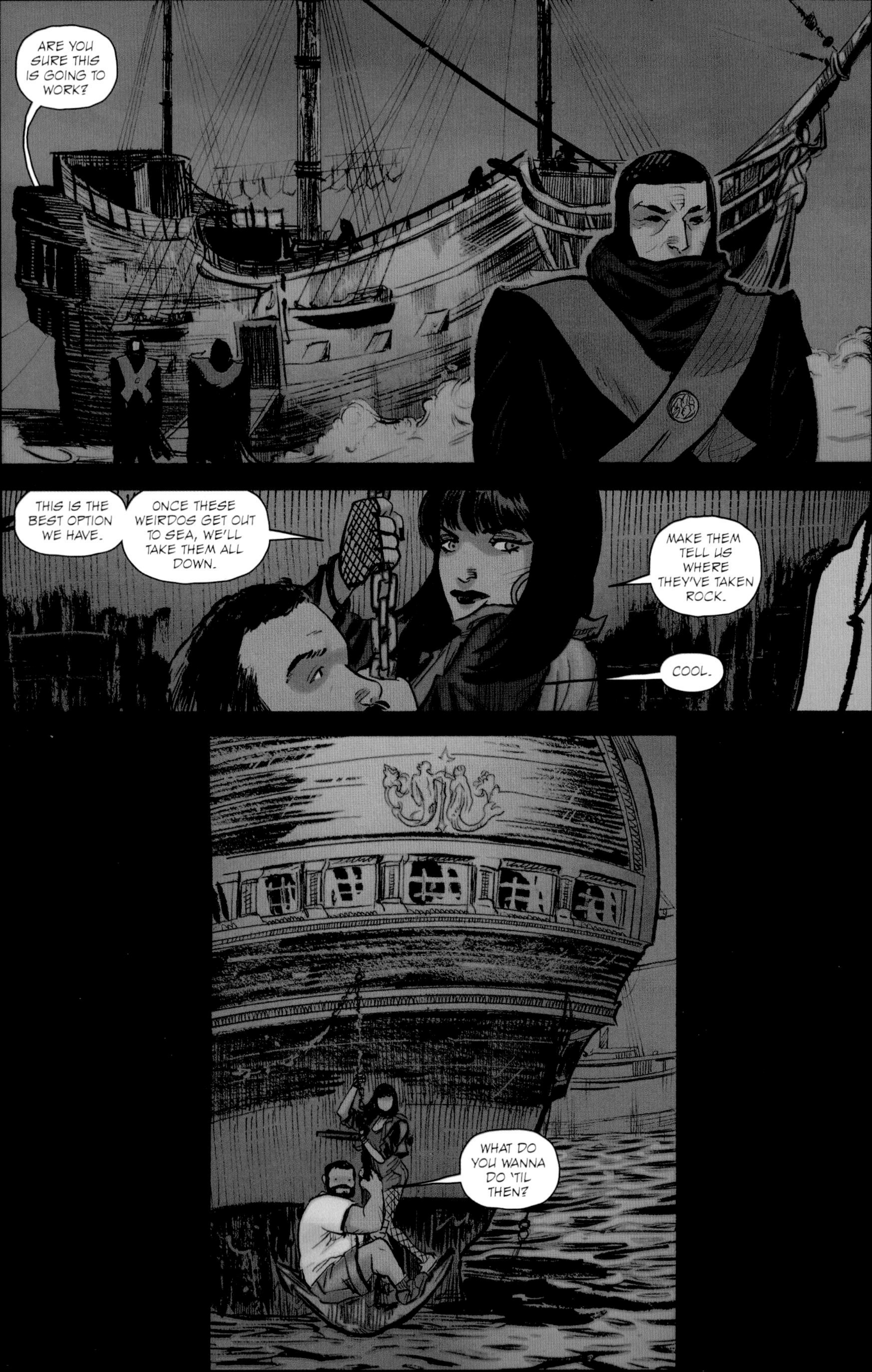
ARE YOU SURE THIS IS GOING TO WORK?
THIS IS THE BEST OPTION WE HAVE.
ONCE THESE WEIRDOS GET OUT TO SEA, WE'LL TAKE THEM ALL DOWN.
MAKE THEM TELL US WHERE THEY'VE TAKEN ROCK.
COOL.
WHAT DO YOU WANNA DO 'TIL THEN?

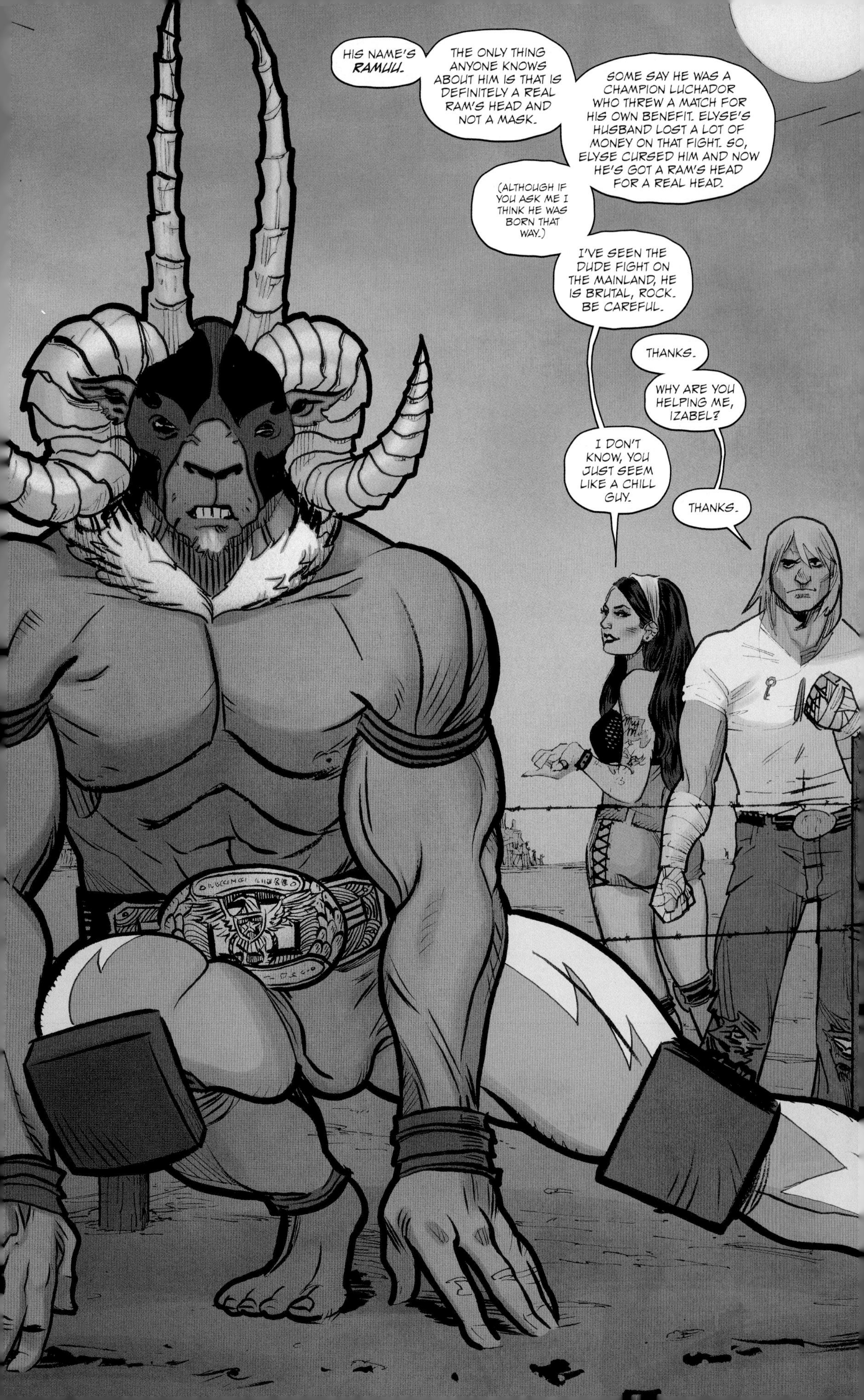
HIS NAME'S RAMUU.
THE ONLY THING ANYONE KNOWS ABOUT HIM IS THAT IS DEFINITELY A REAL RAM'S HEAD AND NOT A MASK.
SOME SAY HE WAS A CHAMPION LUCHADOR WHO THREW A MATCH FOR HIS OWN BENEFIT. ELYSE'S HUSBAND LOST A LOT OF MONEY ON THAT FIGHT. SO, ELYSE CURSED HIM AND NOW HE'S GOT A RAM'S HEAD FOR A REAL HEAD.
(ALTHOUGH IF YOU ASK ME I THINK HE WAS BORN THAT WAY.)
I'VE SEEN THE DUDE FIGHT ON THE MAINLAND, HE IS BRUTAL, ROCK. BE CAREFUL.
THANKS.
WHY ARE YOU HELPING ME, IZABEL?
I DON'T KNOW, YOU JUST SEEM LIKE A CHILL GUY.
THANKS.

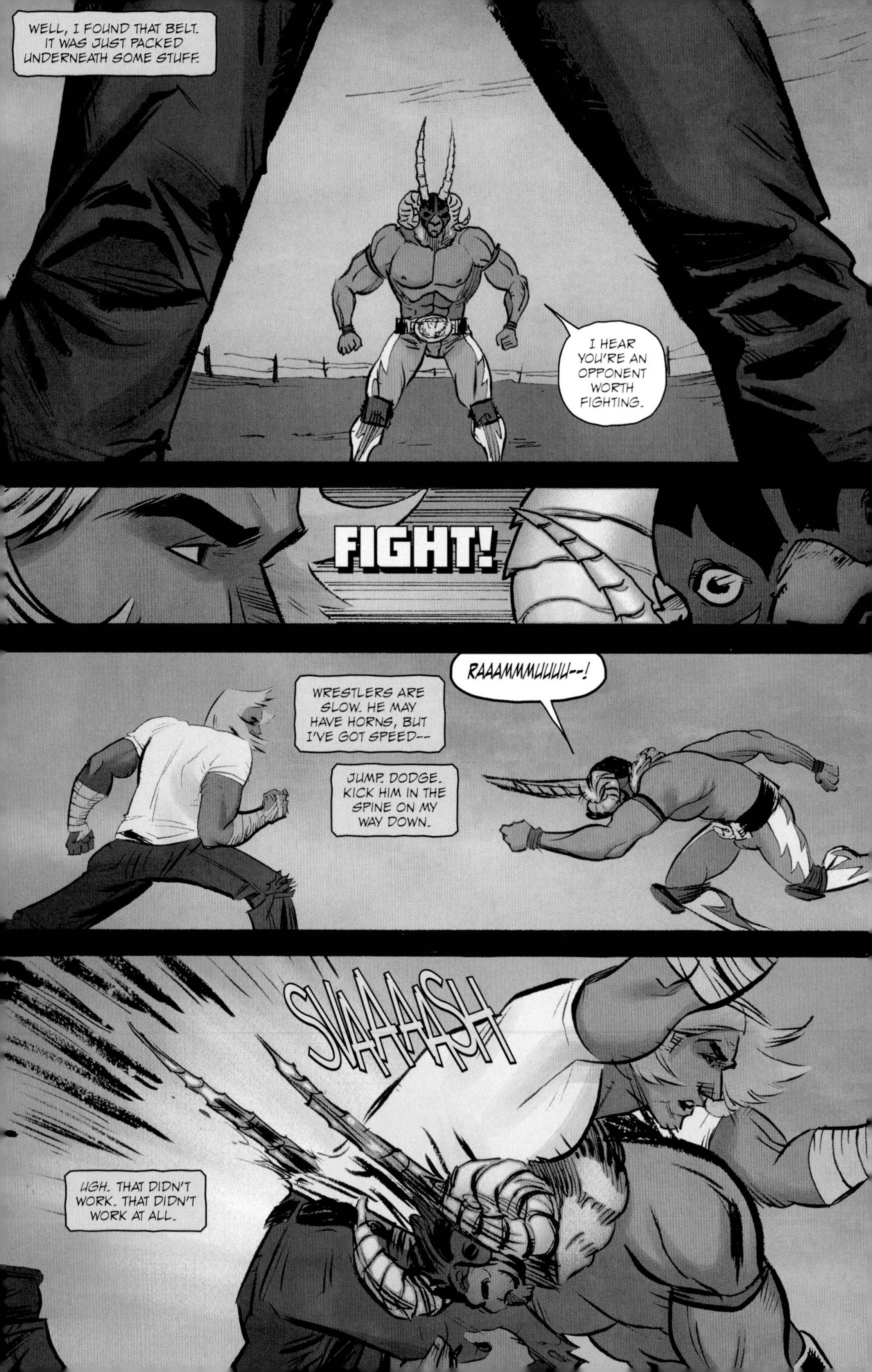
WELL, I FOUND THAT BELT. IT WAS JUST PACKED UNDERNEATH SOME STUFF.
I HEAR YOU'RE AN OPPONENT WORTH FIGHTING.
FIGHT!
WRESTLERS ARE SLOW. HE MAY HAVE HORNS, BUT I'VE GOT SPEED--
RAAAMMMUUUU--!
JUMP. DODGE. KICK HIM IN THE SPINE ON MY WAY DOWN.
SWAAAASH
UGH. THAT DIDN'T WORK. THAT DIDN'T WORK AT ALL.

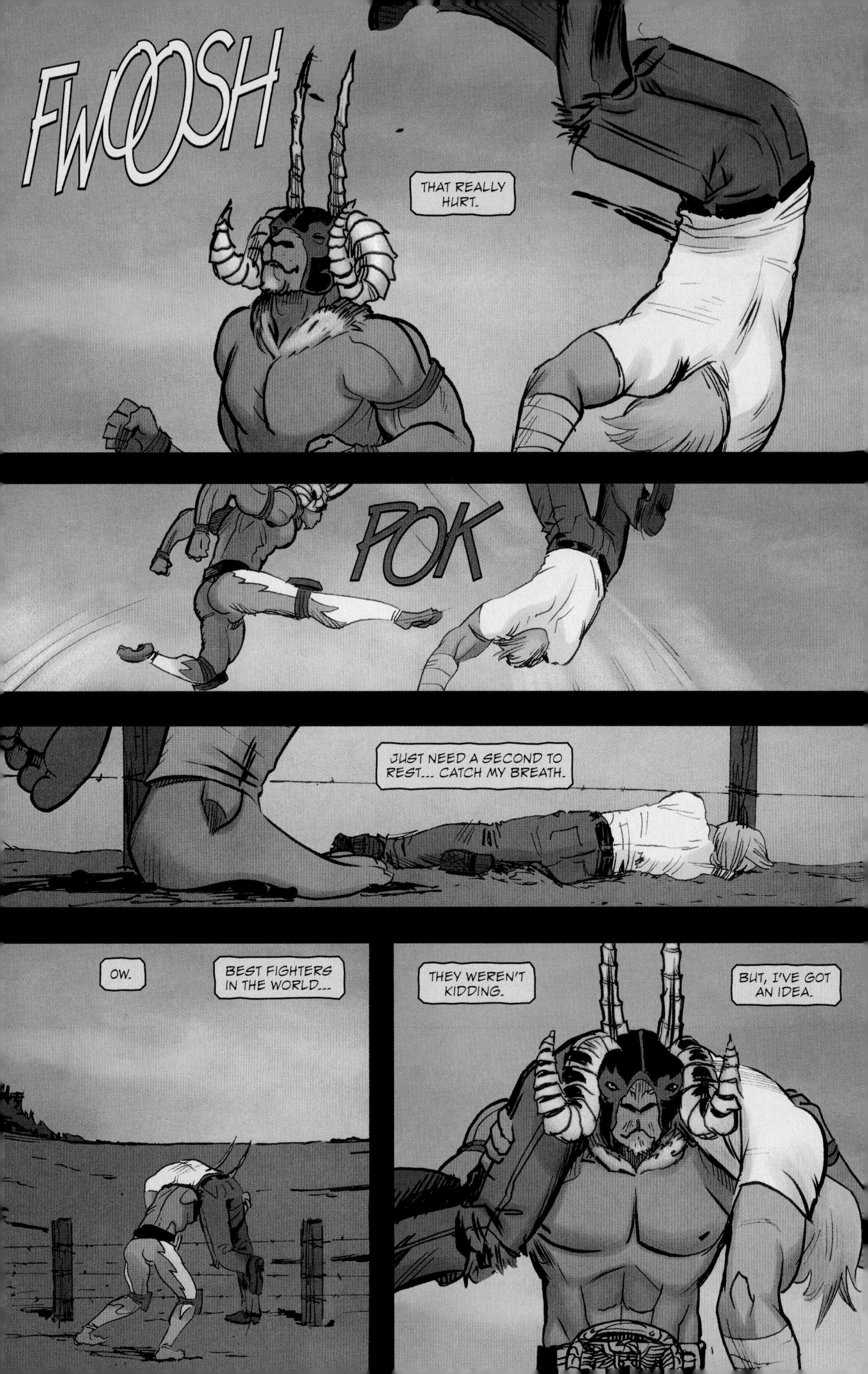
FWOOSH
THAT REALLY HURT.
POK
JUST NEED A SECOND TO REST... CATCH MY BREATH.
OW.
BEST FIGHTERS IN THE WORLD...
THEY WEREN'T KIDDING.
BUT, I'VE GOT AN IDEA.

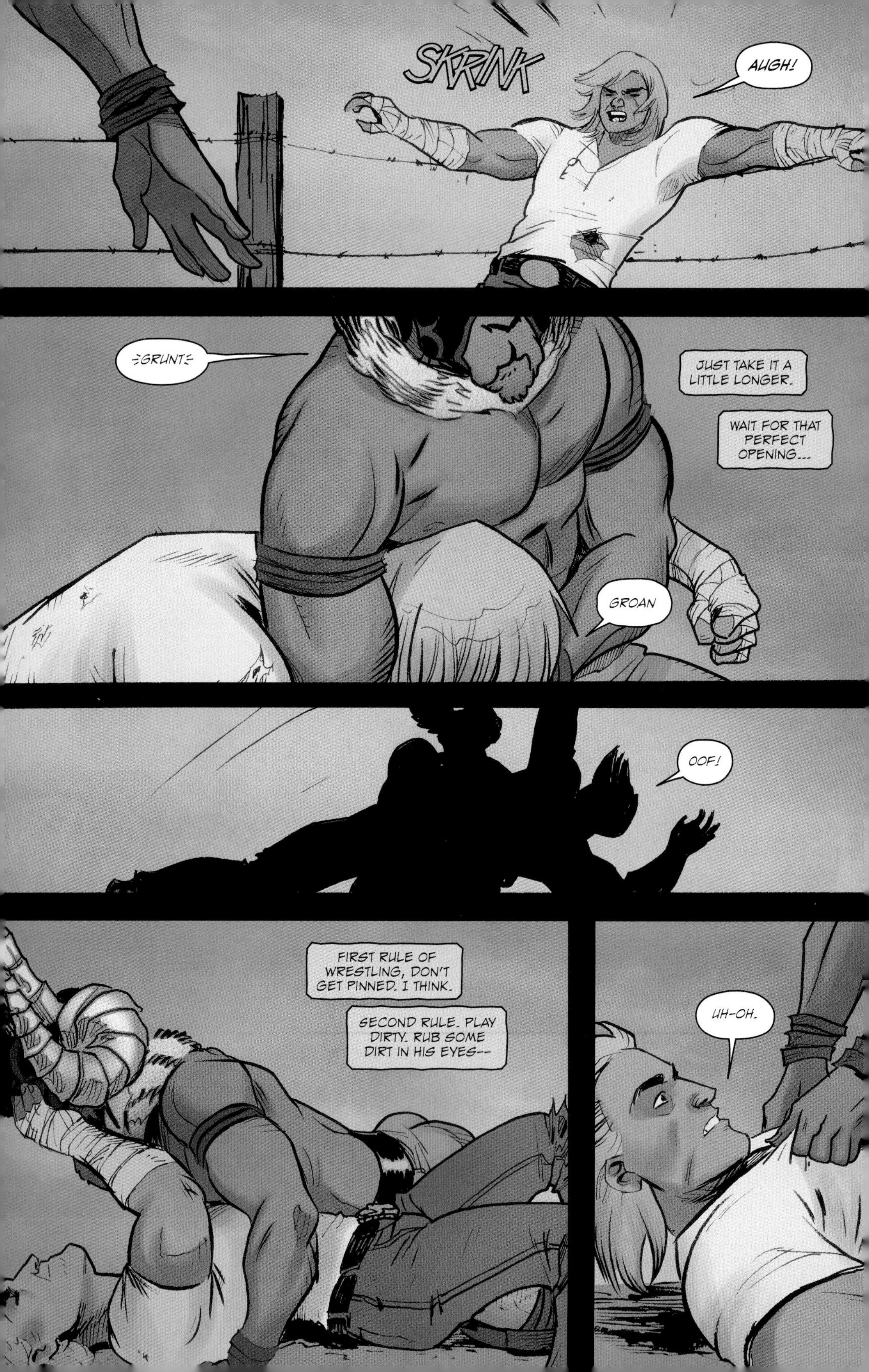
SKRINK
AUGH!
GRUNT
JUST TAKE IT A LITTLE LONGER.
WAIT FOR THAT PERFECT OPENING...
GROAN
OOF!
FIRST RULE OF WRESTLING, DON'T GET PINNED. I THINK.
SECOND RULE. PLAY DIRTY. RUB SOME DIRT IN HIS EYES--
UH-OH.

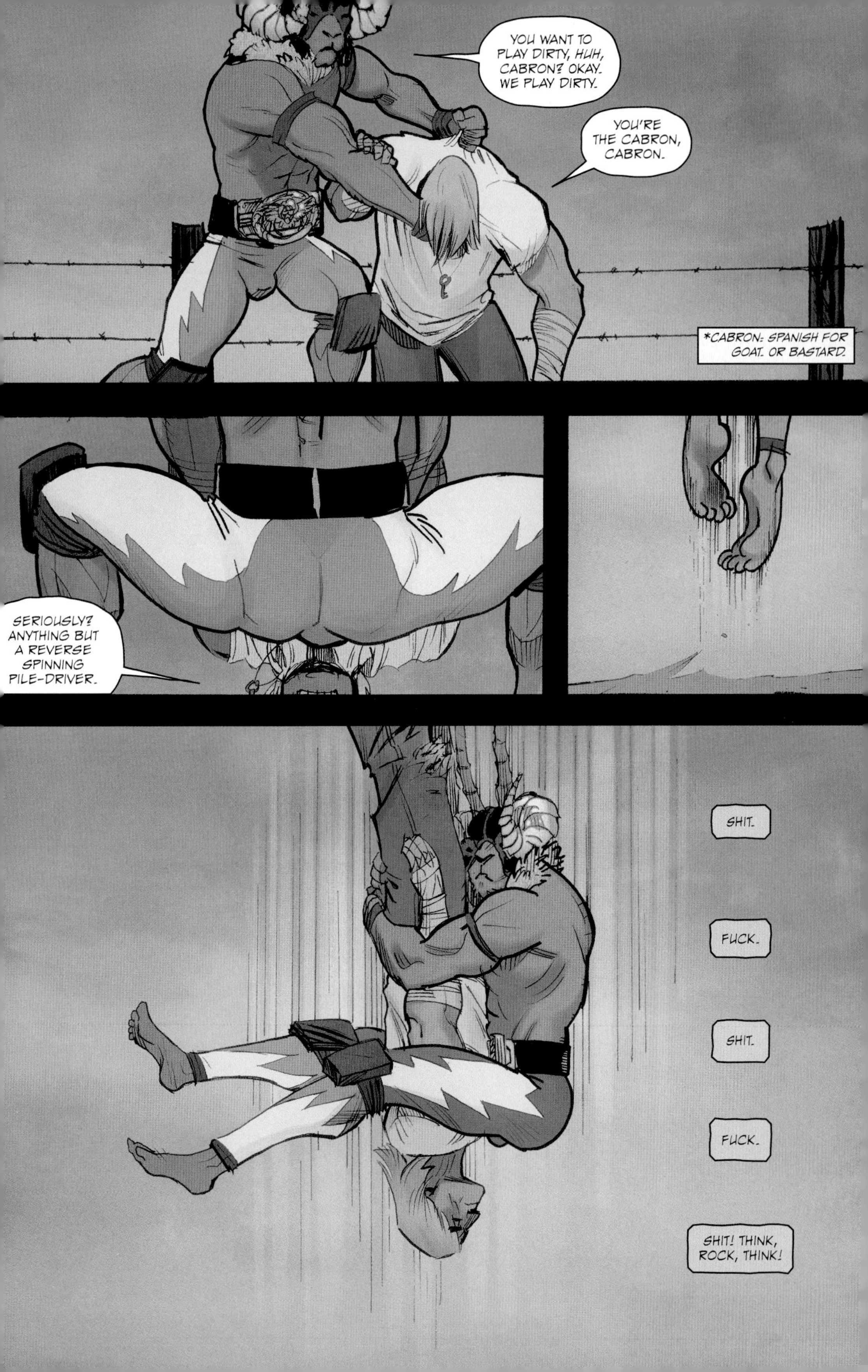

YOU WANT TO PLAY DIRTY, HUH, CABRON? OKAY. WE PLAY DIRTY.
YOU'RE THE CABRON, CABRON.
*CABRON: SPANISH FOR GOAT. OR BASTARD.
SERIOUSLY? ANYTHING BUT A REVERSE SPINNING PILE-DRIVER.
SHIT.
FUCK.
SHIT.
FUCK.
SHIT! THINK, ROCK, THINK!

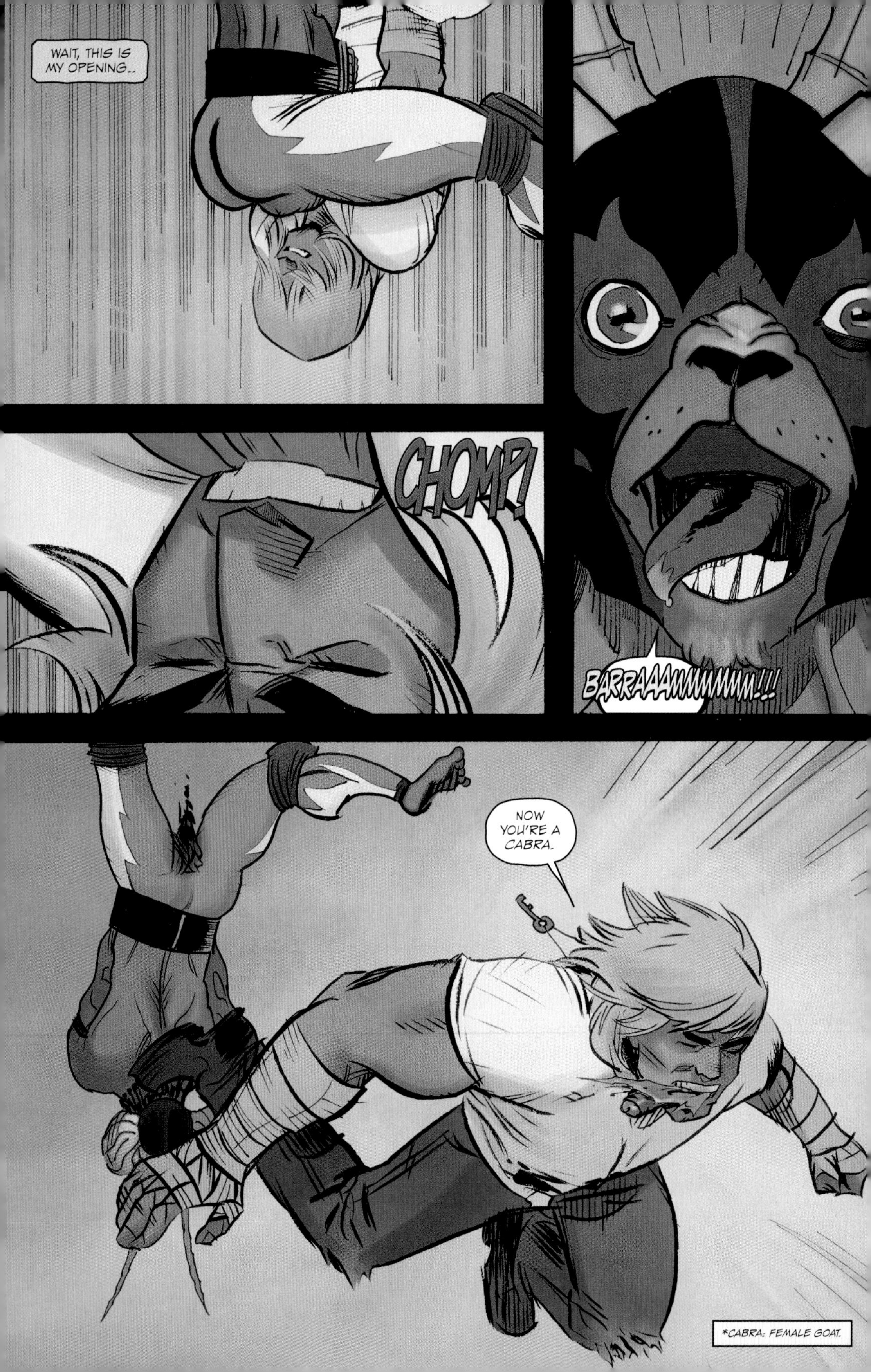
WAIT, THIS IS MY OPENING..
CHOMP!
BARRAAAMMMMMM!!!
NOW YOU'RE A CABRA.
*CABRA: FEMALE GOAT.

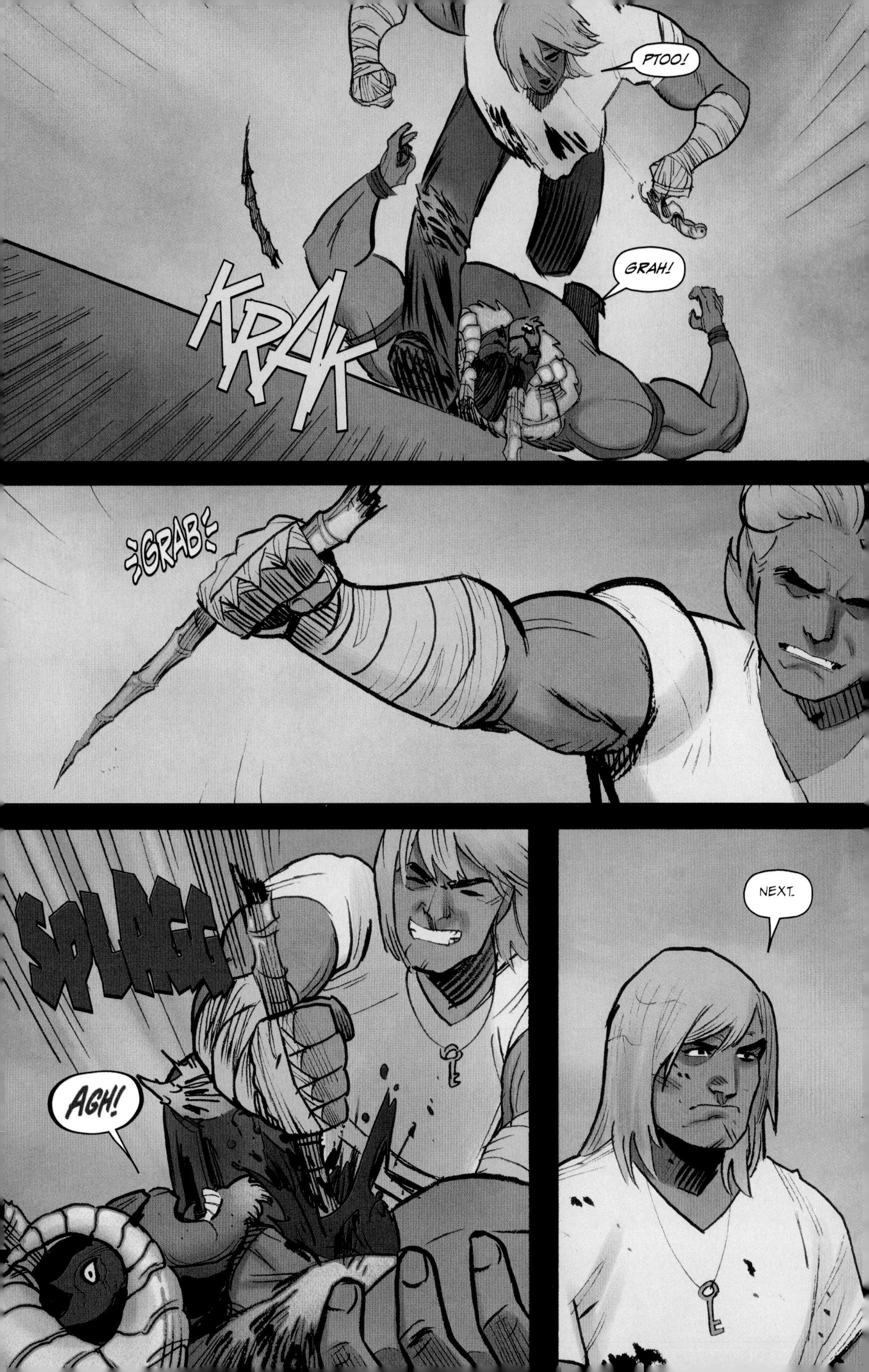
PTOO!
GRAH!
KRAK
GRAB
SPLAGG
AGH!
NEXT.

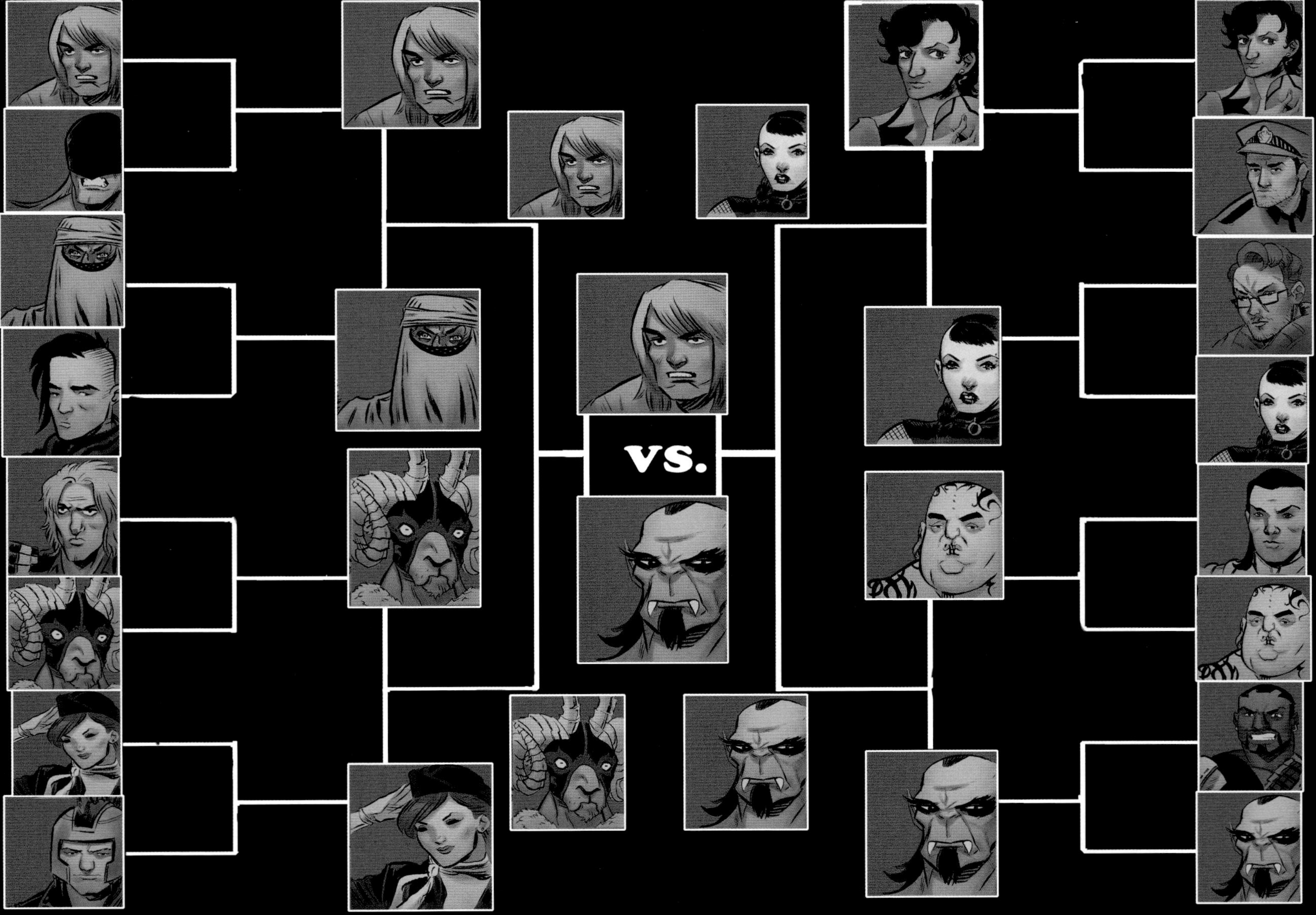
VS.

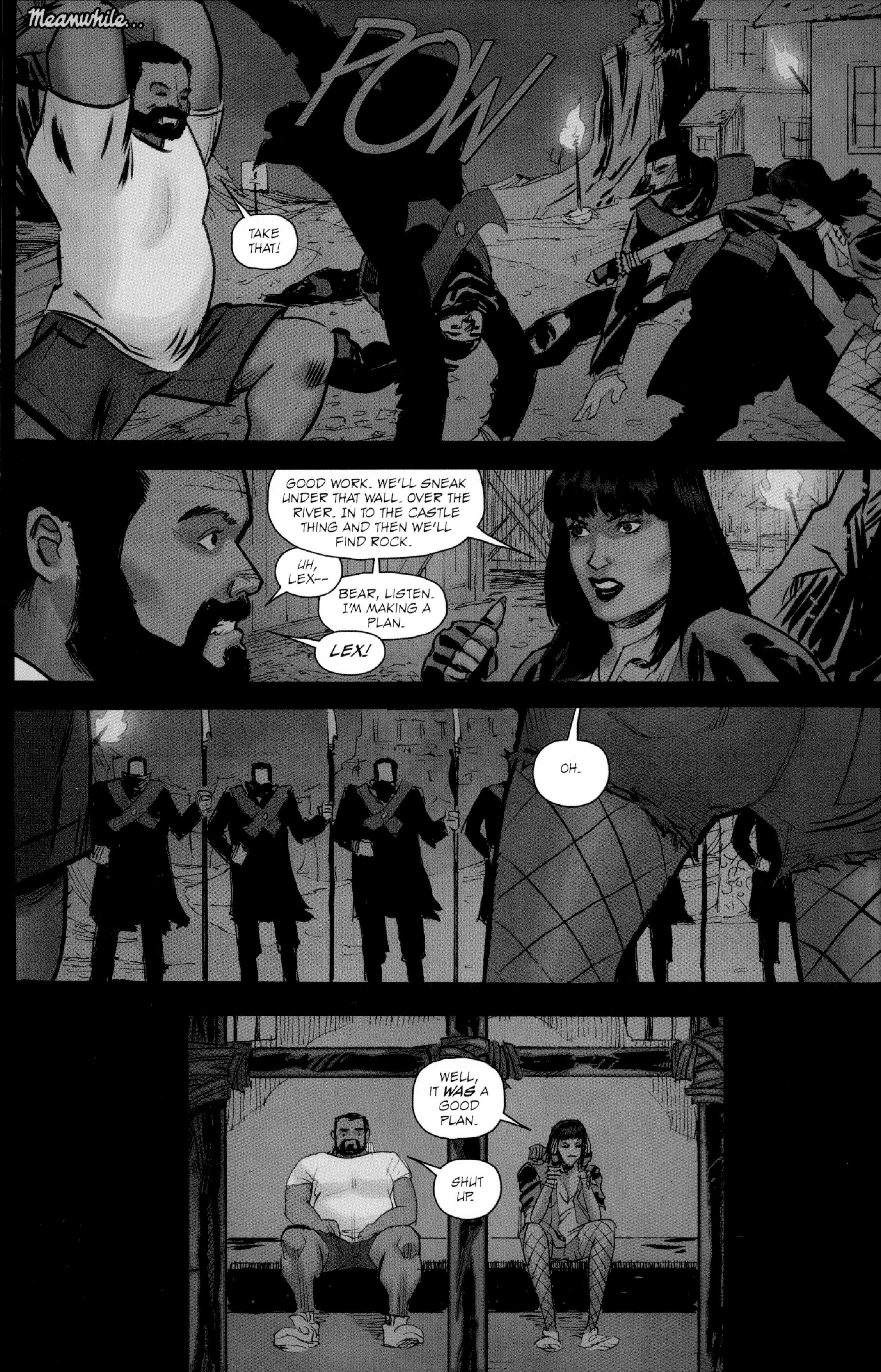
Meanwhile...
POW
TAKE THAT!
GOOD WORK. WE'LL SNEAK UNDER THAT WALL. OVER THE RIVER. IN TO THE CASTLE THING AND THEN WE'LL FIND ROCK.
UH, LEX--
BEAR, LISTEN. I'M MAKING A PLAN.
LEX!
OH.
WELL, IT WAS A GOOD PLAN.
SHUT UP.

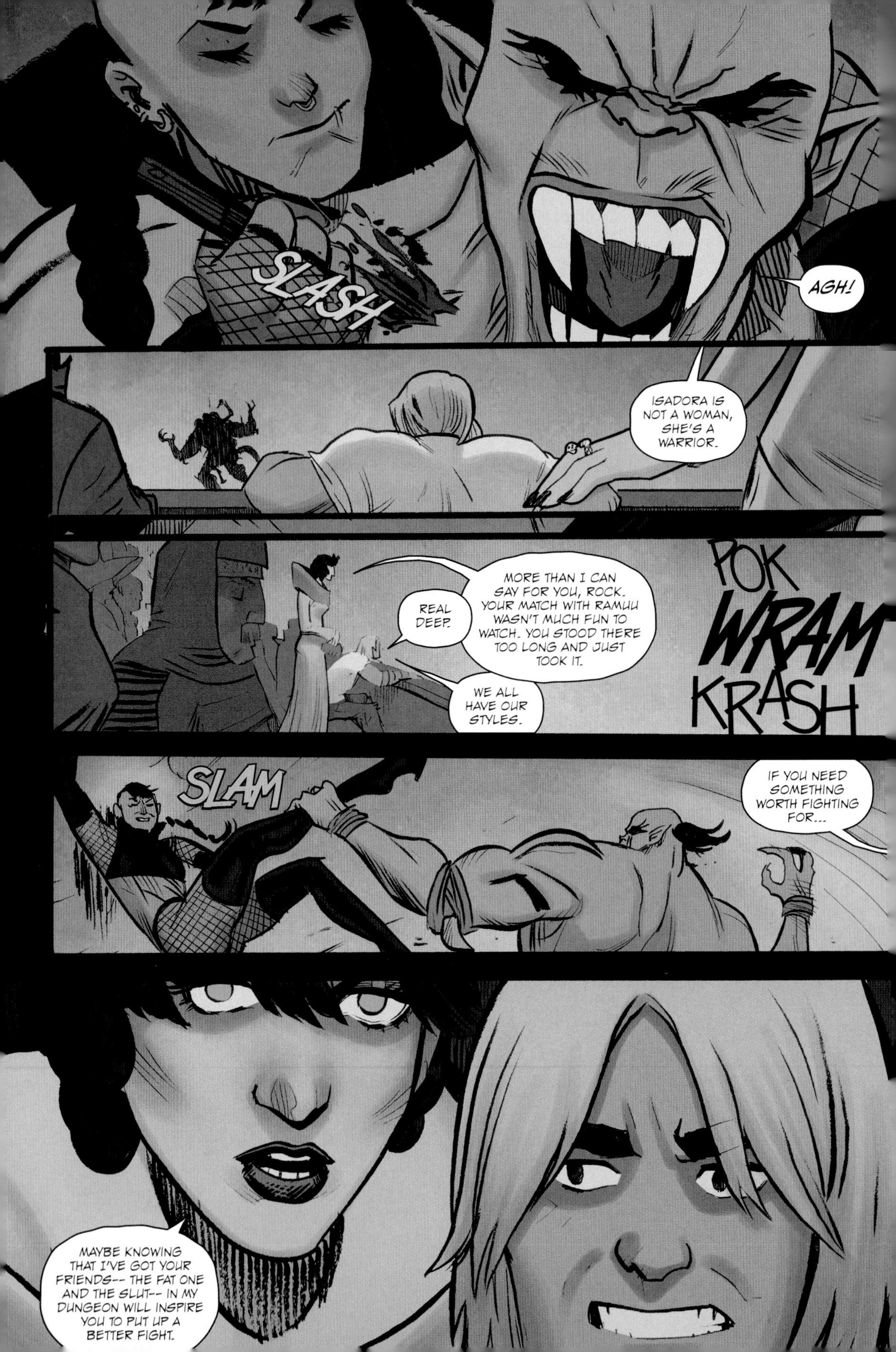
SLASH
AGH!
ISADORA IS NOT A WOMAN, SHE'S A WARRIOR.
REAL DEEP.
MORE THAN I CAN SAY FOR YOU, ROCK. YOUR MATCH WITH RAMUU WASN'T MUCH FUN TO WATCH. YOU STOOD THERE TOO LONG AND JUST TOOK IT.
WE ALL HAVE OUR STYLES.
POK
WRAM
KRASH
SLAM
IF YOU NEED SOMETHING WORTH FIGHTING FOR...
MAYBE KNOWING THAT I'VE GOT YOUR FRIENDS-- THE FAT ONE AND THE SLUT-- IN MY DUNGEON WILL INSPIRE YOU TO PUT UP A BETTER FIGHT.

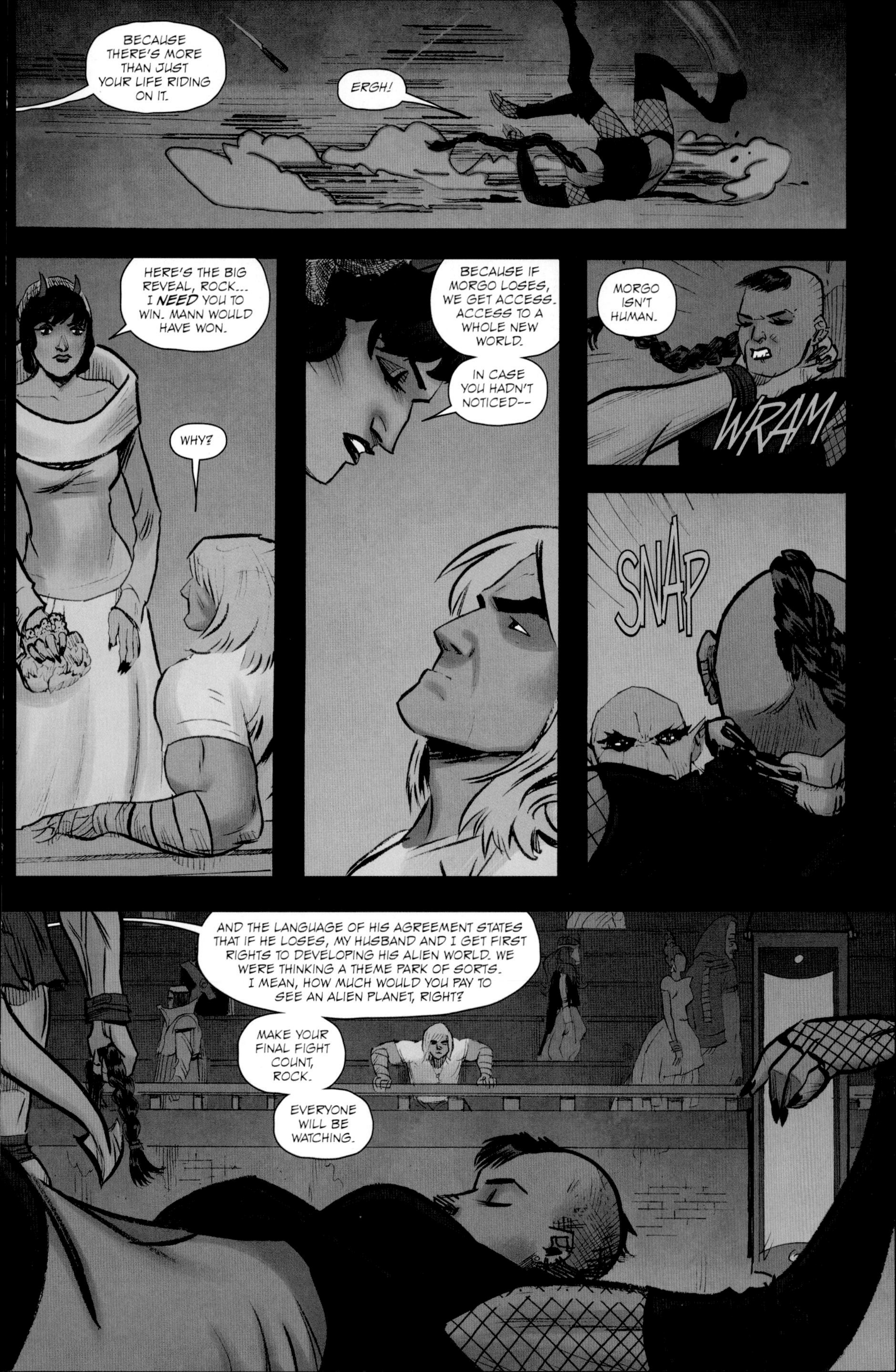
BECAUSE THERE'S MORE THAN JUST YOUR LIFE RIDING ON IT.
ERGH!
HERE'S THE BIG REVEAL, ROCK... I NEED YOU TO WIN. MANN WOULD HAVE WON.
WHY?
BECAUSE IF MORGO LOSES, WE GET ACCESS. ACCESS TO A WHOLE NEW WORLD.
IN CASE YOU HADN'T NOTICED--
MORGO ISN'T HUMAN.
WRAM
SNAP
AND THE LANGUAGE OF HIS AGREEMENT STATES THAT IF HE LOSES, MY HUSBAND AND I GET FIRST RIGHTS TO DEVELOPING HIS ALIEN WORLD. WE WERE THINKING A THEME PARK OF SORTS. I MEAN, HOW MUCH WOULD YOU PAY TO SEE AN ALIEN PLANET, RIGHT?
MAKE YOUR FINAL FIGHT COUNT, ROCK.
EVERYONE WILL BE WATCHING.

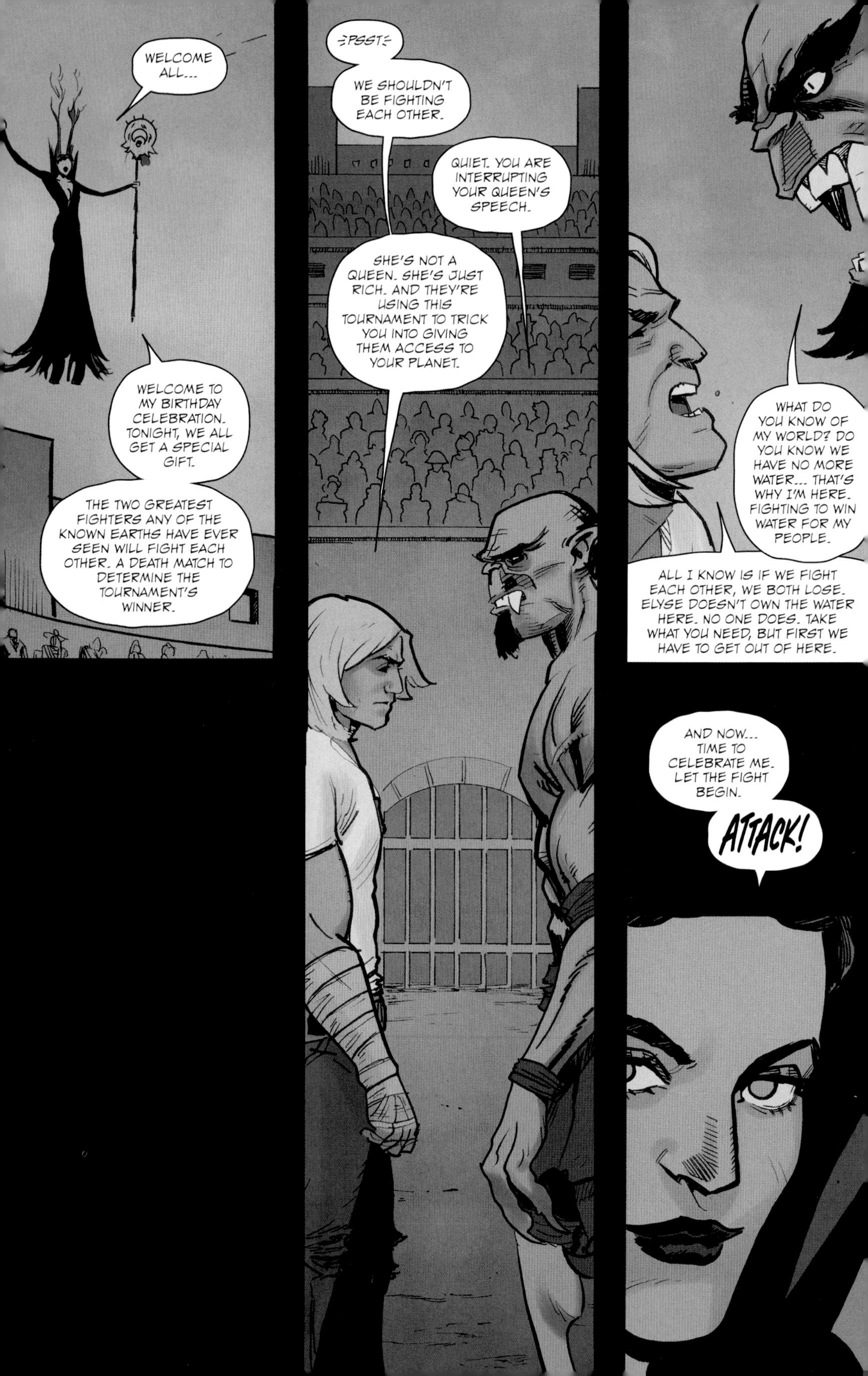
WELCOME ALL...
WELCOME TO MY BIRTHDAY CELEBRATION. TONIGHT, WE ALL GET A SPECIAL GIFT.
THE TWO GREATEST FIGHTERS ANY OF THE KNOWN EARTHS HAVE EVER SEEN WILL FIGHT EACH OTHER. A DEATH MATCH TO DETERMINE THE TOURNAMENT'S WINNER.
PSST
WE SHOULDN'T BE FIGHTING EACH OTHER.
QUIET. YOU ARE INTERRUPTING YOUR QUEEN'S SPEECH.
SHE'S NOT A QUEEN. SHE'S JUST RICH. AND THEY'RE USING THIS TOURNAMENT TO TRICK YOU INTO GIVING THEM ACCESS TO YOUR PLANET.
WHAT DO YOU KNOW OF MY WORLD? DO YOU KNOW WE HAVE NO MORE WATER... THAT'S WHY I'M HERE. FIGHTING TO WIN WATER FOR MY PEOPLE.
ALL I KNOW IS IF WE FIGHT EACH OTHER, WE BOTH LOSE. ELYSE DOESN'T OWN THE WATER HERE. NO ONE DOES. TAKE WHAT YOU NEED, BUT FIRST WE HAVE TO GET OUT OF HERE.
AND NOW... TIME TO CELEBRATE ME. LET THE FIGHT BEGIN.
ATTACK!

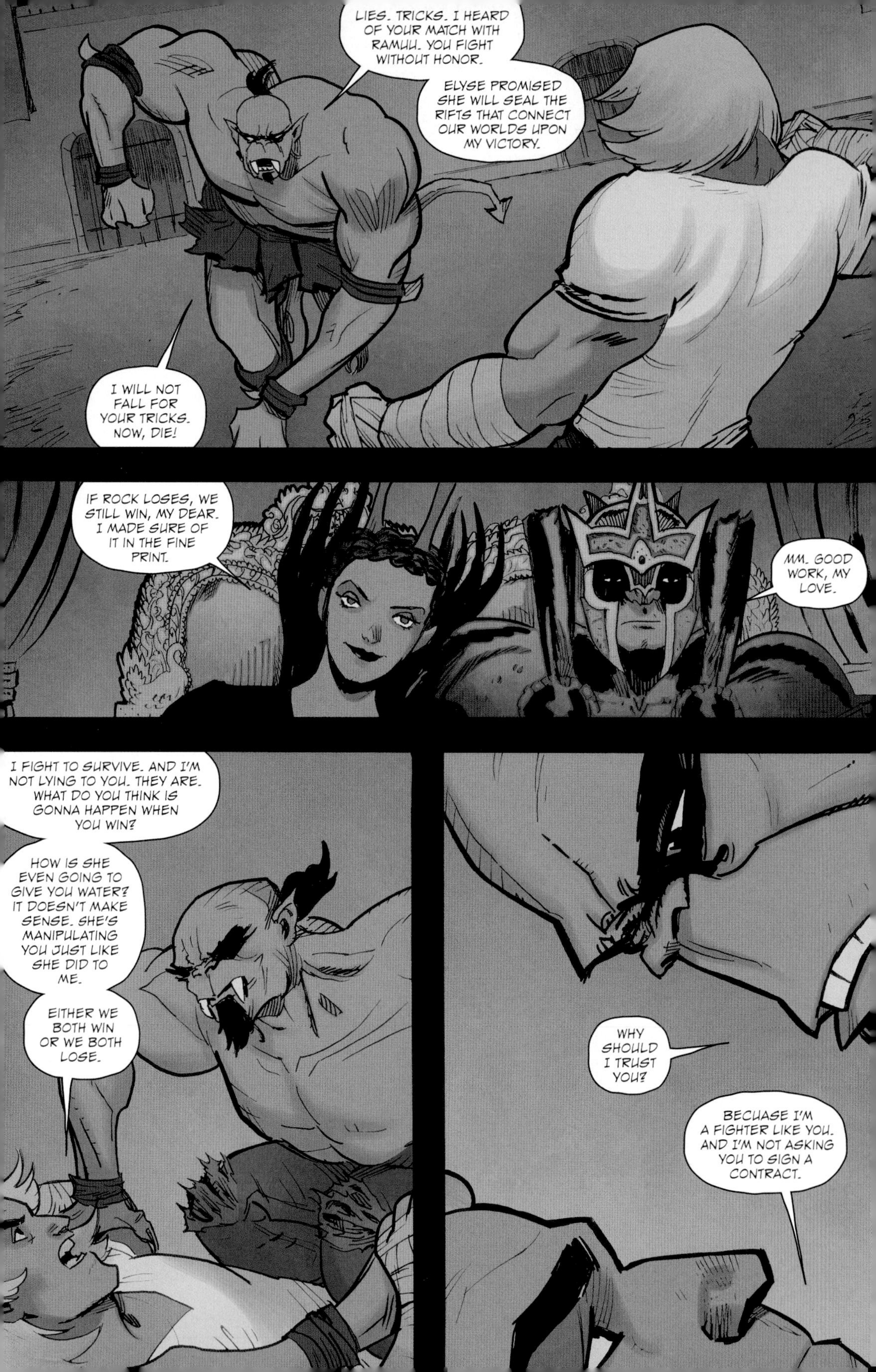
LIES. TRICKS. I HEARD OF YOUR MATCH WITH RAMUU. YOU FIGHT WITHOUT HONOR.
ELYSE PROMISED SHE WILL SEAL THE RIFTS THAT CONNECT OUR WORLDS UPON MY VICTORY.
I WILL NOT FALL FOR YOUR TRICKS. NOW, DIE!
IF ROCK LOSES, WE STILL WIN, MY DEAR. I MADE SURE OF IT IN THE FINE PRINT.
MM. GOOD WORK, MY LOVE.
I FIGHT TO SURVIVE. AND I'M NOT LYING TO YOU. THEY ARE. WHAT DO YOU THINK IS GONNA HAPPEN WHEN YOU WIN?
HOW IS SHE EVEN GOING TO GIVE YOU WATER? IT DOESN'T MAKE SENSE. SHE'S MANIPULATING YOU JUST LIKE SHE DID TO ME.
EITHER WE BOTH WIN OR WE BOTH LOSE.
WHY SHOULD I TRUST YOU?
BECUASE I'M A FIGHTER LIKE YOU. AND I'M NOT ASKING YOU TO SIGN A CONTRACT.

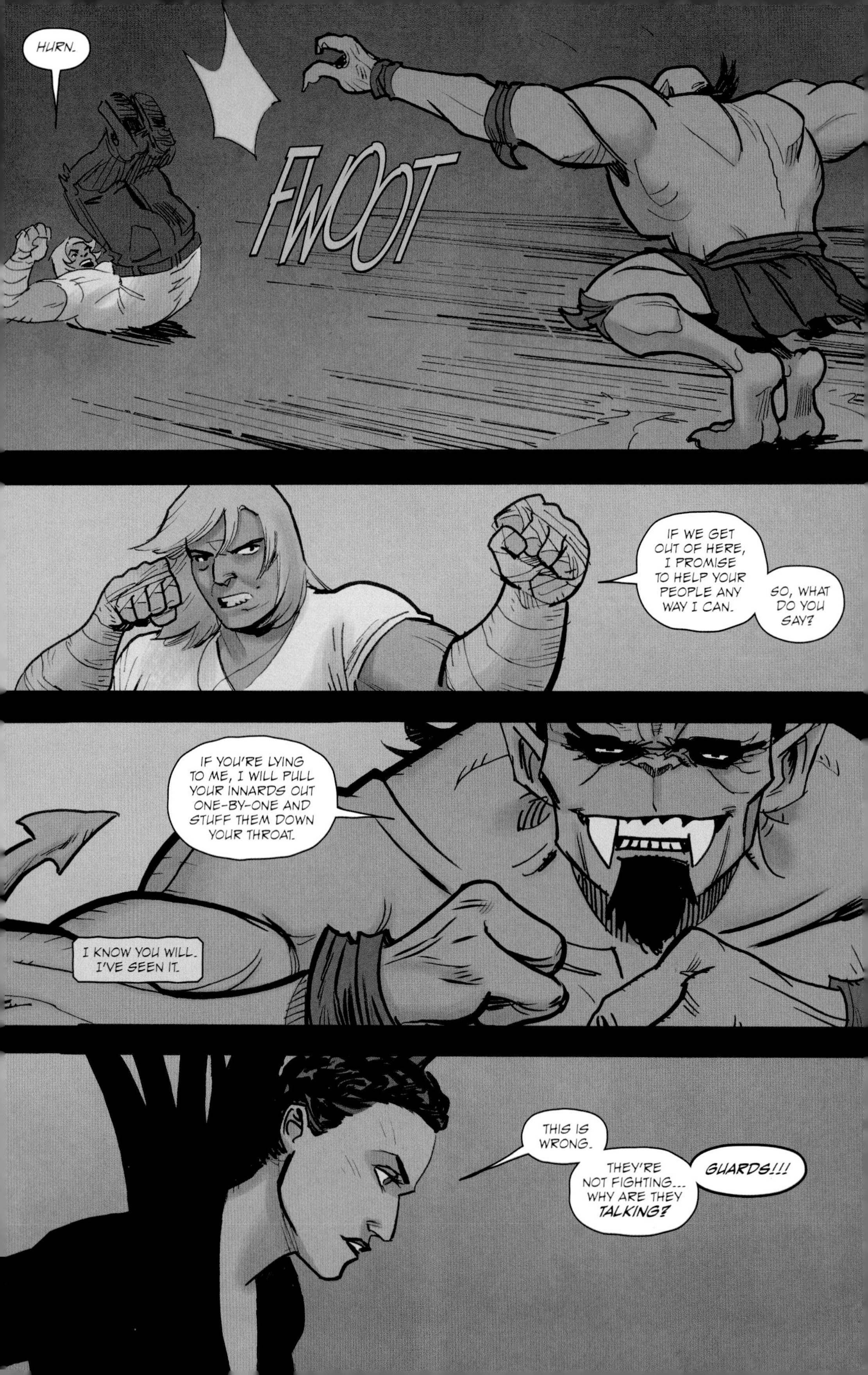
HURN.
FWOOT
IF WE GET OUT OF HERE, I PROMISE TO HELP YOUR PEOPLE ANY WAY I CAN.
SO, WHAT DO YOU SAY?
IF YOU'RE LYING TO ME, I WILL PULL YOUR INNARDS OUT ONE-BY-ONE AND STUFF THEM DOWN YOUR THROAT.
I KNOW YOU WILL. I'VE SEEN IT.
THIS IS WRONG.
THEY'RE NOT FIGHTING... WHY ARE THEY *TALKING?*
GUARDS!!!

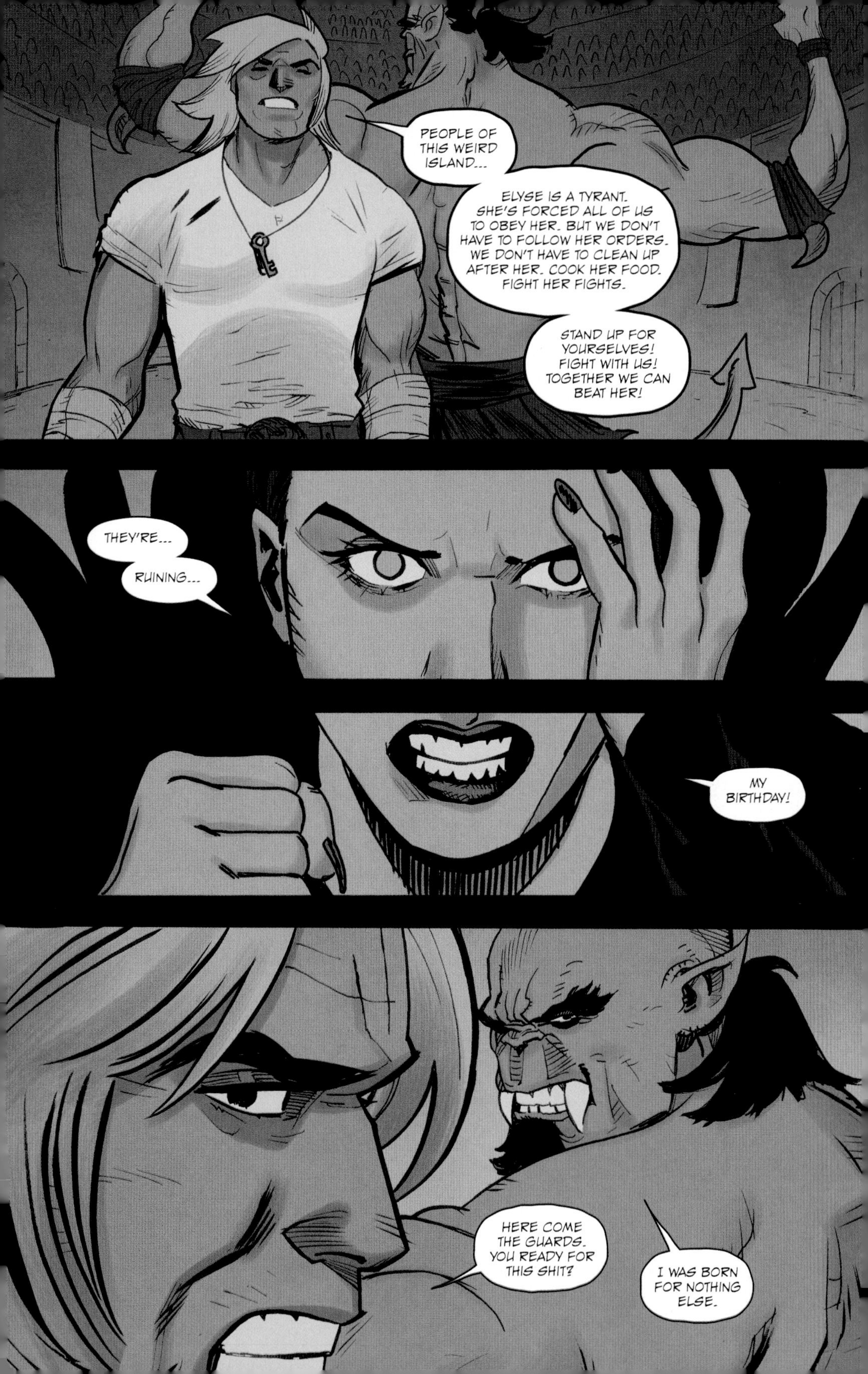

PEOPLE OF THIS WEIRD ISLAND...
ELYSE IS A TYRANT. SHE'S FORCED ALL OF US TO OBEY HER. BUT WE DON'T HAVE TO FOLLOW HER ORDERS. WE DON'T HAVE TO CLEAN UP AFTER HER. COOK HER FOOD. FIGHT HER FIGHTS.
STAND UP FOR YOURSELVES! FIGHT WITH US! TOGETHER WE CAN BEAT HER!
THEY'RE...
RUINING...
MY BIRTHDAY!
HERE COME THE GUARDS. YOU READY FOR THIS SHIT?
I WAS BORN FOR NOTHING ELSE.

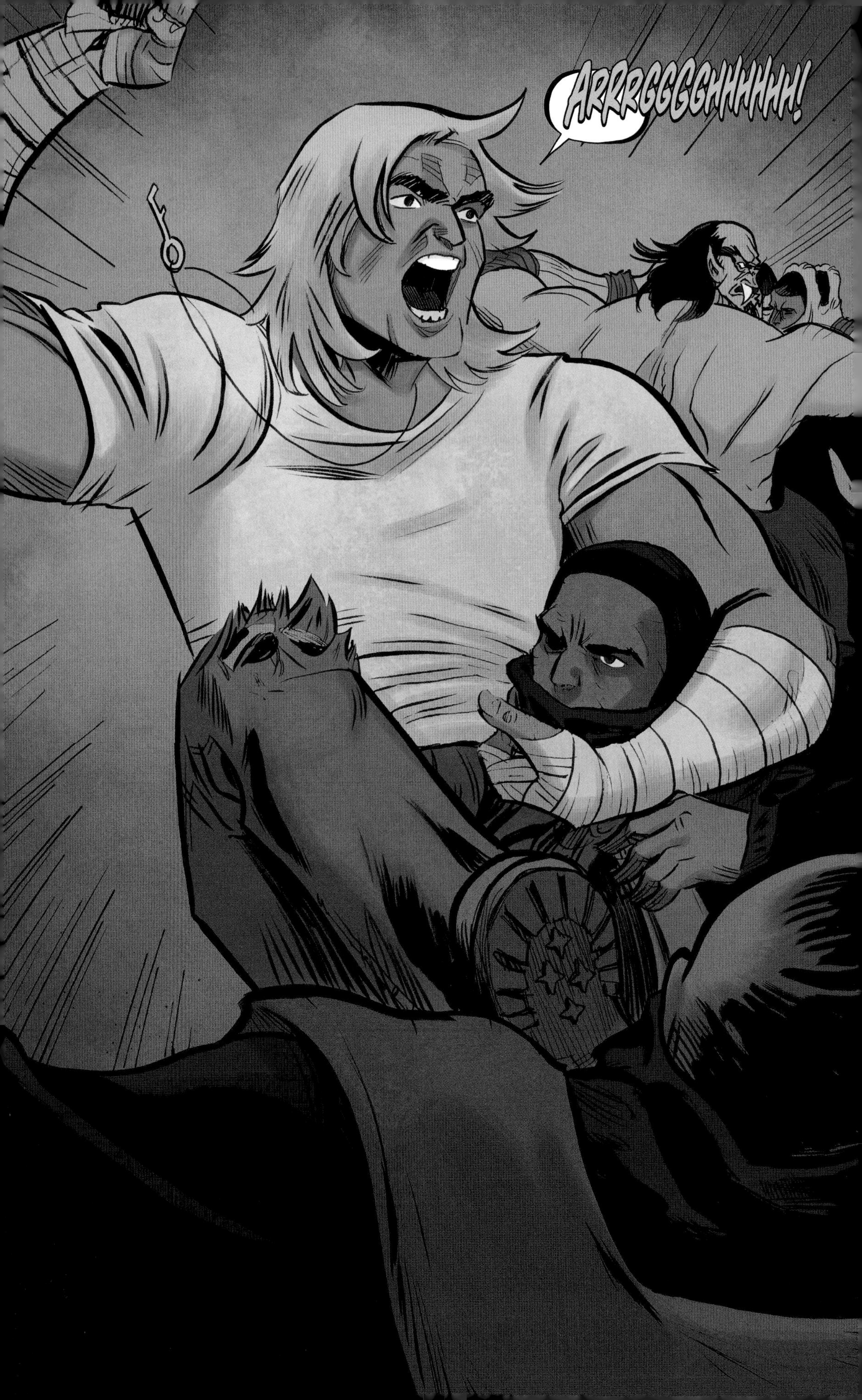
ARRRGGGGHHHHHH!

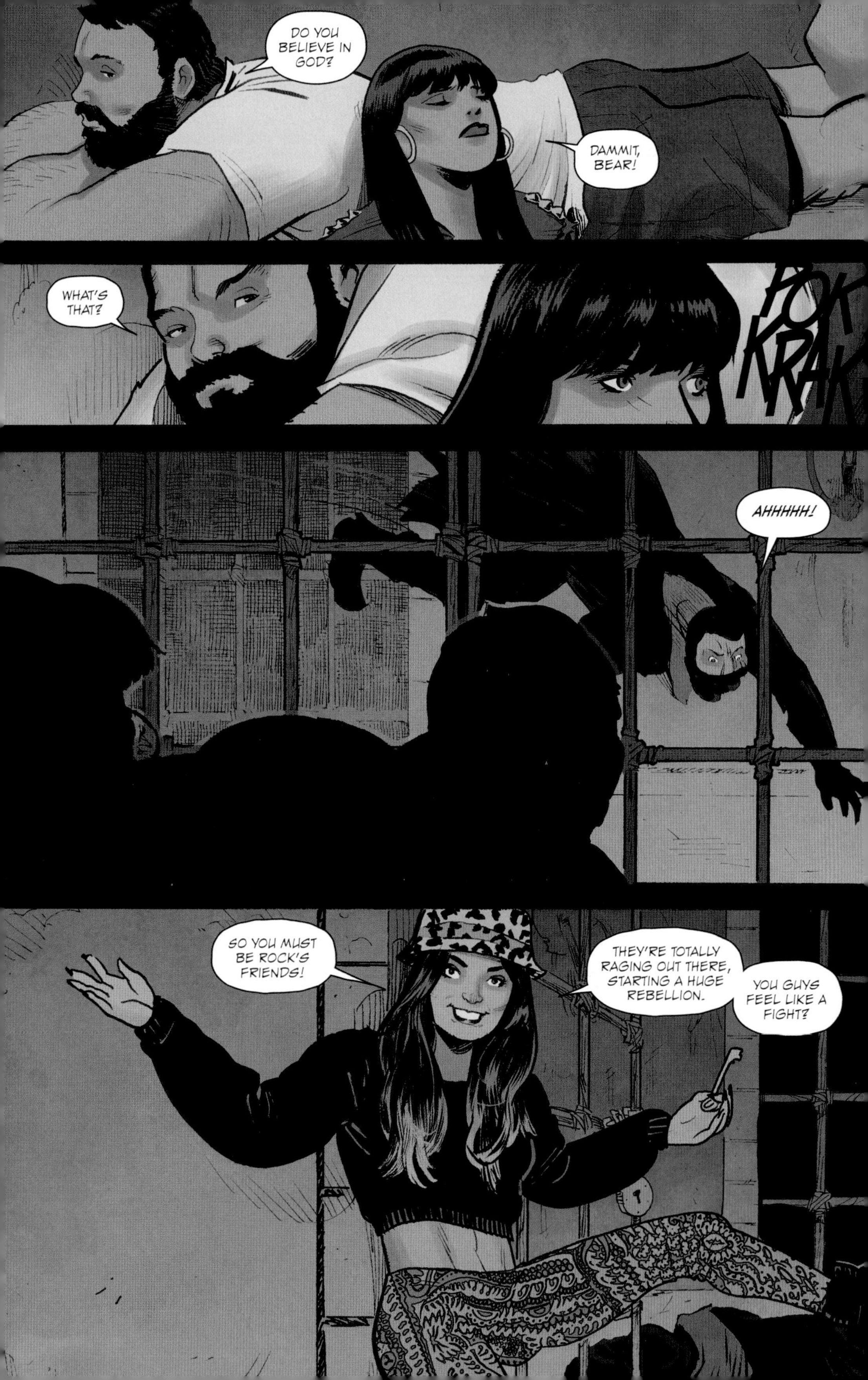
DO YOU BELIEVE IN GOD?
DAMMIT, BEAR!
WHAT'S THAT?
POK
KRAK
AHHHHH!
SO YOU MUST BE ROCK'S FRIENDS!
THEY'RE TOTALLY RAGING OUT THERE, STARTING A HUGE REBELLION.
YOU GUYS FEEL LIKE A FIGHT?

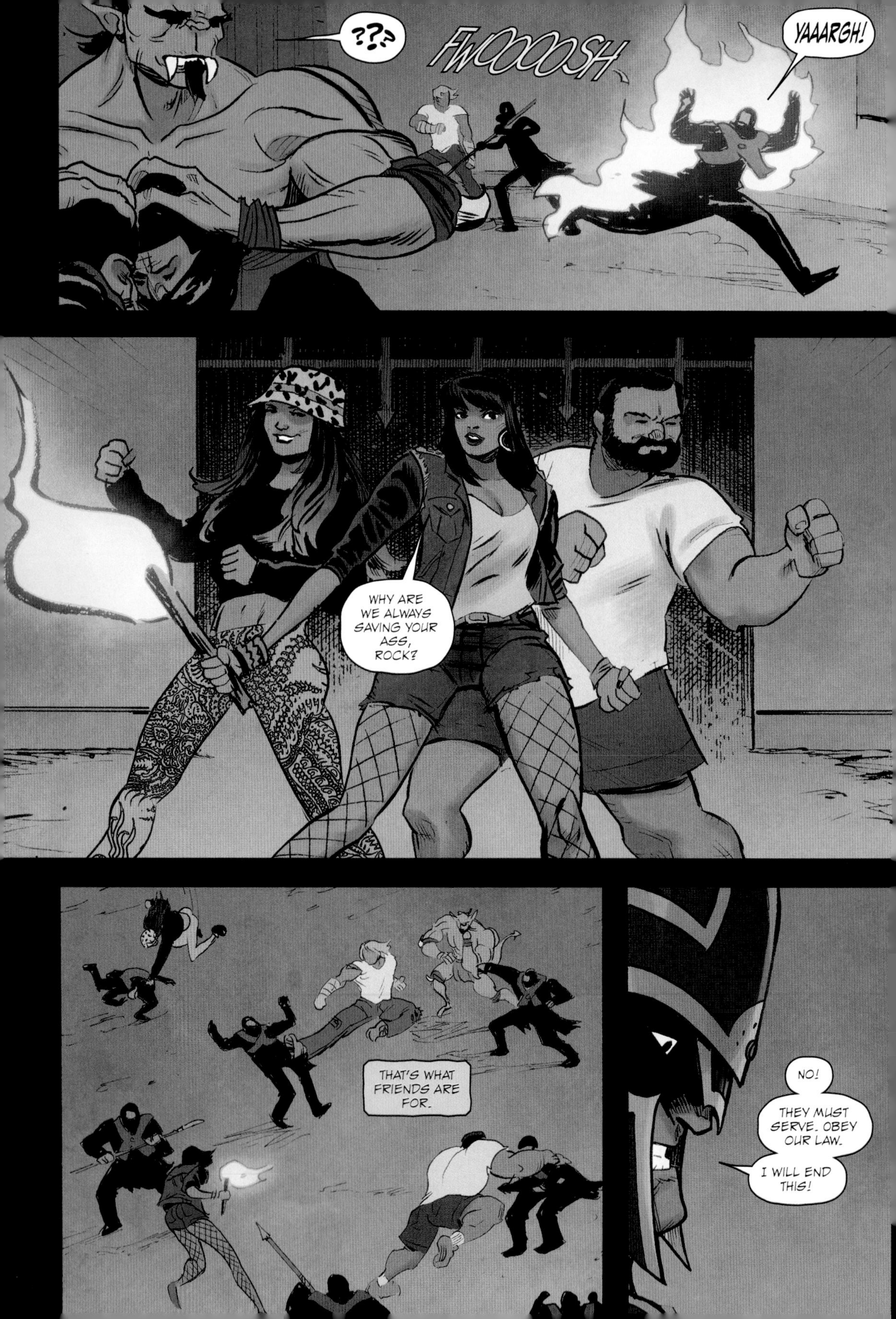

???
FWOOOOSH
YAAARGH!
WHY ARE WE ALWAYS SAVING YOUR ASS, ROCK?
THAT'S WHAT FRIENDS ARE FOR.
NO!
THEY MUST SERVE. OBEY OUR LAW.
I WILL END THIS!

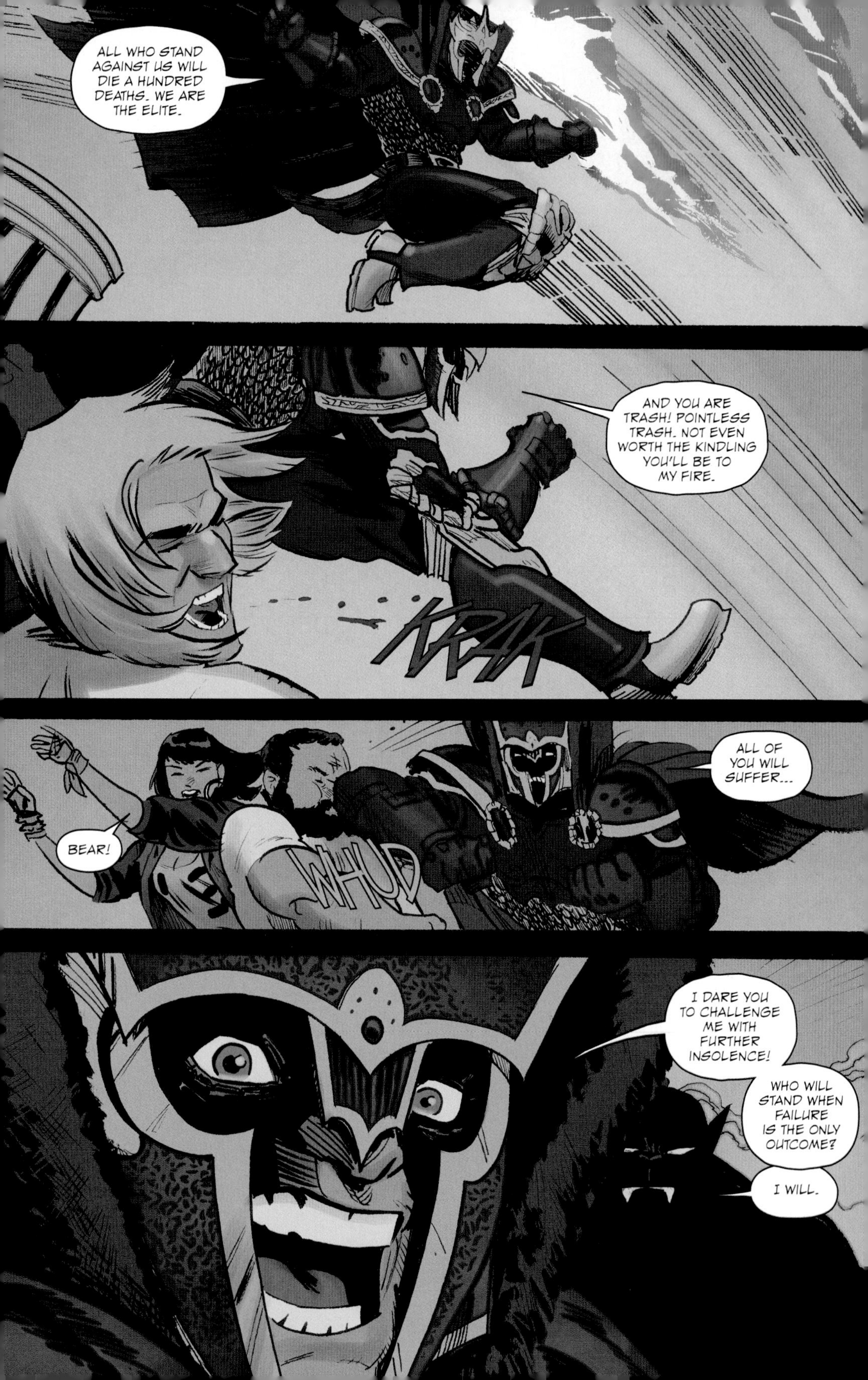
ALL WHO STAND AGAINST US WILL DIE A HUNDRED DEATHS. WE ARE THE ELITE.
AND YOU ARE TRASH! POINTLESS TRASH. NOT EVEN WORTH THE KINDLING YOU'LL BE TO MY FIRE.
KRAK
ALL OF YOU WILL SUFFER...
BEAR!
WHUD
I DARE YOU TO CHALLENGE ME WITH FURTHER INSOLENCE!
WHO WILL STAND WHEN FAILURE IS THE ONLY OUTCOME?
I WILL.

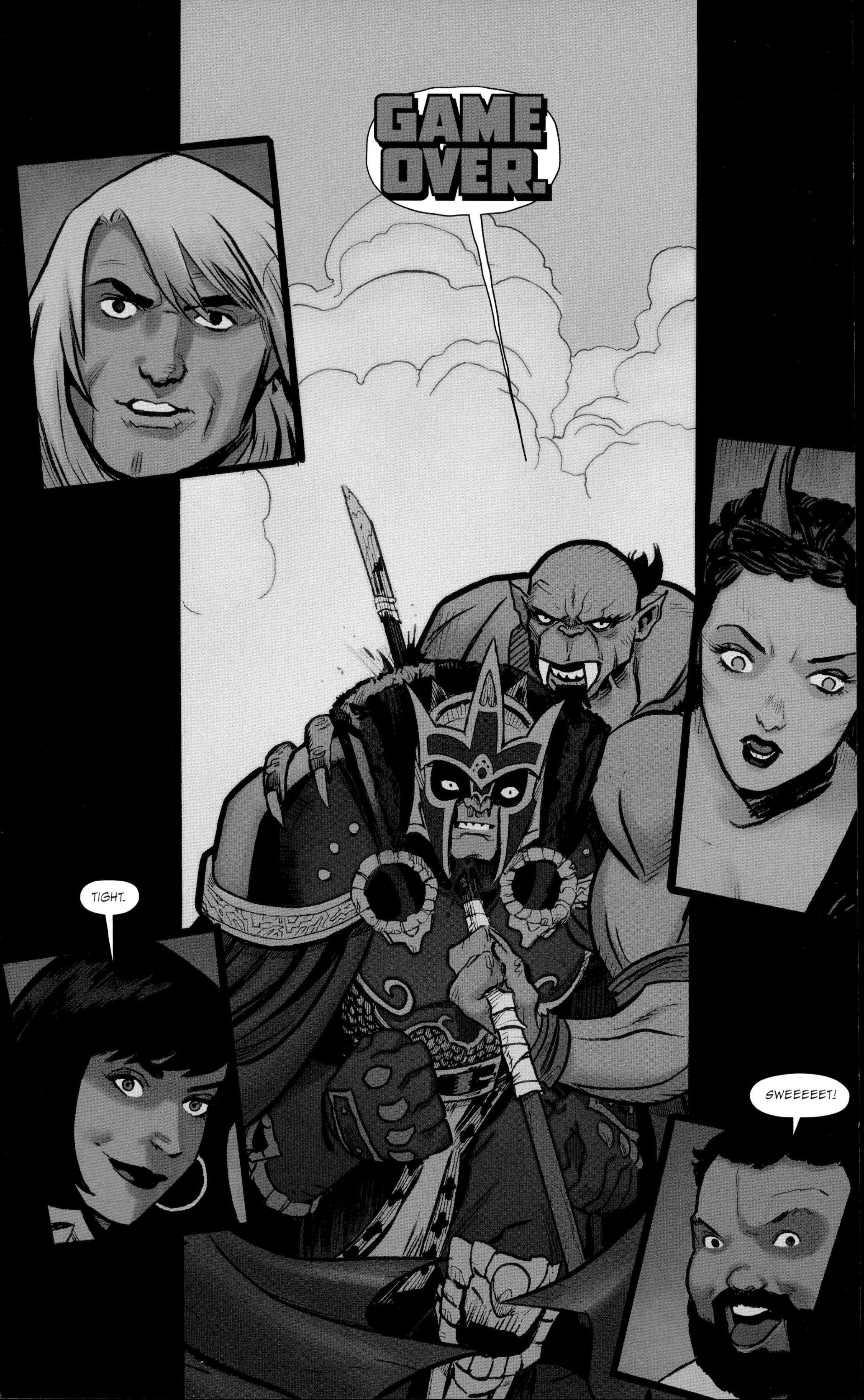
GAME OVER.
TIGHT.
SWEEEEEET!

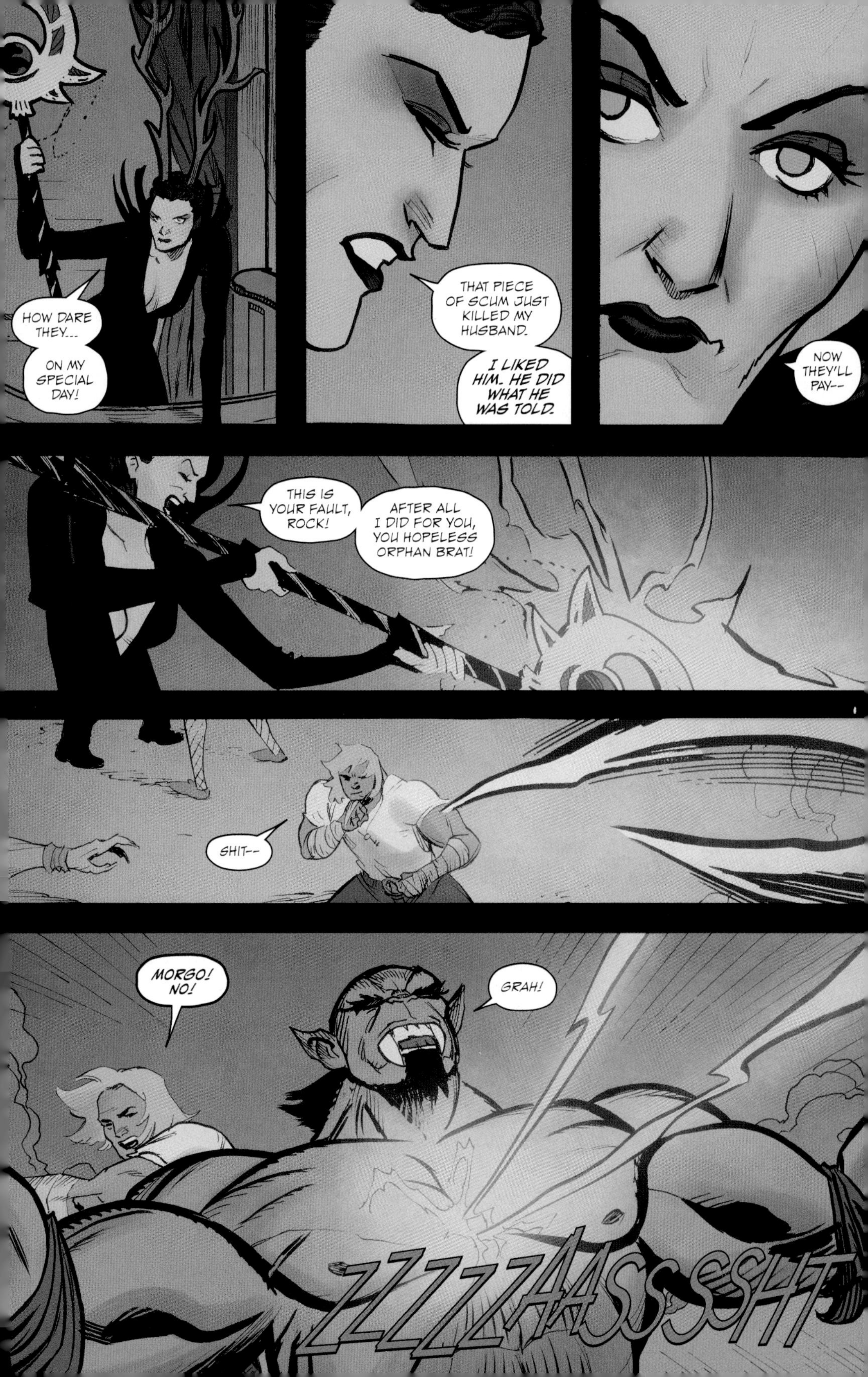
HOW DARE THEY...
ON MY SPECIAL DAY!
THAT PIECE OF SCUM JUST KILLED MY HUSBAND.
I LIKED HIM. HE DID WHAT HE WAS TOLD.
NOW THEY'LL PAY--
THIS IS YOUR FAULT, ROCK!
AFTER ALL I DID FOR YOU, YOU HOPELESS ORPHAN BRAT!
SHIT--
MORGO! NO!
GRAH!
ZZZZZZAASSSSHT

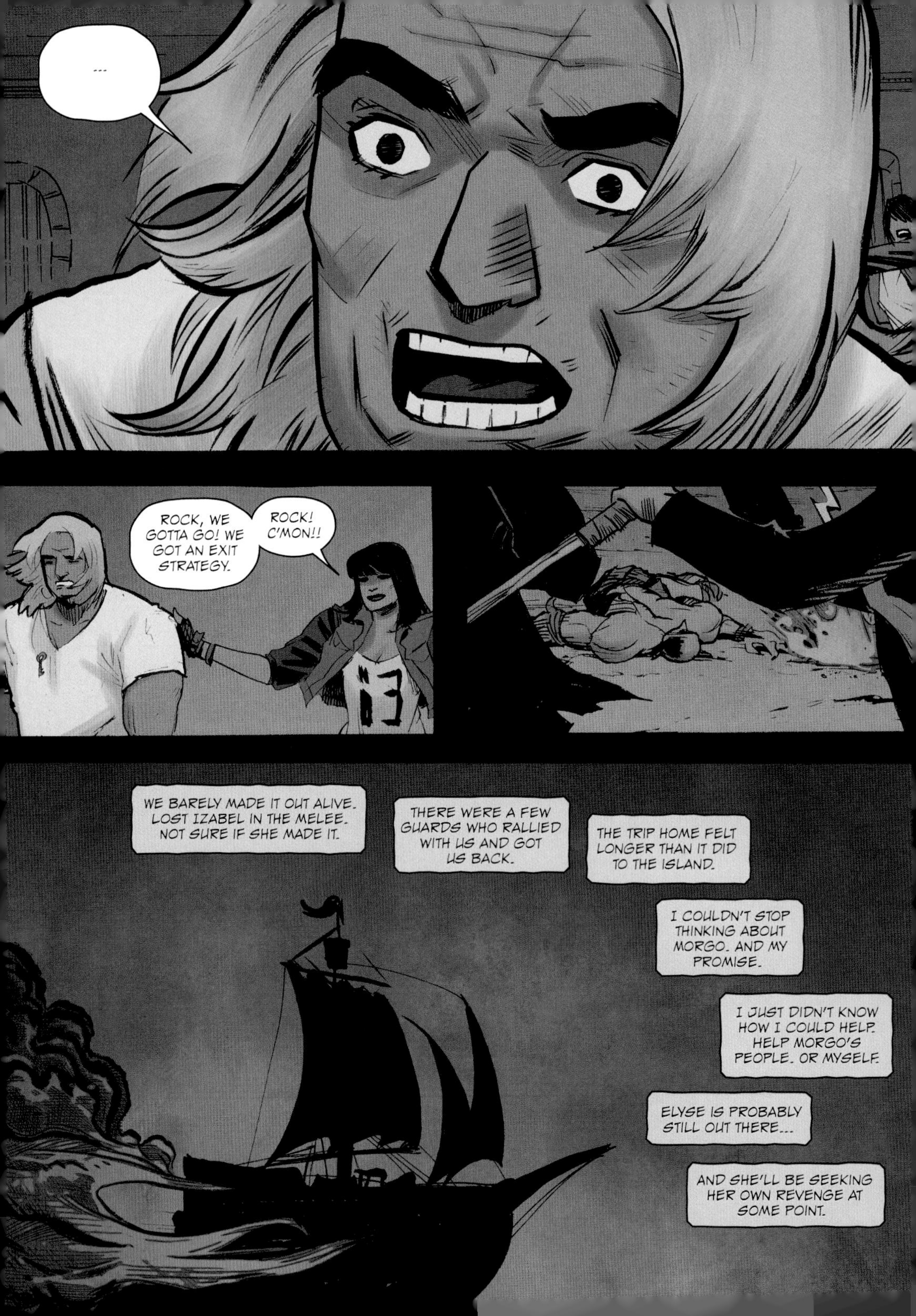
...
ROCK, WE GOTTA GO! WE GOT AN EXIT STRATEGY.
ROCK! C'MON!!
WE BARELY MADE IT OUT ALIVE. LOST IZABEL IN THE MELEE. NOT SURE IF SHE MADE IT.
THERE WERE A FEW GUARDS WHO RALLIED WITH US AND GOT US BACK.
THE TRIP HOME FELT LONGER THAN IT DID TO THE ISLAND.
I COULDN'T STOP THINKING ABOUT MORGO. AND MY PROMISE.
I JUST DIDN'T KNOW HOW I COULD HELP. HELP MORGO'S PEOPLE. OR MYSELF.
ELYSE IS PROBABLY STILL OUT THERE...
AND SHE'LL BE SEEKING HER OWN REVENGE AT SOME POINT.

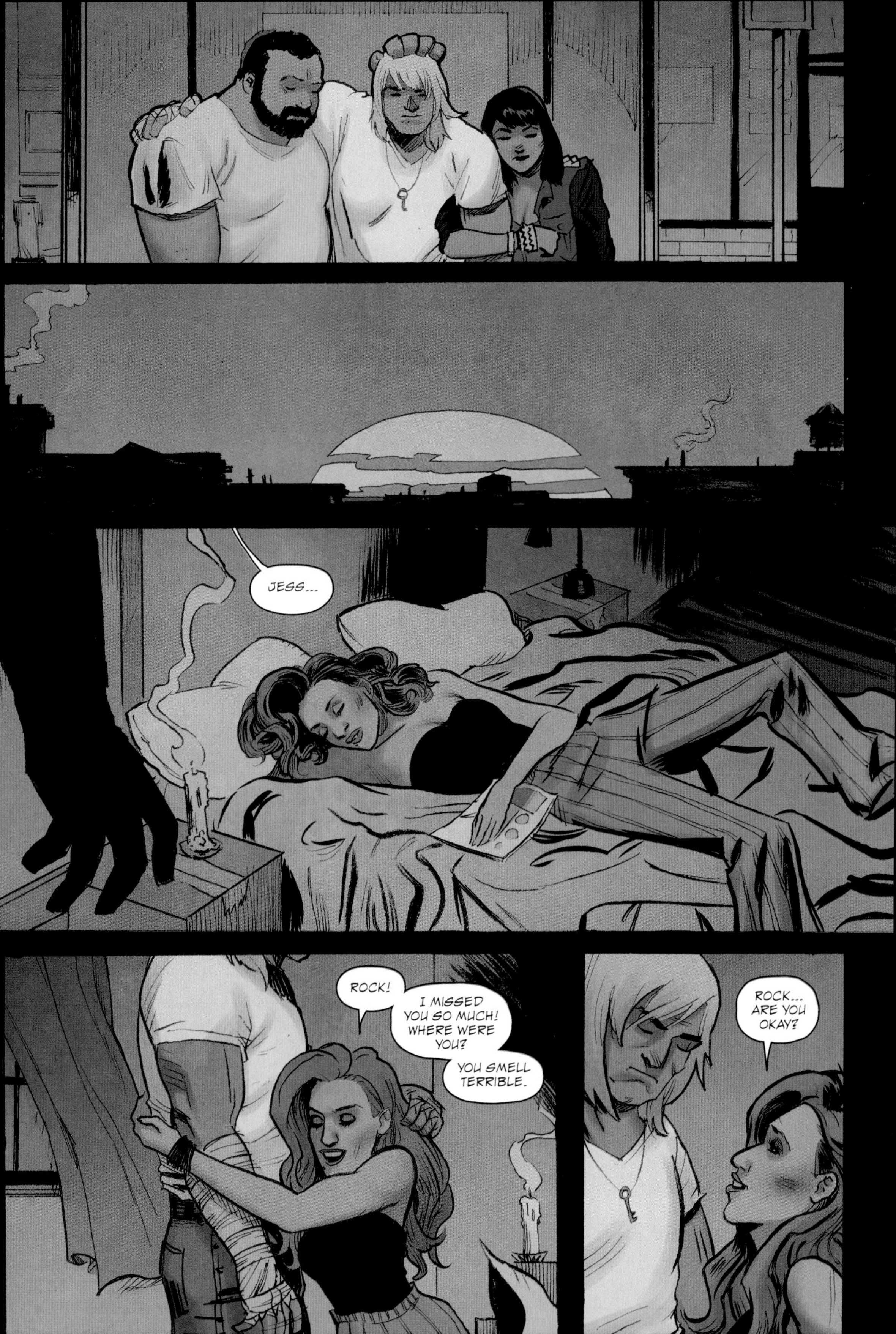
JESS...
ROCK!
I MISSED YOU SO MUCH! WHERE WERE YOU?
YOU SMELL TERRIBLE.
ROCK... ARE YOU OKAY?

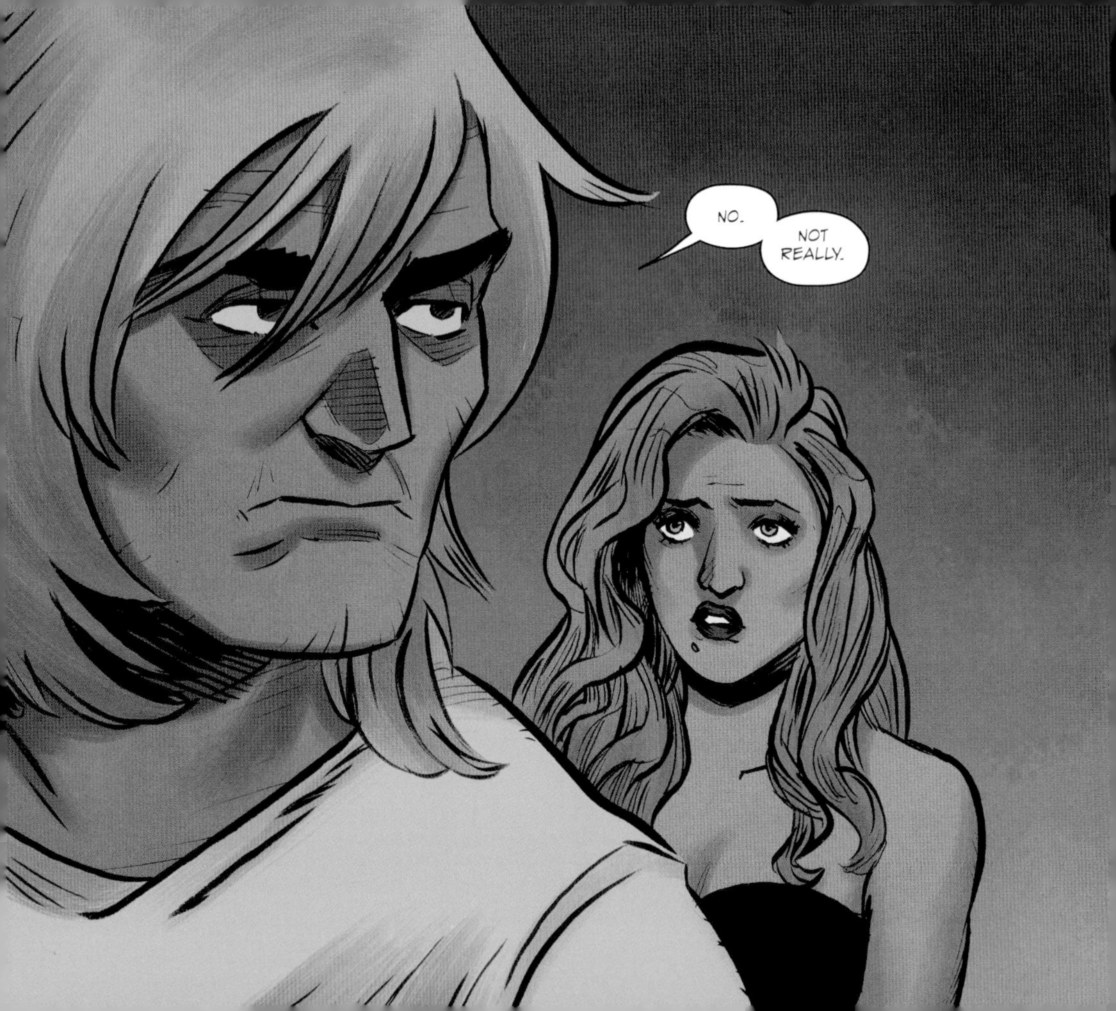
NO.
NOT REALLY.

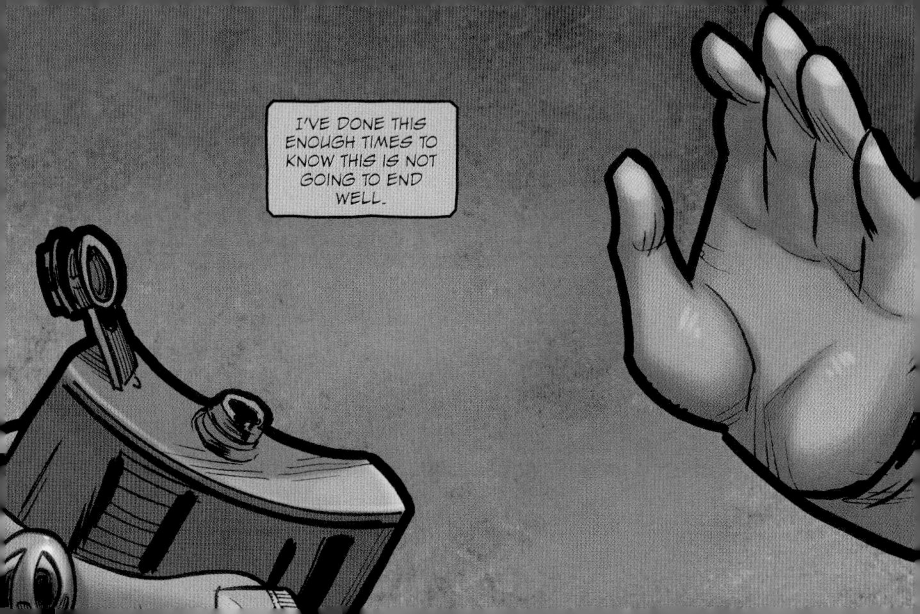
I'VE DONE THIS ENOUGH TIMES TO KNOW THIS IS NOT GOING TO END WELL.

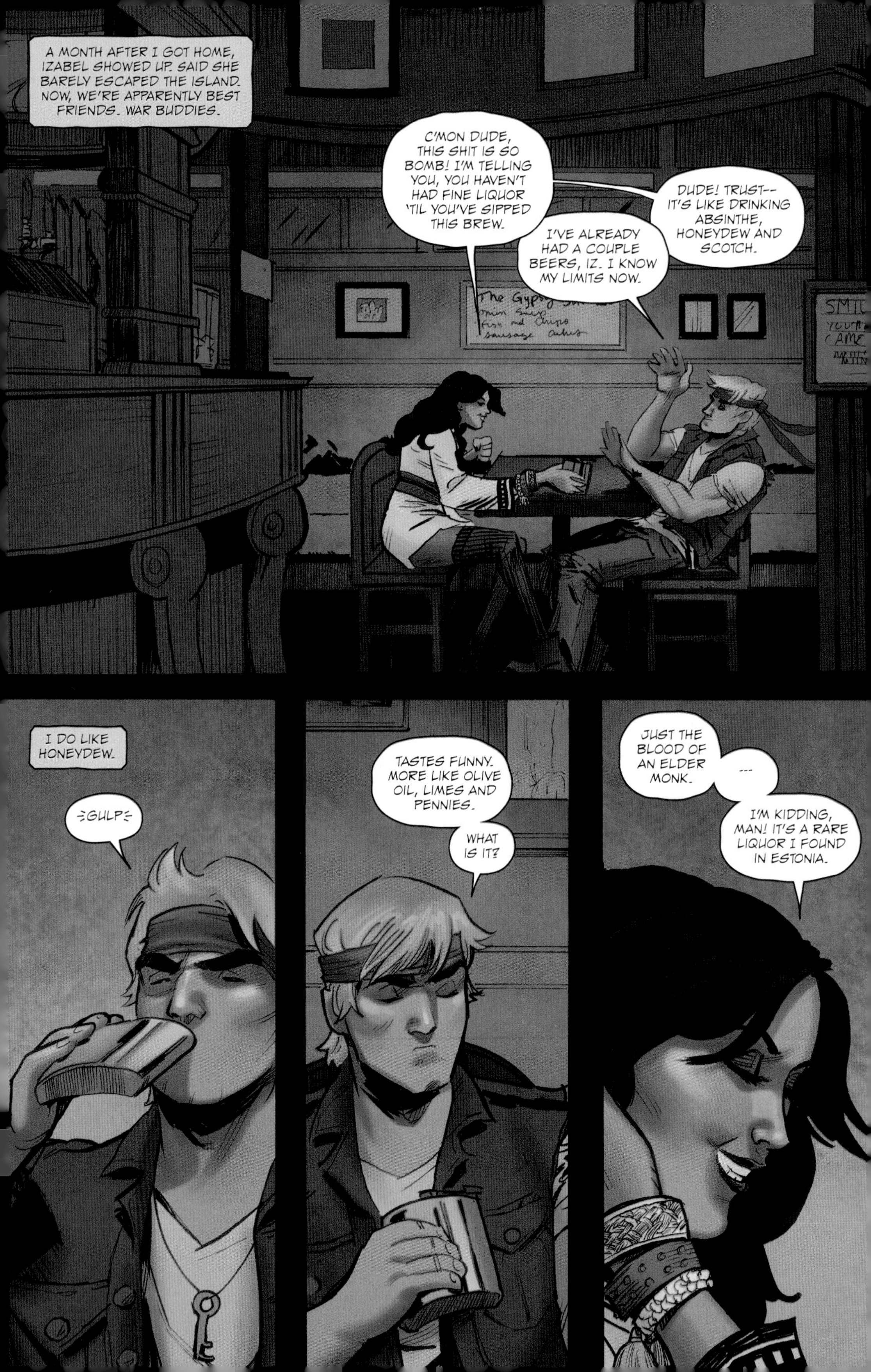

A MONTH AFTER I GOT HOME, IZABEL SHOWED UP. SAID SHE BARELY ESCAPED THE ISLAND. NOW, WE'RE APPARENTLY BEST FRIENDS. WAR BUDDIES.
C'MON DUDE, THIS SHIT IS SO BOMB! I'M TELLING YOU, YOU HAVEN'T HAD FINE LIQUOR 'TIL YOU'VE SIPPED THIS BREW.
I'VE ALREADY HAD A COUPLE BEERS, IZ. I KNOW MY LIMITS NOW.
DUDE! TRUST-- IT'S LIKE DRINKING ABSINTHE, HONEYDEW AND SCOTCH.
I DO LIKE HONEYDEW.
GULP
TASTES FUNNY. MORE LIKE OLIVE OIL, LIMES AND PENNIES.
WHAT IS IT?
JUST THE BLOOD OF AN ELDER MONK.
...
I'M KIDDING, MAN! IT'S A RARE LIQUOR I FOUND IN ESTONIA.

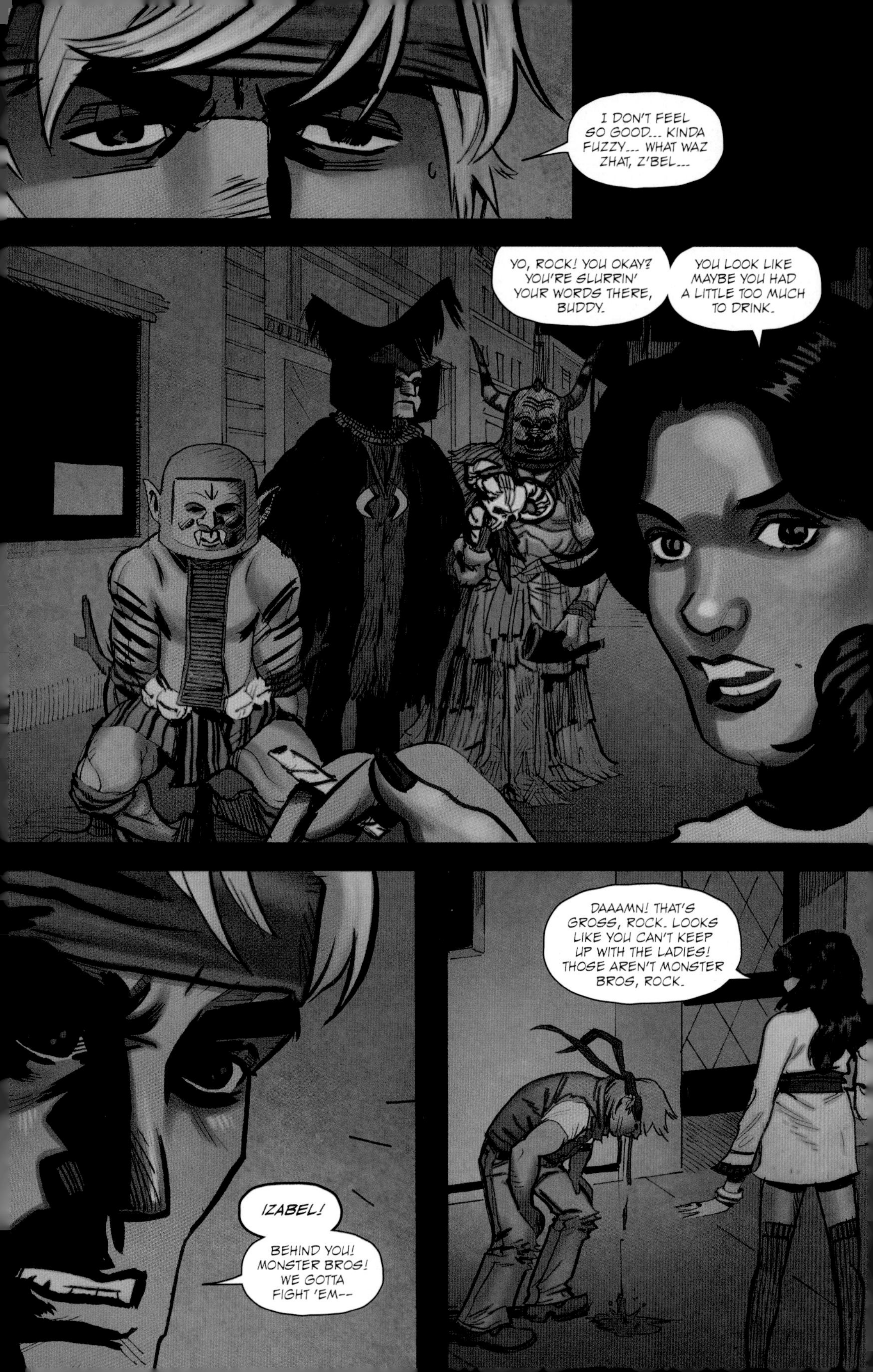
I DON'T FEEL SO GOOD... KINDA FUZZY... WHAT WAZ ZHAT, Z'BEL...
YO, ROCK! YOU OKAY? YOU'RE SLURRIN' YOUR WORDS THERE, BUDDY.
YOU LOOK LIKE MAYBE YOU HAD A LITTLE TOO MUCH TO DRINK.
IZABEL!
BEHIND YOU! MONSTER BROS! WE GOTTA FIGHT 'EM--
DAAAMN! THAT'S GROSS, ROCK. LOOKS LIKE YOU CAN'T KEEP UP WITH THE LADIES! THOSE AREN'T MONSTER BROS, ROCK.

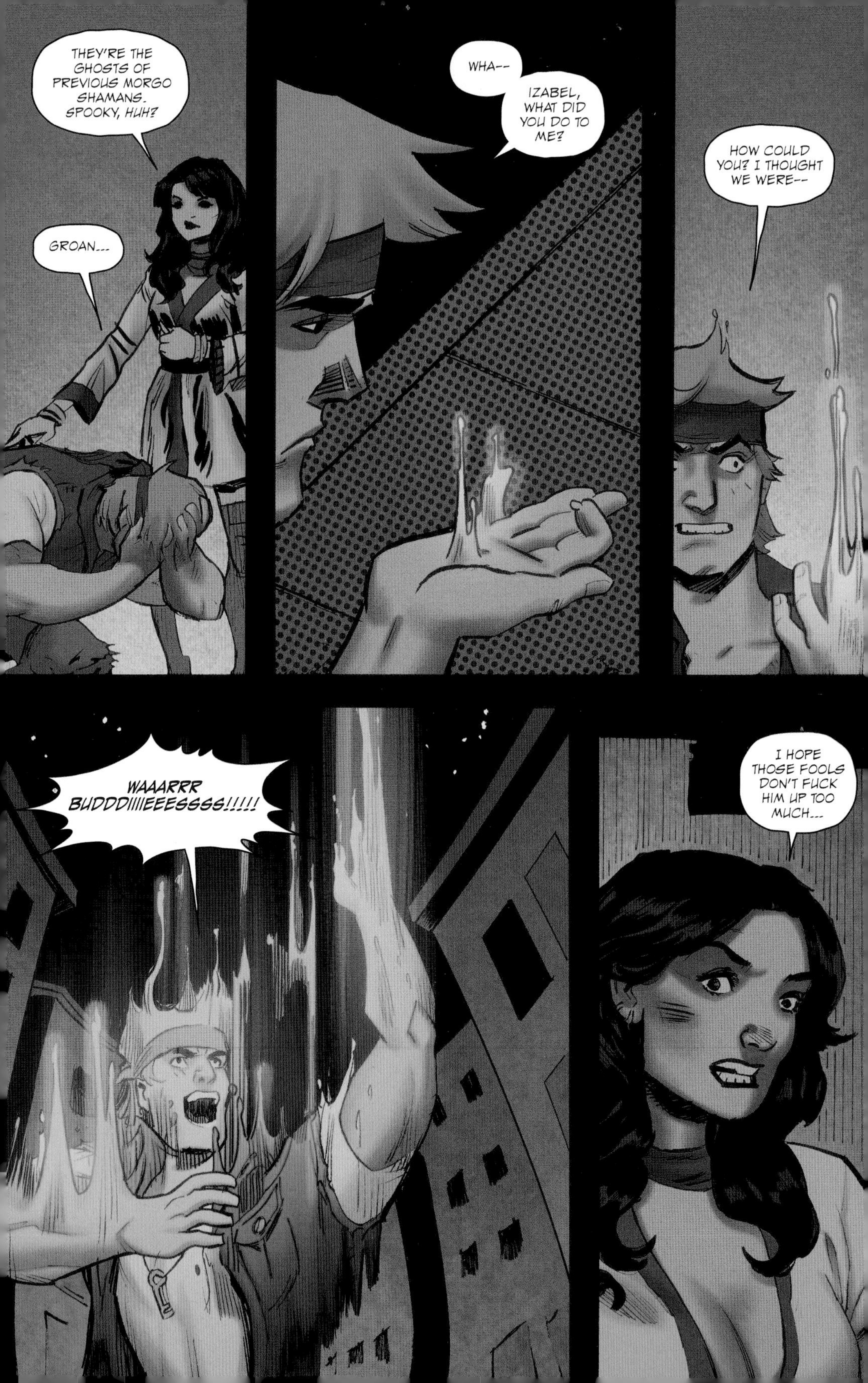
THEY'RE THE GHOSTS OF PREVIOUS MORGO SHAMANS. SPOOKY, HUH?
GROAN...
WHA--
IZABEL, WHAT DID YOU DO TO ME?
HOW COULD YOU? I THOUGHT WE WERE--
WAAARRR BUDDDIIIIEEESSSS!!!!!
I HOPE THOSE FOOLS DON'T FUCK HIM UP TOO MUCH...

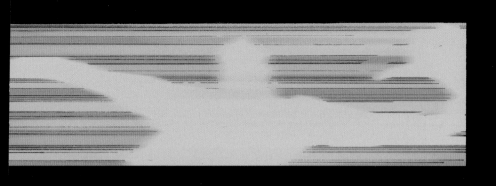

OUR CHAMPION... WHO IS RESPONSIBLE FOR HIS DEATH?

WE MADE A DEAL WITH ELYSE. SHE ASSURED US OUR CHAMPION WOULD WIN. WHY WOULD SHE BETRAY US?

IT WAS NOT HER. IT WAS ONE OF YOU.

TECHNICALLY IT WAS THE WITCH ELYSE. SHE'S RESPONSIBLE FOR THIS WHOLE TOURNAMENT.

WELL...THERE MAY HAVE BEEN THIS GUY WHO STARTED A REBELLION... NOTSAYINGIKNOWHIM...

BUT IF I DID...

PROMISE NOT TO KILL ME?

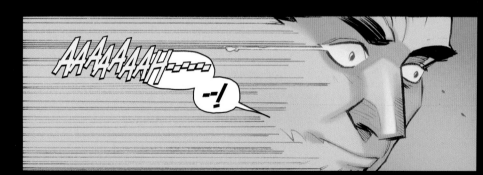

AAAAAAAH----!

THIS BETRAYAL REQUIRES AN OBLATION. MAKE THE BETRAYER DRINK THIS. IT WILL BRING HIM TO US. YOU DO THIS, AND YOUR LIFE WILL BE SPARED.

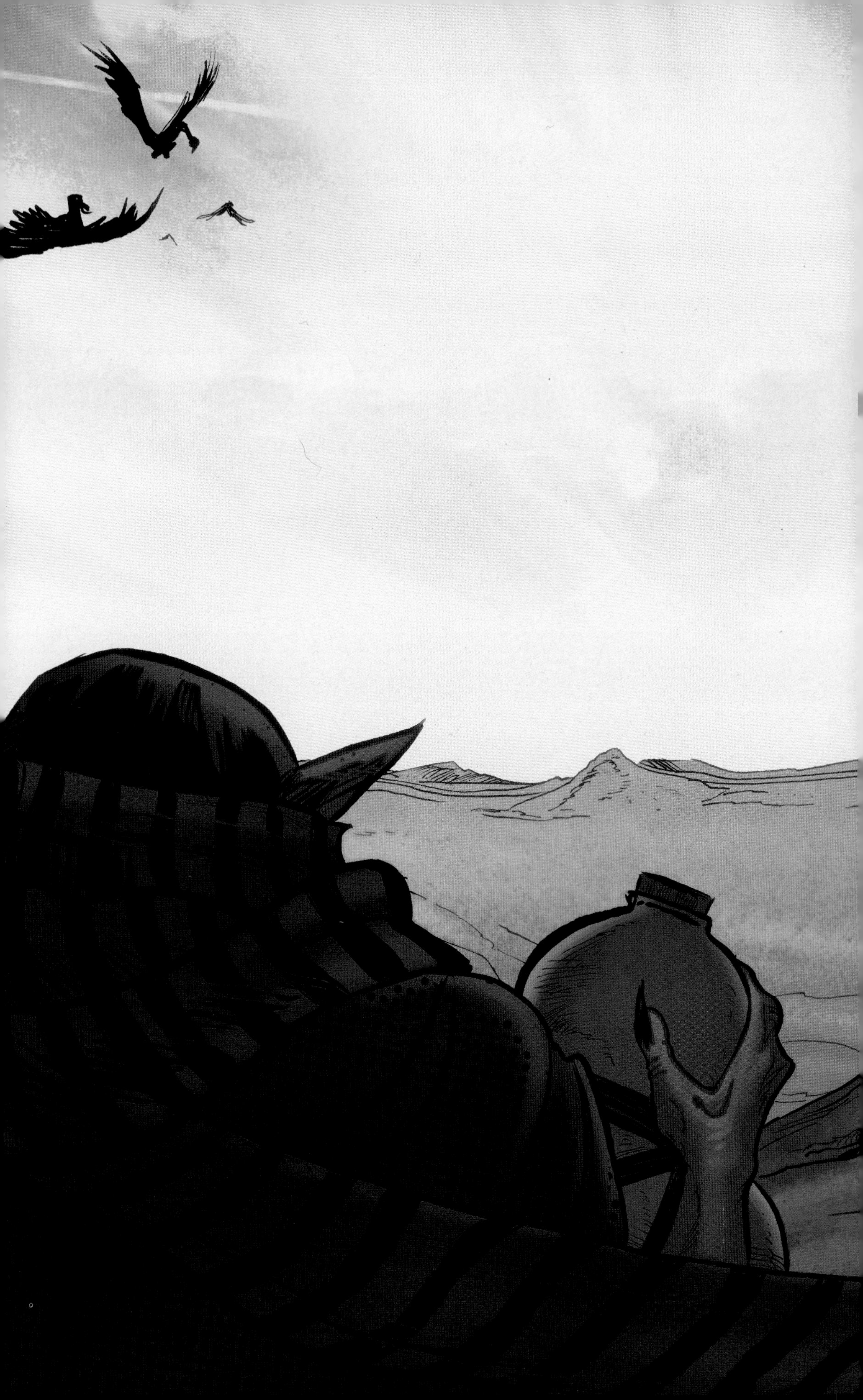

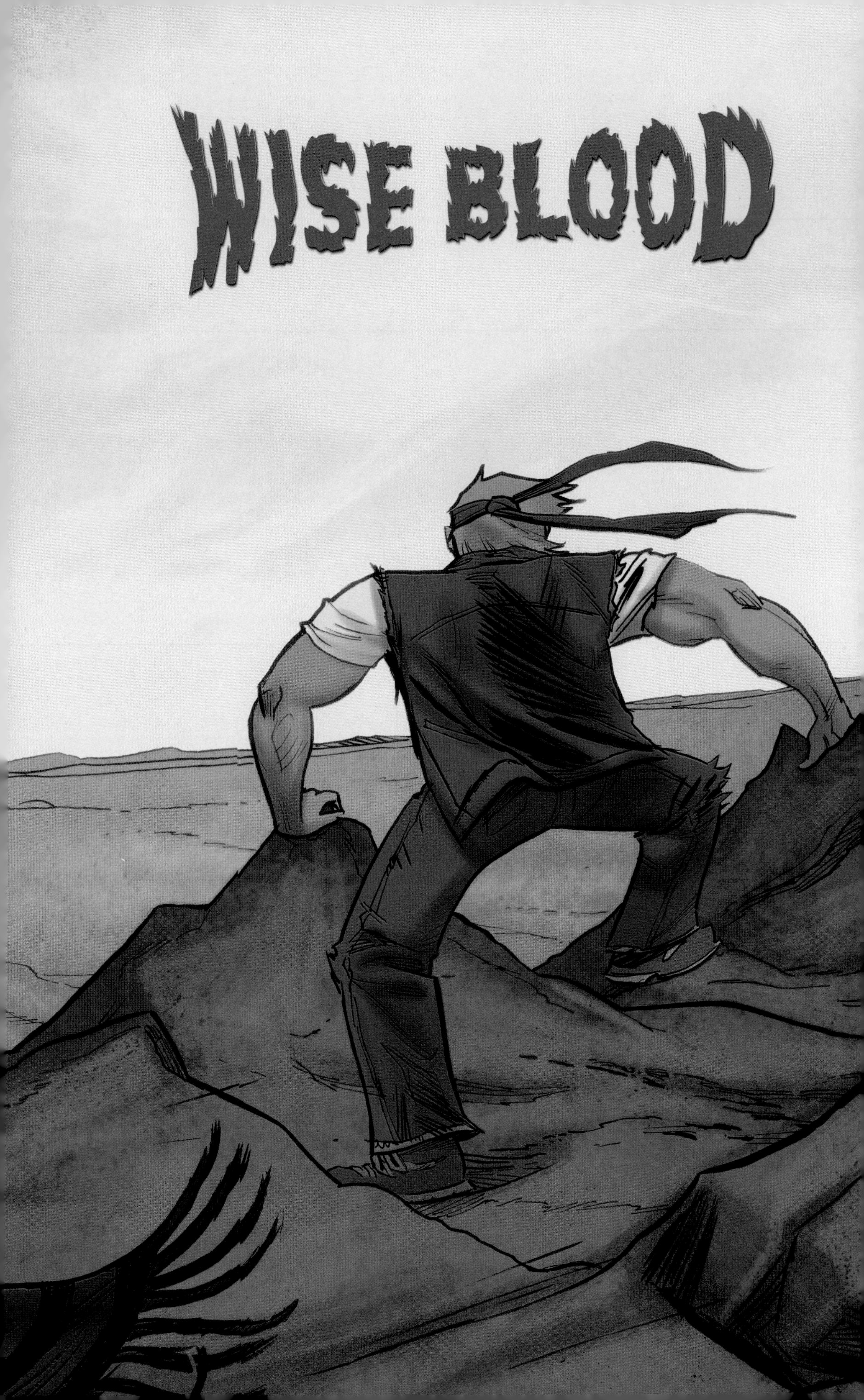
WISE BLOOD

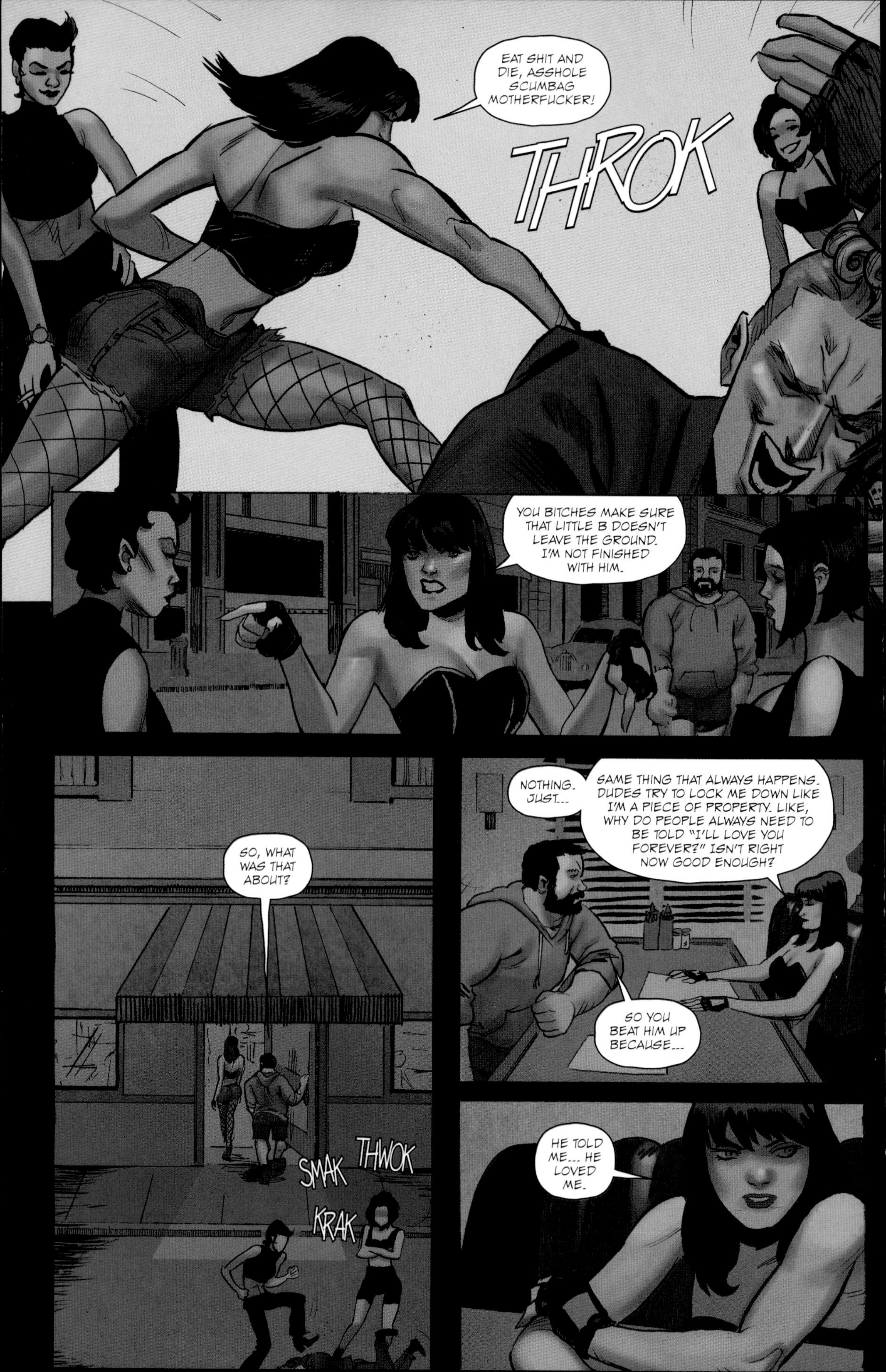
EAT SHIT AND DIE, ASSHOLE SCUMBAG MOTHERFUCKER!
THROK
YOU BITCHES MAKE SURE THAT LITTLE B DOESN'T LEAVE THE GROUND. I'M NOT FINISHED WITH HIM.
SO, WHAT WAS THAT ABOUT?
SMAK
THWOK
KRAK
NOTHING. JUST...
SAME THING THAT ALWAYS HAPPENS. DUDES TRY TO LOCK ME DOWN LIKE I'M A PIECE OF PROPERTY. LIKE, WHY DO PEOPLE ALWAYS NEED TO BE TOLD "I'LL LOVE YOU FOREVER?" ISN'T RIGHT NOW GOOD ENOUGH?
SO YOU BEAT HIM UP BECAUSE...
HE TOLD ME... HE LOVED ME.

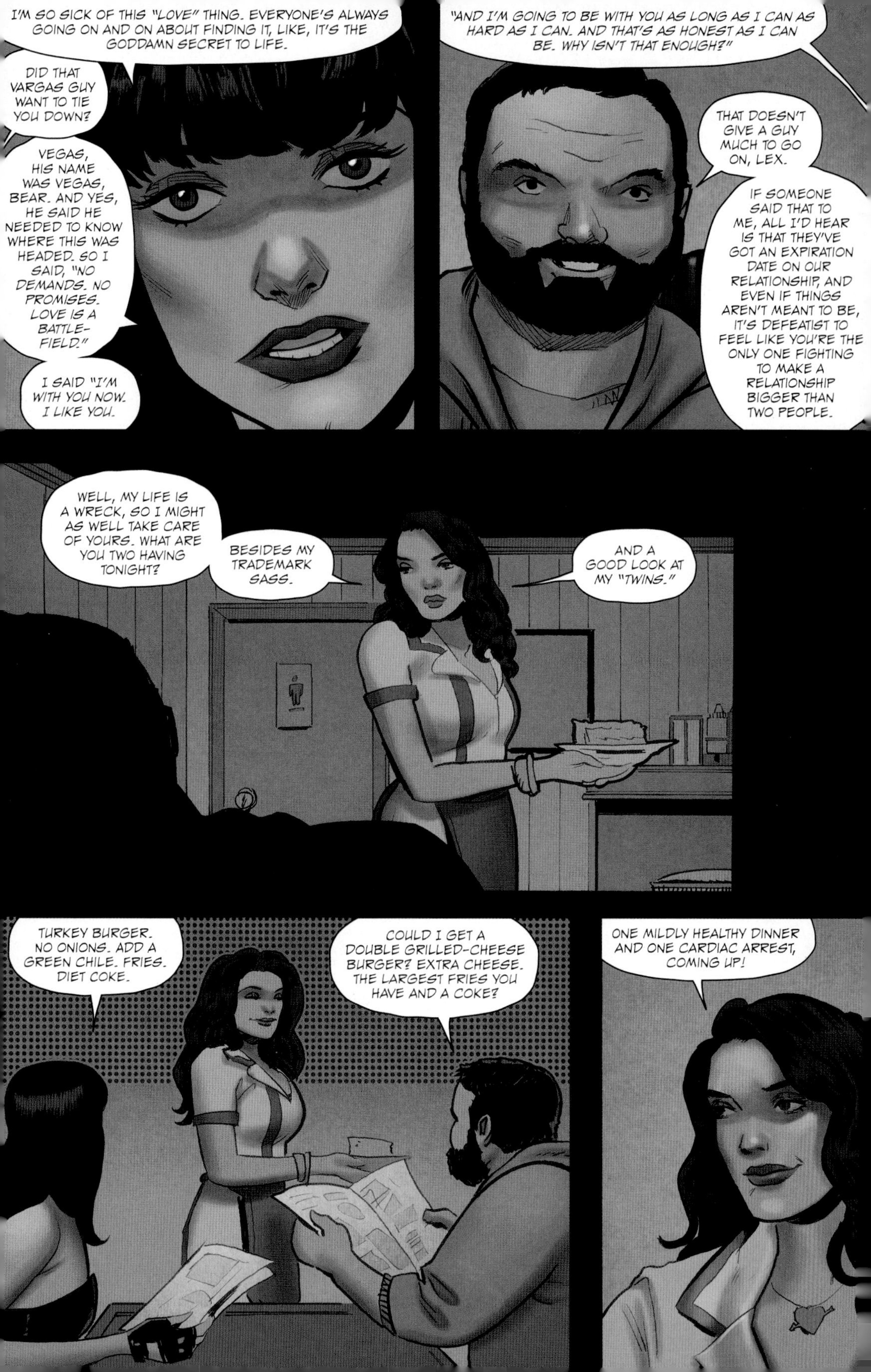
I'M SO SICK OF THIS "LOVE" THING. EVERYONE'S ALWAYS GOING ON AND ON ABOUT FINDING IT, LIKE, IT'S THE GODDAMN SECRET TO LIFE.
DID THAT VARGAS GUY WANT TO TIE YOU DOWN?
VEGAS, HIS NAME WAS VEGAS, BEAR. AND YES, HE SAID HE NEEDED TO KNOW WHERE THIS WAS HEADED. SO I SAID, "NO DEMANDS. NO PROMISES. LOVE IS A BATTLE-FIELD."
I SAID "I'M WITH YOU NOW. I LIKE YOU.
"AND I'M GOING TO BE WITH YOU AS LONG AS I CAN AS HARD AS I CAN. AND THAT'S AS HONEST AS I CAN BE. WHY ISN'T THAT ENOUGH?"
THAT DOESN'T GIVE A GUY MUCH TO GO ON, LEX.
IF SOMEONE SAID THAT TO ME, ALL I'D HEAR IS THAT THEY'VE GOT AN EXPIRATION DATE ON OUR RELATIONSHIP, AND EVEN IF THINGS AREN'T MEANT TO BE, IT'S DEFEATIST TO FEEL LIKE YOU'RE THE ONLY ONE FIGHTING TO MAKE A RELATIONSHIP BIGGER THAN TWO PEOPLE.
WELL, MY LIFE IS A WRECK, SO I MIGHT AS WELL TAKE CARE OF YOURS. WHAT ARE YOU TWO HAVING TONIGHT?
BESIDES MY TRADEMARK SASS.
AND A GOOD LOOK AT MY "TWINS."
TURKEY BURGER. NO ONIONS. ADD A GREEN CHILE. FRIES. DIET COKE.
COULD I GET A DOUBLE GRILLED-CHEESE BURGER? EXTRA CHEESE. THE LARGEST FRIES YOU HAVE AND A COKE?
ONE MILDLY HEALTHY DINNER AND ONE CARDIAC ARREST, COMING UP!

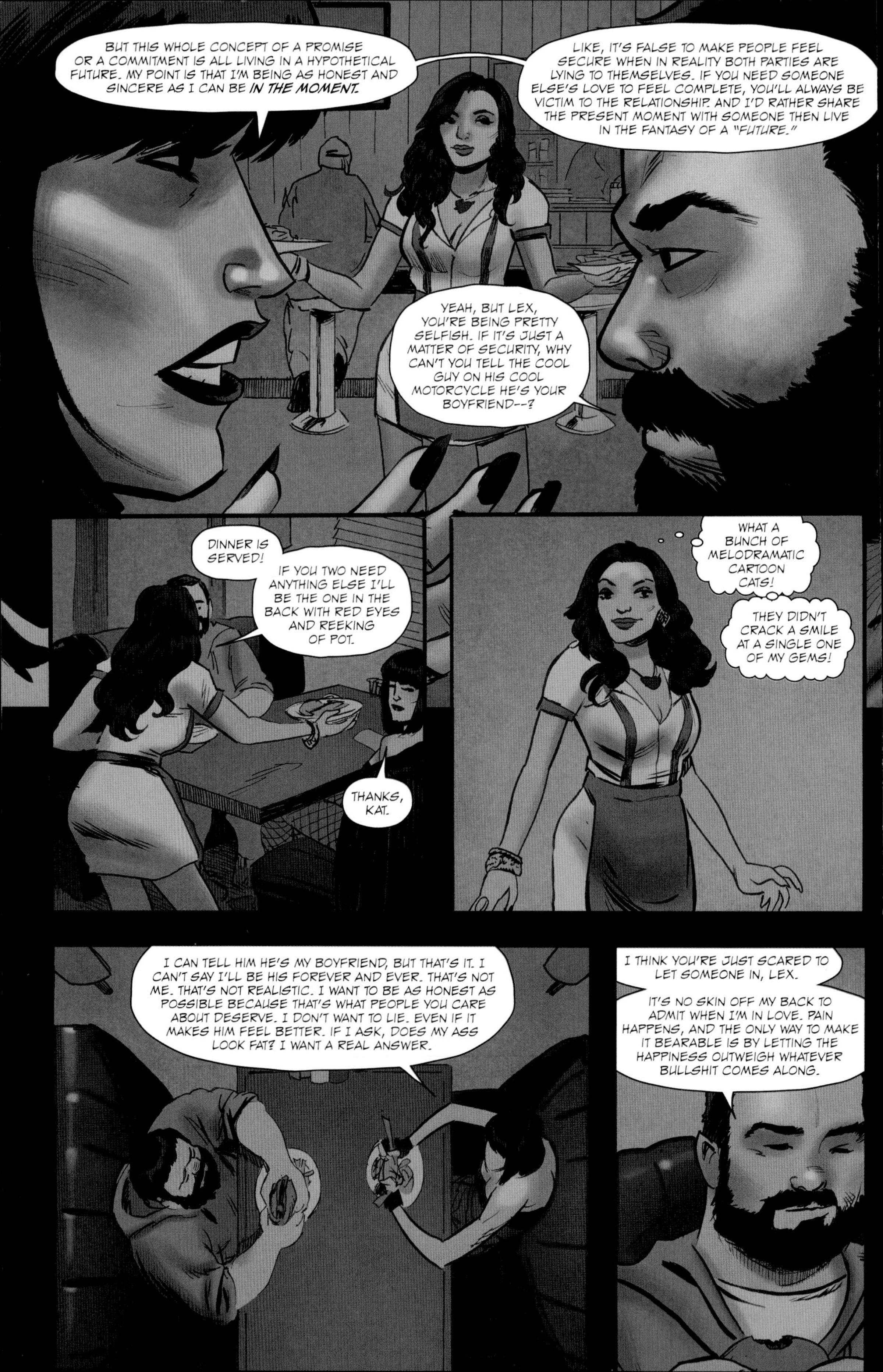
BUT THIS WHOLE CONCEPT OF A PROMISE OR A COMMITMENT IS ALL LIVING IN A HYPOTHETICAL FUTURE. MY POINT IS THAT I'M BEING AS HONEST AND SINCERE AS I CAN BE IN THE MOMENT.
LIKE, IT'S FALSE TO MAKE PEOPLE FEEL SECURE WHEN IN REALITY BOTH PARTIES ARE LYING TO THEMSELVES. IF YOU NEED SOMEONE ELSE'S LOVE TO FEEL COMPLETE, YOU'LL ALWAYS BE VICTIM TO THE RELATIONSHIP. AND I'D RATHER SHARE THE PRESENT MOMENT WITH SOMEONE THEN LIVE IN THE FANTASY OF A "FUTURE."
YEAH, BUT LEX, YOU'RE BEING PRETTY SELFISH. IF IT'S JUST A MATTER OF SECURITY, WHY CAN'T YOU TELL THE COOL GUY ON HIS COOL MOTORCYCLE HE'S YOUR BOYFRIEND--?
DINNER IS SERVED!
IF YOU TWO NEED ANYTHING ELSE I'LL BE THE ONE IN THE BACK WITH RED EYES AND REEKING OF POT.
THANKS, KAT.
WHAT A BUNCH OF MELODRAMATIC CARTOON CATS!
THEY DIDN'T CRACK A SMILE AT A SINGLE ONE OF MY GEMS!
I CAN TELL HIM HE'S MY BOYFRIEND, BUT THAT'S IT. I CAN'T SAY I'LL BE HIS FOREVER AND EVER. THAT'S NOT ME. THAT'S NOT REALISTIC. I WANT TO BE AS HONEST AS POSSIBLE BECAUSE THAT'S WHAT PEOPLE YOU CARE ABOUT DESERVE. I DON'T WANT TO LIE. EVEN IF IT MAKES HIM FEEL BETTER. IF I ASK, DOES MY ASS LOOK FAT? I WANT A REAL ANSWER.
I THINK YOU'RE JUST SCARED TO LET SOMEONE IN, LEX.
IT'S NO SKIN OFF MY BACK TO ADMIT WHEN I'M IN LOVE. PAIN HAPPENS, AND THE ONLY WAY TO MAKE IT BEARABLE IS BY LETTING THE HAPPINESS OUTWEIGH WHATEVER BULLSHIT COMES ALONG.

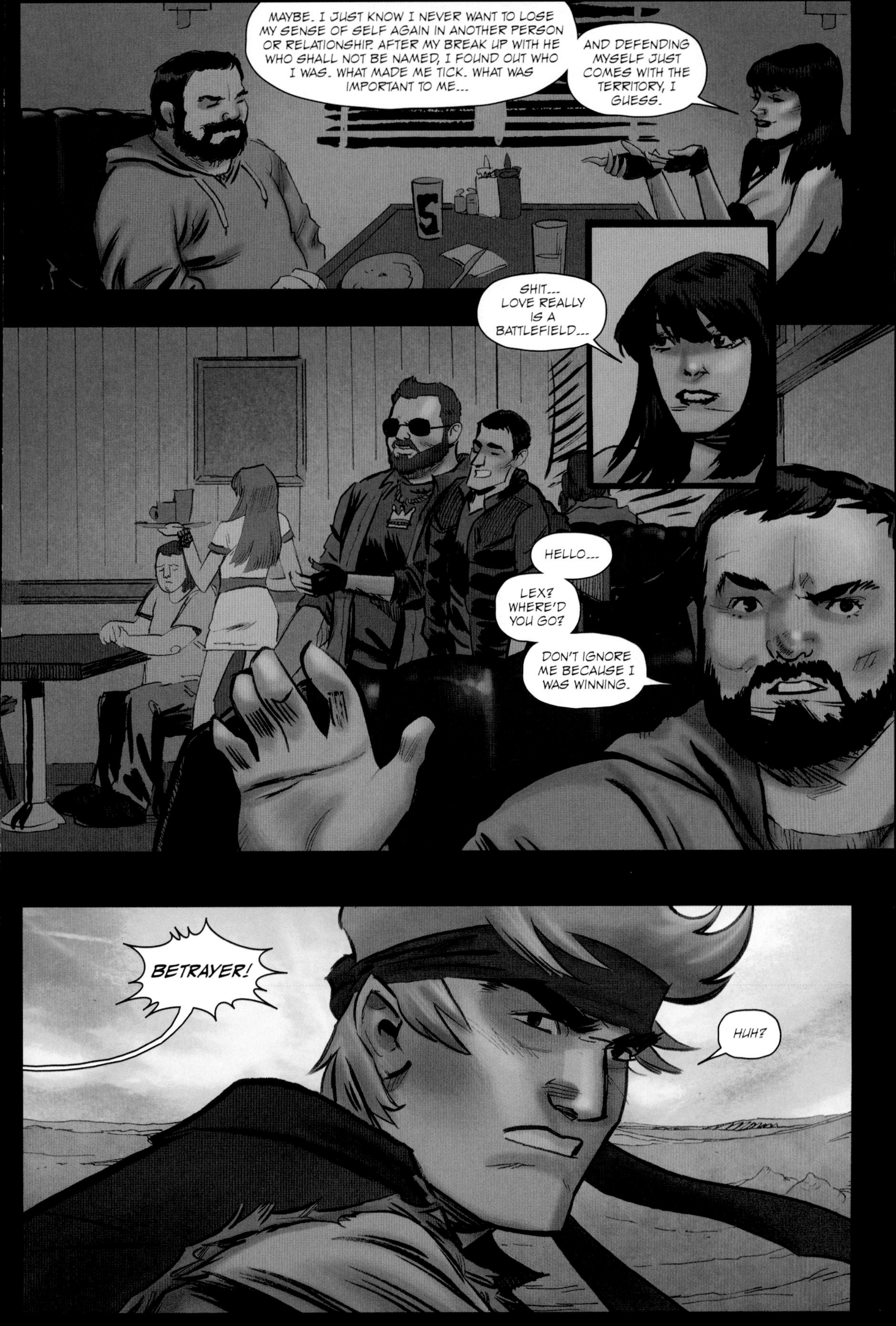
MAYBE. I JUST KNOW I NEVER WANT TO LOSE MY SENSE OF SELF AGAIN IN ANOTHER PERSON OR RELATIONSHIP. AFTER MY BREAK UP WITH HE WHO SHALL NOT BE NAMED, I FOUND OUT WHO I WAS. WHAT MADE ME TICK. WHAT WAS IMPORTANT TO ME...
AND DEFENDING MYSELF JUST COMES WITH THE TERRITORY, I GUESS.
SHIT... LOVE REALLY IS A BATTLEFIELD...
HELLO...
LEX? WHERE'D YOU GO?
DON'T IGNORE ME BECAUSE I WAS WINNING.
BETRAYER!
HUH?

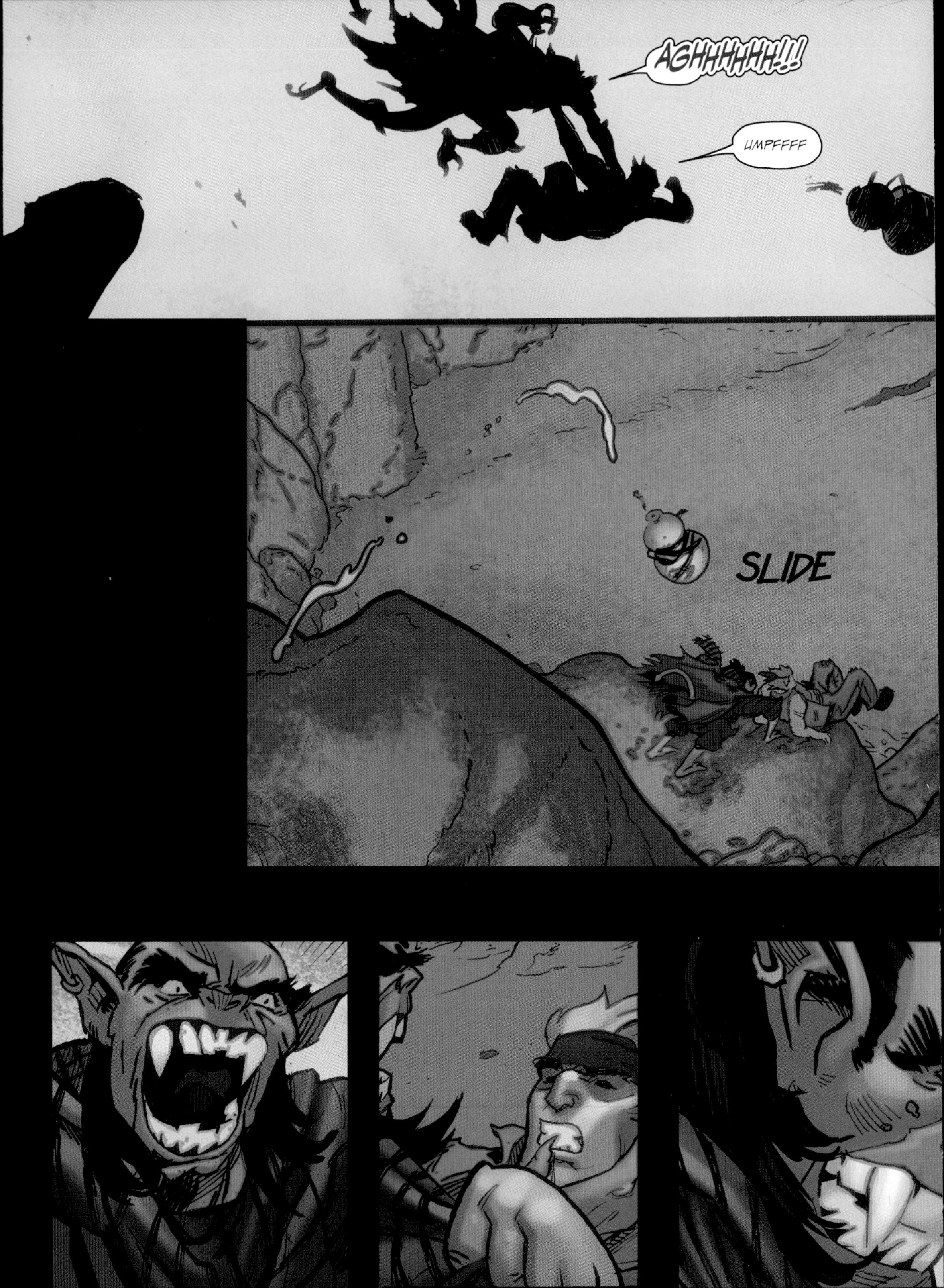
AGHHHHHH!!!
UMPFFFF
SLIDE

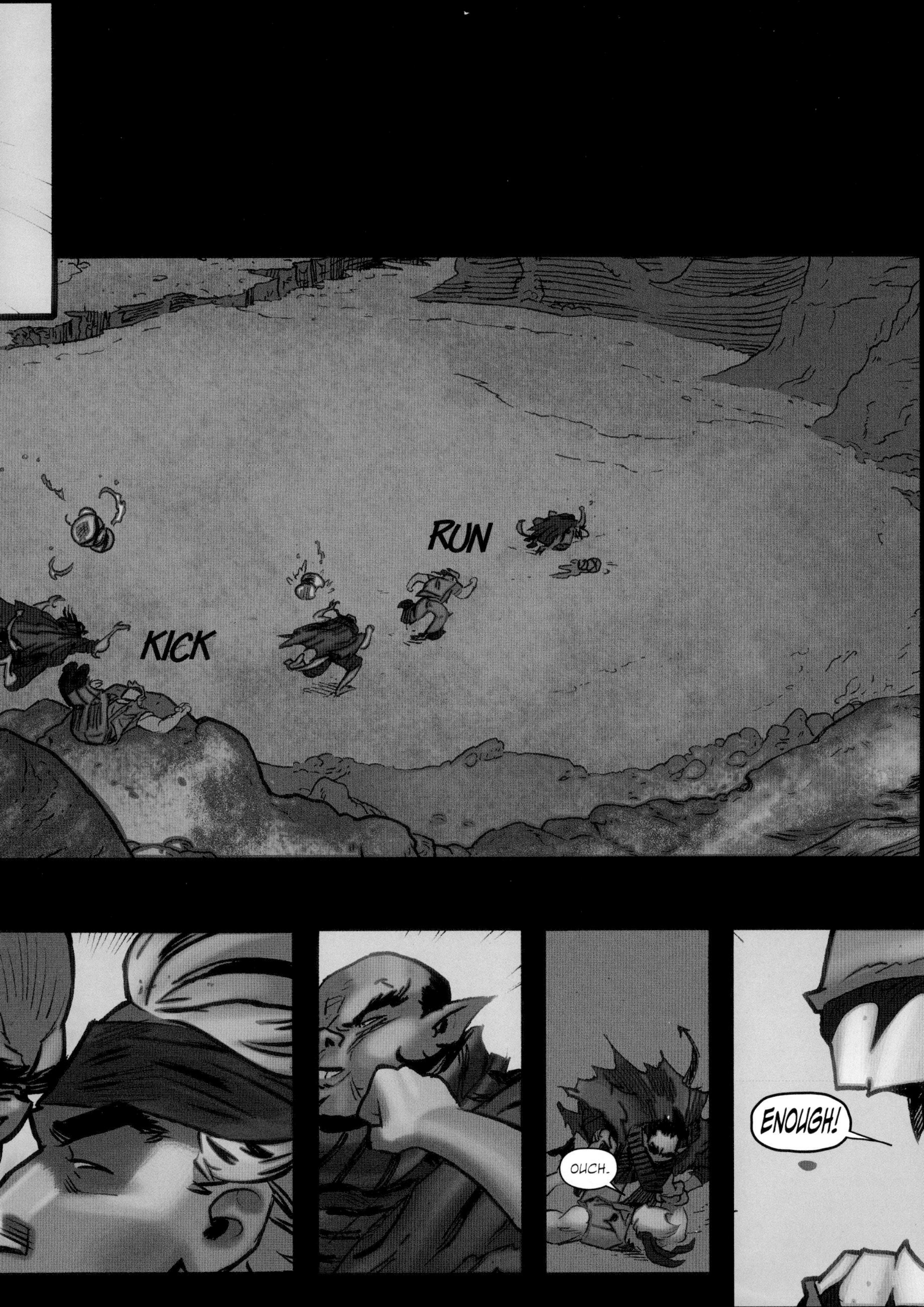
RUN
KICK
OUCH.
ENOUGH!

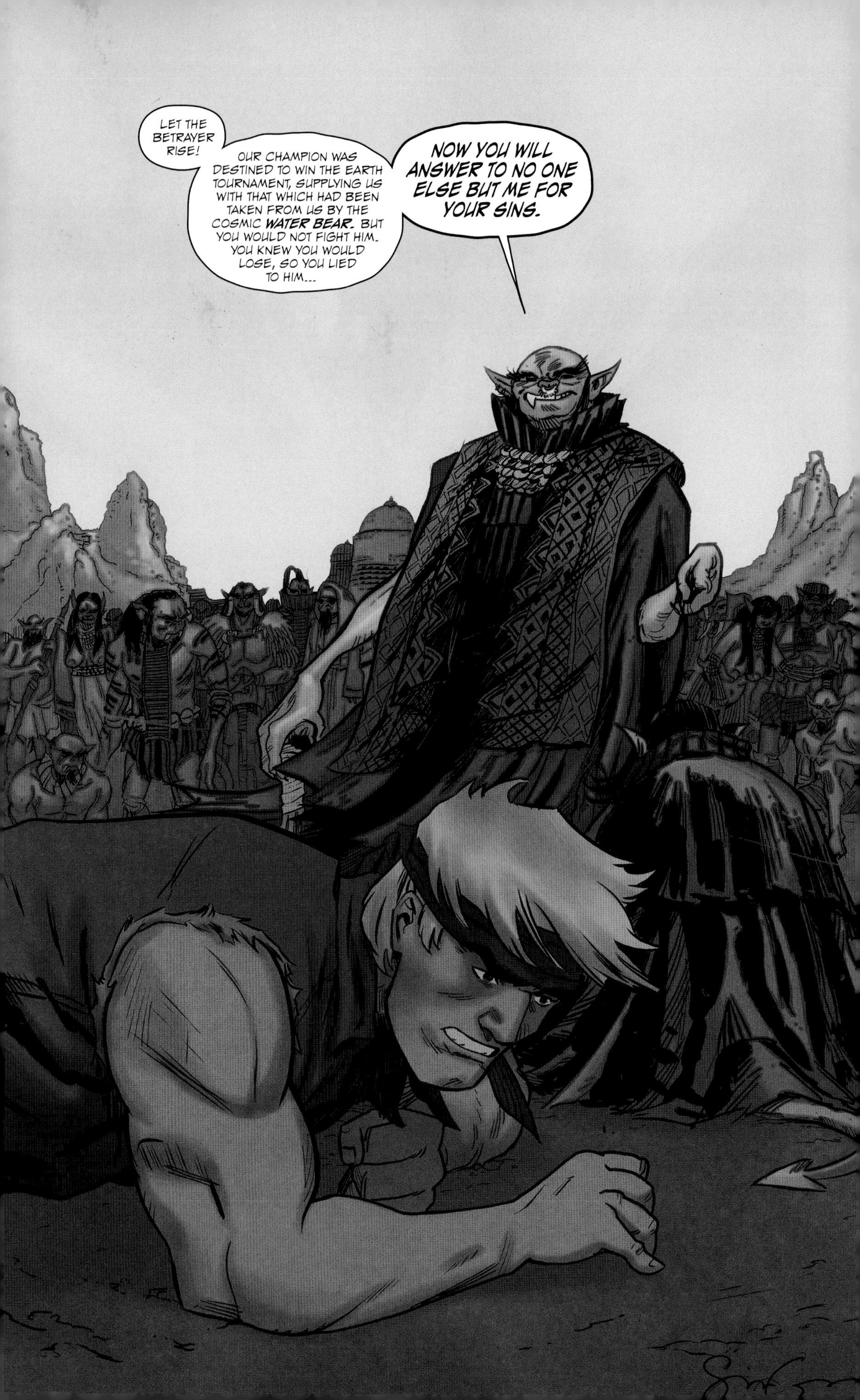
LET THE BETRAYER RISE!
OUR CHAMPION WAS DESTINED TO WIN THE EARTH TOURNAMENT, SUPPLYING US WITH THAT WHICH HAD BEEN TAKEN FROM US BY THE COSMIC WATER BEAR. BUT YOU WOULD NOT FIGHT HIM. YOU KNEW YOU WOULD LOSE, SO YOU LIED TO HIM...
NOW YOU WILL ANSWER TO NO ONE ELSE BUT ME FOR YOUR SINS.

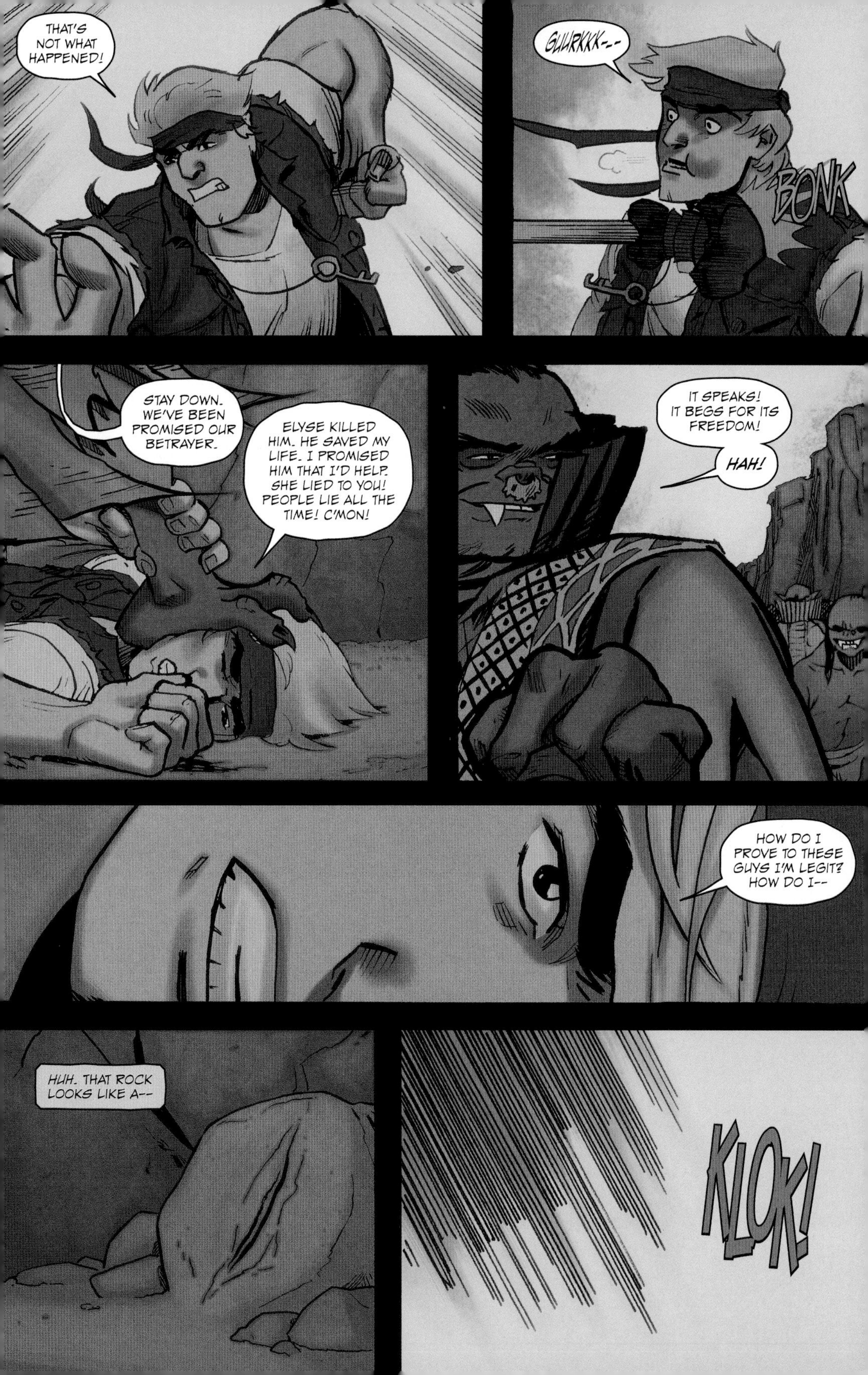
THAT'S NOT WHAT HAPPENED!
GUURKKK--
BONK
STAY DOWN. WE'VE BEEN PROMISED OUR BETRAYER.
ELYSE KILLED HIM. HE SAVED MY LIFE. I PROMISED HIM THAT I'D HELP. SHE LIED TO YOU! PEOPLE LIE ALL THE TIME! C'MON!
IT SPEAKS! IT BEGS FOR ITS FREEDOM!
HAH!
HOW DO I PROVE TO THESE GUYS I'M LEGIT? HOW DO I--
HUH. THAT ROCK LOOKS LIKE A--
KLOK!

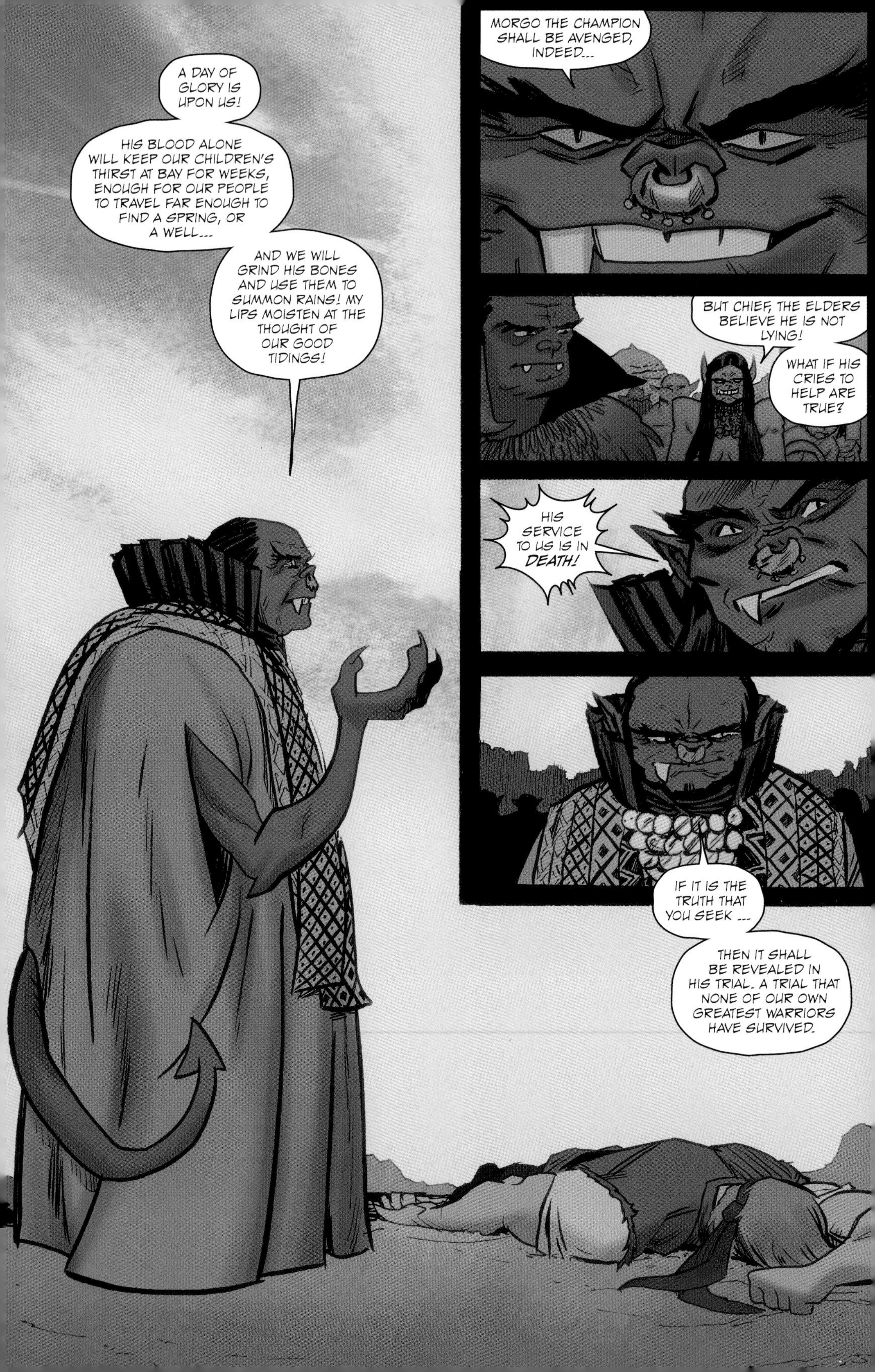
A DAY OF GLORY IS UPON US!
HIS BLOOD ALONE WILL KEEP OUR CHILDREN'S THIRST AT BAY FOR WEEKS, ENOUGH FOR OUR PEOPLE TO TRAVEL FAR ENOUGH TO FIND A SPRING, OR A WELL...
AND WE WILL GRIND HIS BONES AND USE THEM TO SUMMON RAINS! MY LIPS MOISTEN AT THE THOUGHT OF OUR GOOD TIDINGS!
MORGO THE CHAMPION SHALL BE AVENGED, INDEED...
BUT CHIEF, THE ELDERS BELIEVE HE IS NOT LYING!
WHAT IF HIS CRIES TO HELP ARE TRUE?
HIS SERVICE TO US IS IN DEATH!
IF IT IS THE TRUTH THAT YOU SEEK ...
THEN IT SHALL BE REVEALED IN HIS TRIAL. A TRIAL THAT NONE OF OUR OWN GREATEST WARRIORS HAVE SURVIVED.

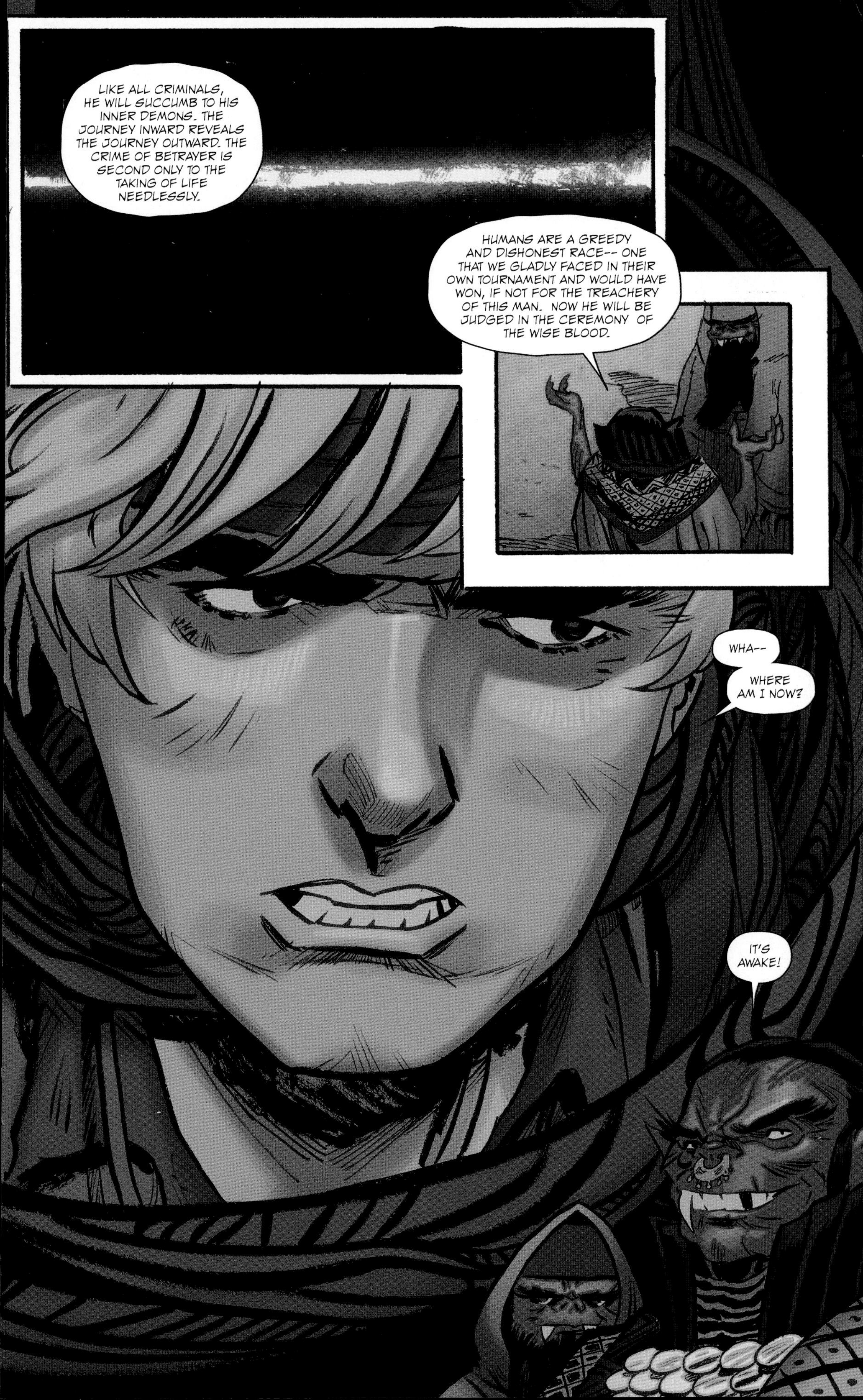
LIKE ALL CRIMINALS, HE WILL SUCCUMB TO HIS INNER DEMONS. THE JOURNEY INWARD REVEALS THE JOURNEY OUTWARD. THE CRIME OF BETRAYER IS SECOND ONLY TO THE TAKING OF LIFE NEEDLESSLY.
HUMANS ARE A GREEDY AND DISHONEST RACE-- ONE THAT WE GLADLY FACED IN THEIR OWN TOURNAMENT AND WOULD HAVE WON, IF NOT FOR THE TREACHERY OF THIS MAN. NOW HE WILL BE JUDGED IN THE CEREMONY OF THE WISE BLOOD.
WHA--
WHERE AM I NOW?
IT'S AWAKE!

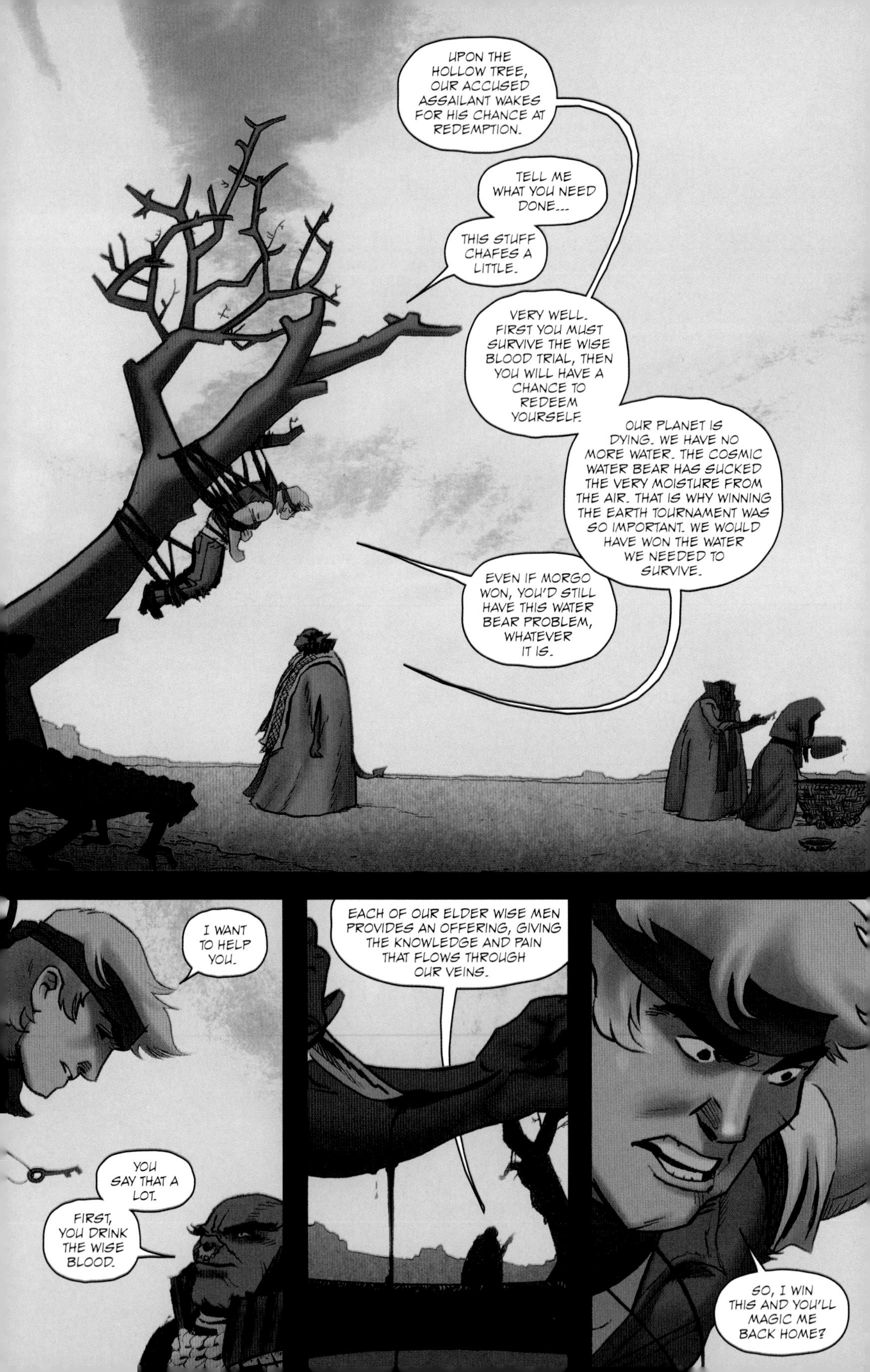
UPON THE HOLLOW TREE, OUR ACCUSED ASSAILANT WAKES FOR HIS CHANCE AT REDEMPTION.
TELL ME WHAT YOU NEED DONE...
THIS STUFF CHAFES A LITTLE.
VERY WELL. FIRST YOU MUST SURVIVE THE WISE BLOOD TRIAL, THEN YOU WILL HAVE A CHANCE TO REDEEM YOURSELF.
OUR PLANET IS DYING. WE HAVE NO MORE WATER. THE COSMIC WATER BEAR HAS SUCKED THE VERY MOISTURE FROM THE AIR. THAT IS WHY WINNING THE EARTH TOURNAMENT WAS SO IMPORTANT. WE WOULD HAVE WON THE WATER WE NEEDED TO SURVIVE.
EVEN IF MORGO WON, YOU'D STILL HAVE THIS WATER BEAR PROBLEM, WHATEVER IT IS.
I WANT TO HELP YOU.
YOU SAY THAT A LOT.
FIRST, YOU DRINK THE WISE BLOOD.
EACH OF OUR ELDER WISE MEN PROVIDES AN OFFERING, GIVING THE KNOWLEDGE AND PAIN THAT FLOWS THROUGH OUR VEINS.
SO, I WIN THIS AND YOU'LL MAGIC ME BACK HOME?

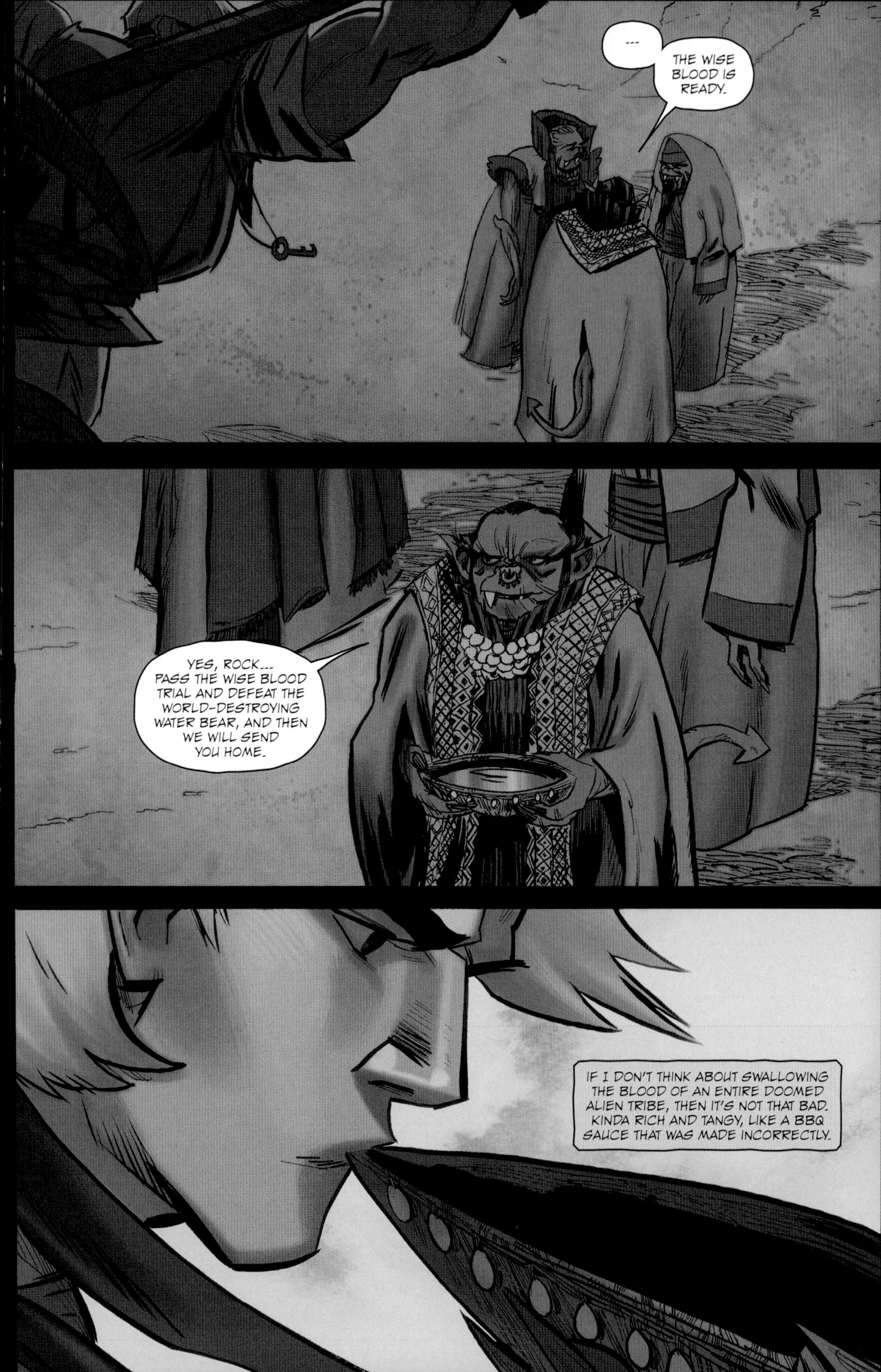
...
THE WISE BLOOD IS READY.
YES, ROCK... PASS THE WISE BLOOD TRIAL AND DEFEAT THE WORLD-DESTROYING WATER BEAR, AND THEN WE WILL SEND YOU HOME.
IF I DON'T THINK ABOUT SWALLOWING THE BLOOD OF AN ENTIRE DOOMED ALIEN TRIBE, THEN IT'S NOT THAT BAD. KINDA RICH AND TANGY, LIKE A BBQ SAUCE THAT WAS MADE INCORRECTLY.

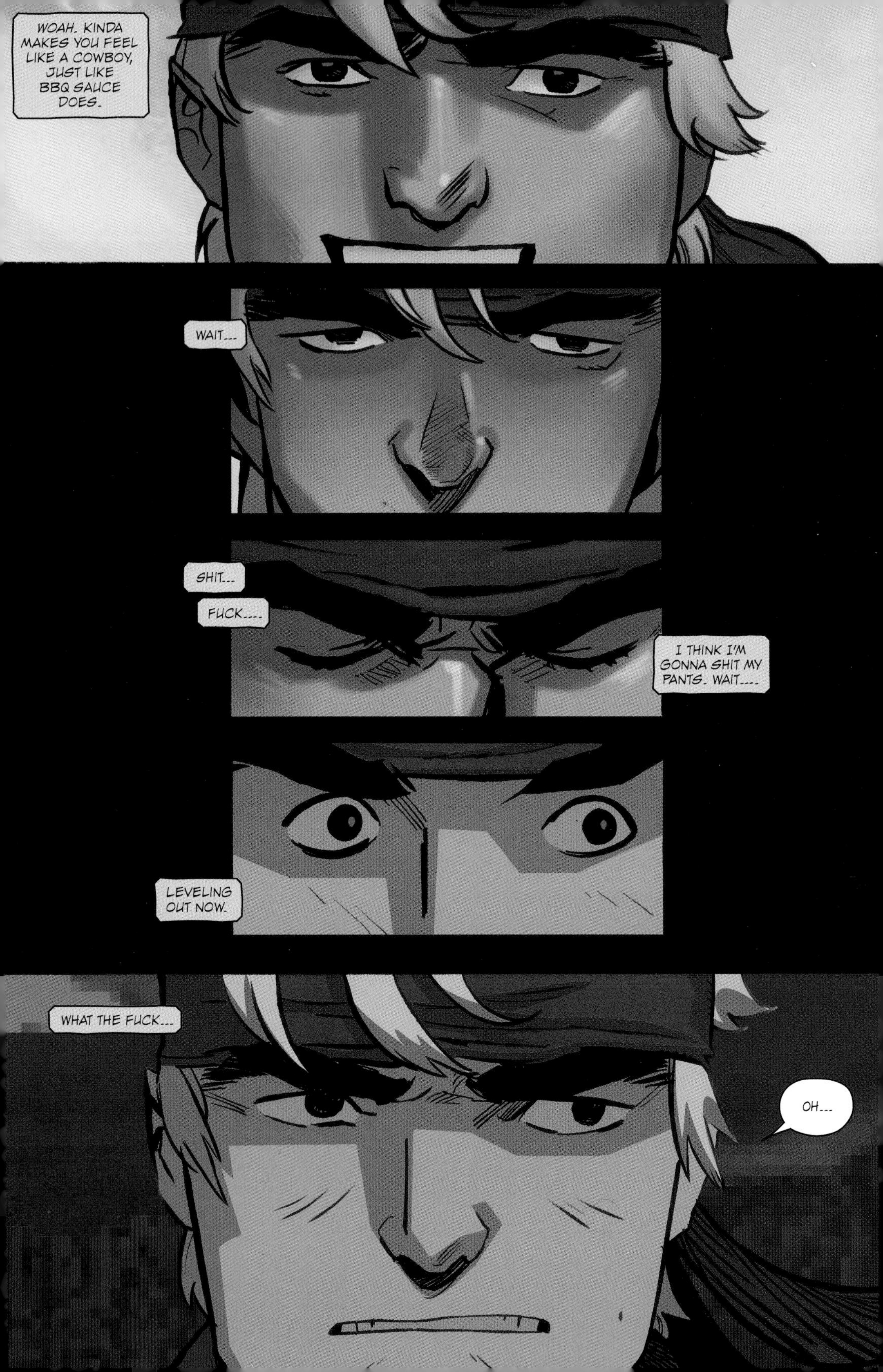
WOAH. KINDA MAKES YOU FEEL LIKE A COWBOY, JUST LIKE BBQ SAUCE DOES.
WAIT...
SHIT...
FUCK....
I THINK I'M GONNA SHIT MY PANTS. WAIT....
LEVELING OUT NOW.
WHAT THE FUCK...
OH...

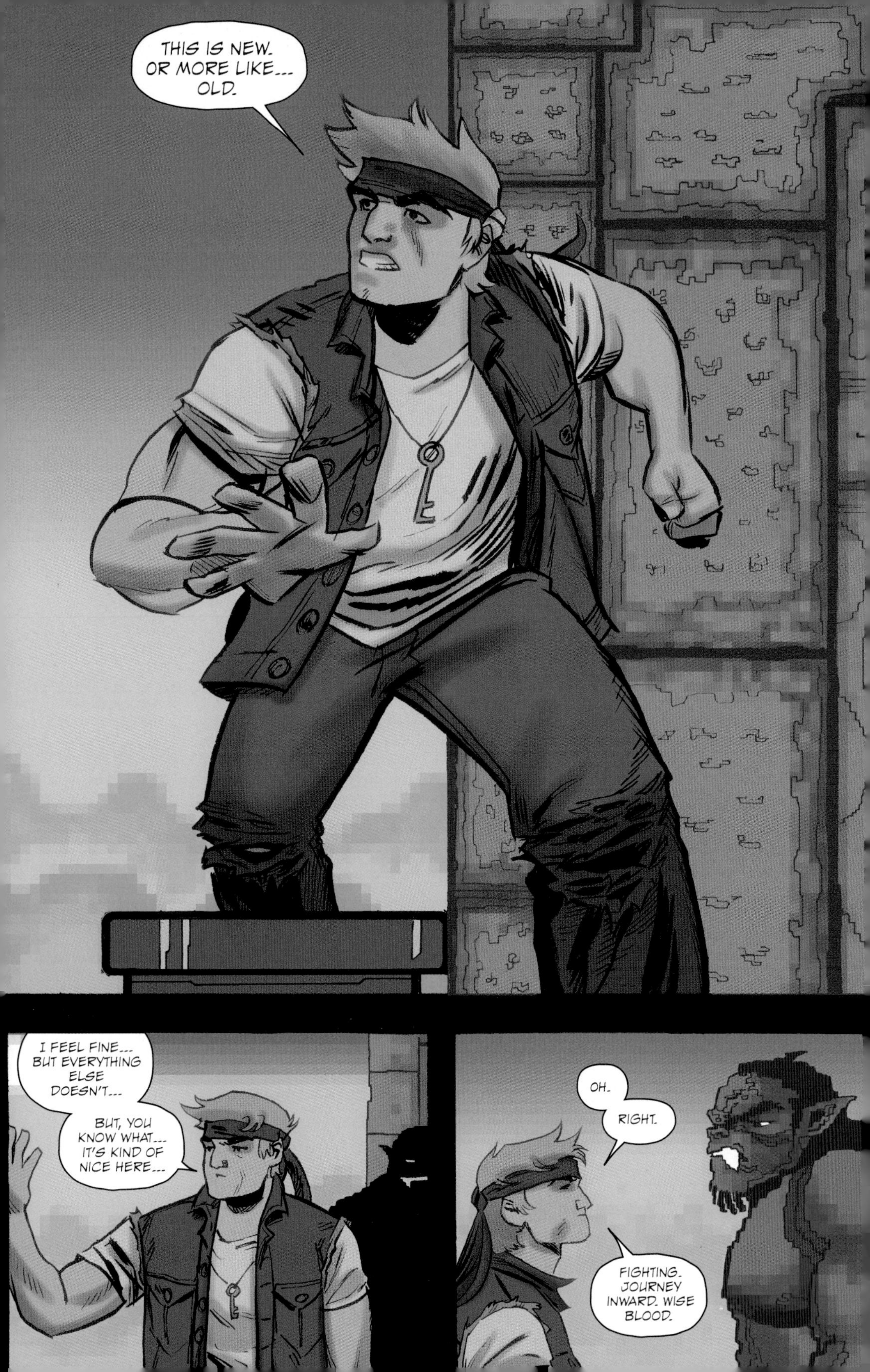
THIS IS NEW. OR MORE LIKE... OLD.
I FEEL FINE... BUT EVERYTHING ELSE DOESN'T...
BUT, YOU KNOW WHAT... IT'S KIND OF NICE HERE...
OH.
RIGHT.
FIGHTING. JOURNEY INWARD. WISE BLOOD.

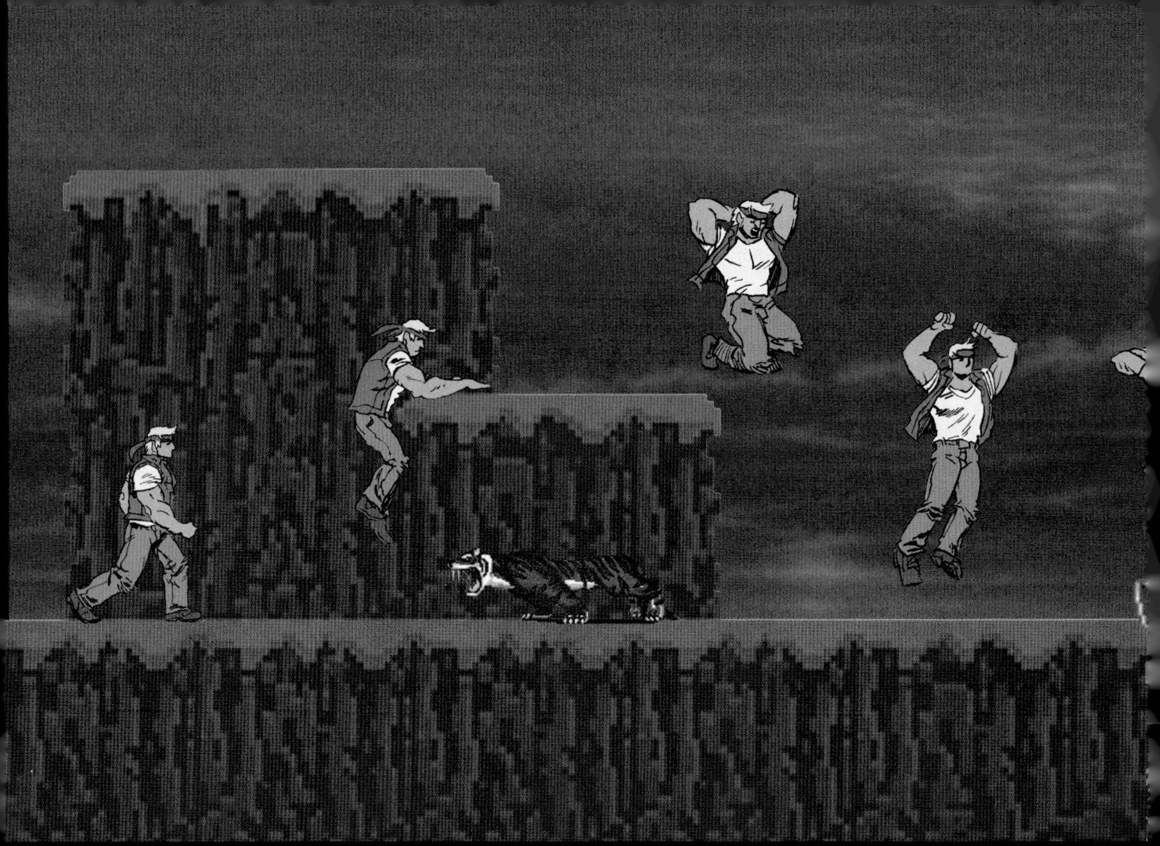

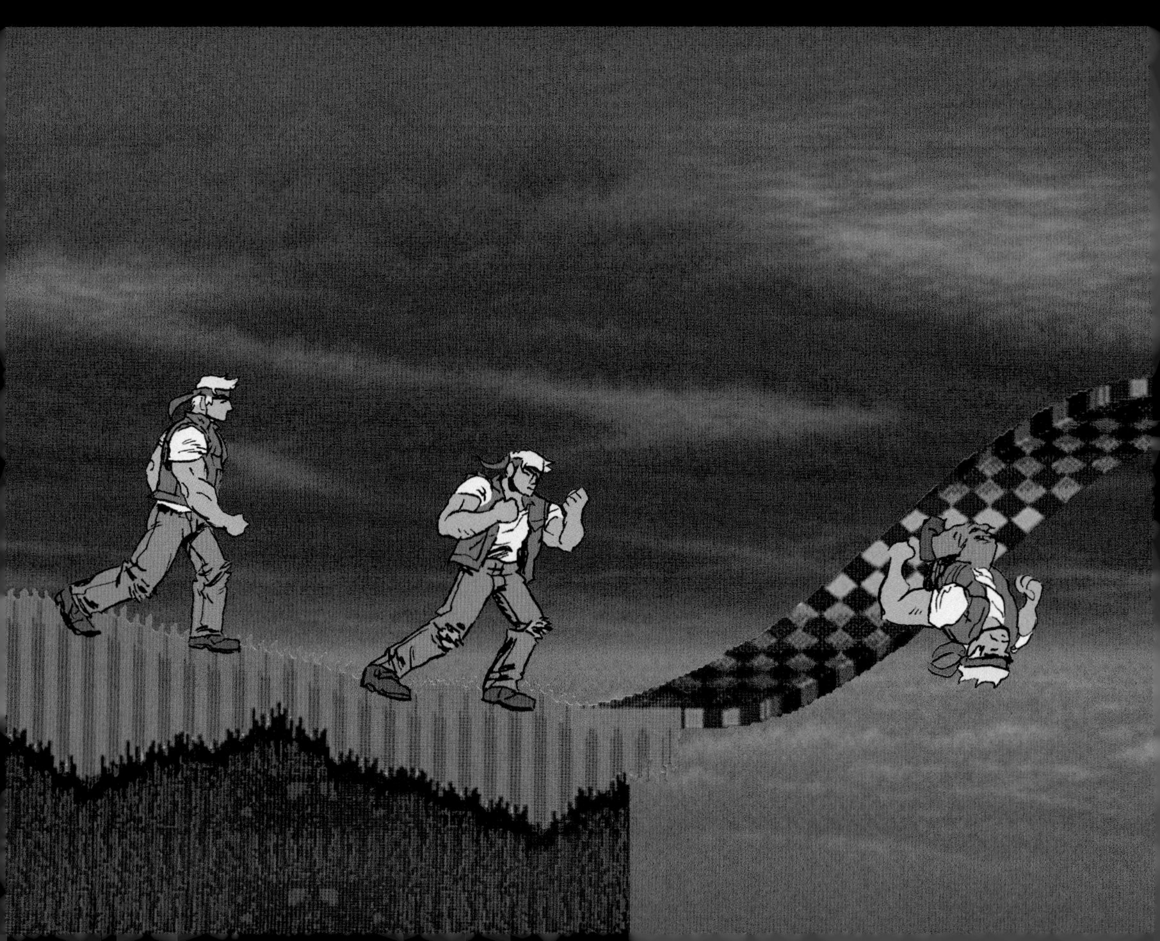

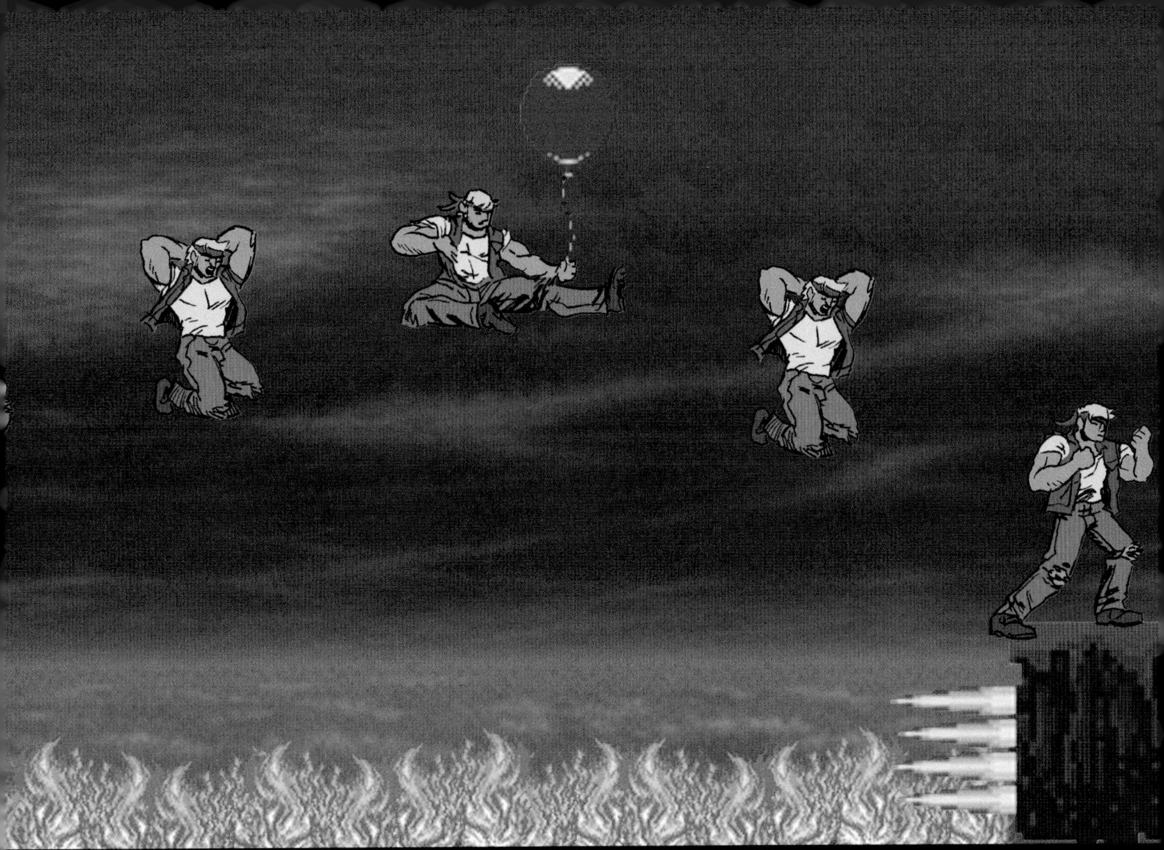

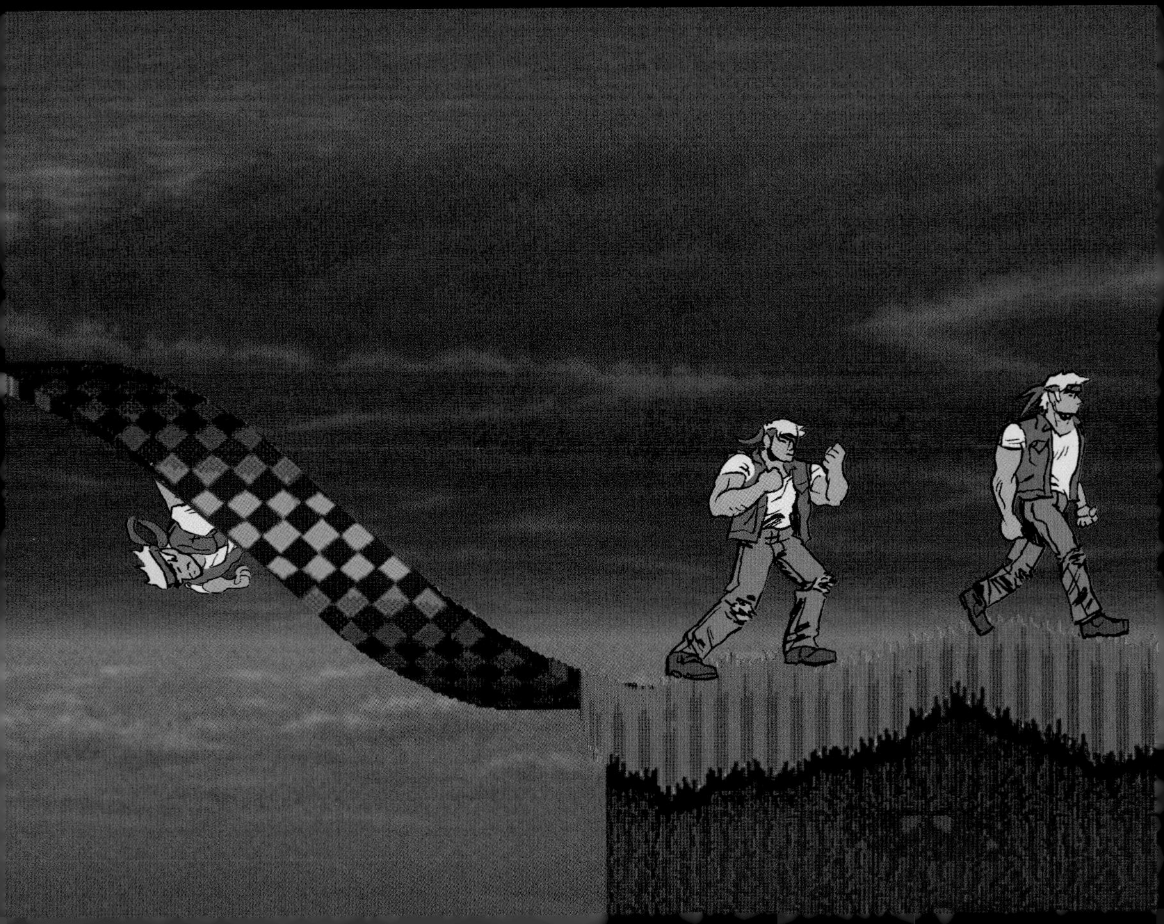

WELL, WELL, WELL, IF IT ISN'T HOME TOWN HERO, ROCK.THE LITTLE STREET RAT THAT COULD.

WHAT ARE YOU DOING HERE? I THOUGHT I KICKED YOUR HEAD OFF.

YES, I DO!
I HAVE A FAMILY NOW.

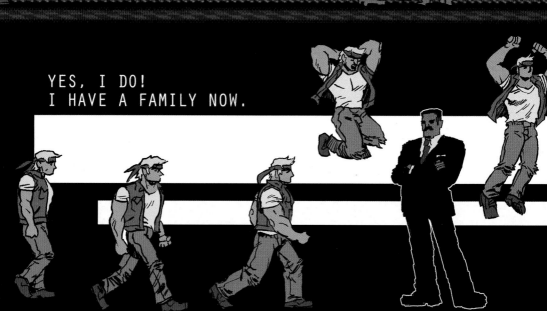

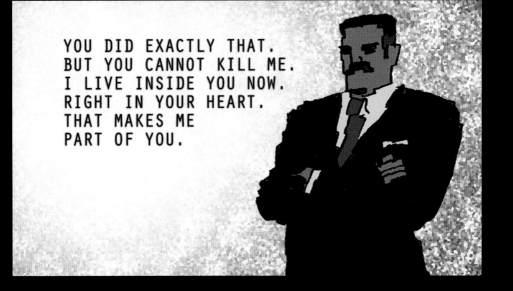

YOU DID EXACTLY THAT.
BUT YOU CANNOT KILL ME.
I LIVE INSIDE YOU NOW.
RIGHT IN YOUR HEART.
THAT MAKES ME
PART OF YOU.

NEVER. I DON'T NEED YOU
ANYMORE, MANN. I LIVE
FOR MORE NOW THAN JUST
ENDING YOU.

NO YOU DON'T.
YOU HAVE NOTHING,
ORPHAN SCUM--

SOME FAMILY.
A BUNCH OF
MISCREANTS AND
DEGENERATES.

MORE THAN YOU
EVER DID.

AND MORE THAN
ENOUGH FOR ME.

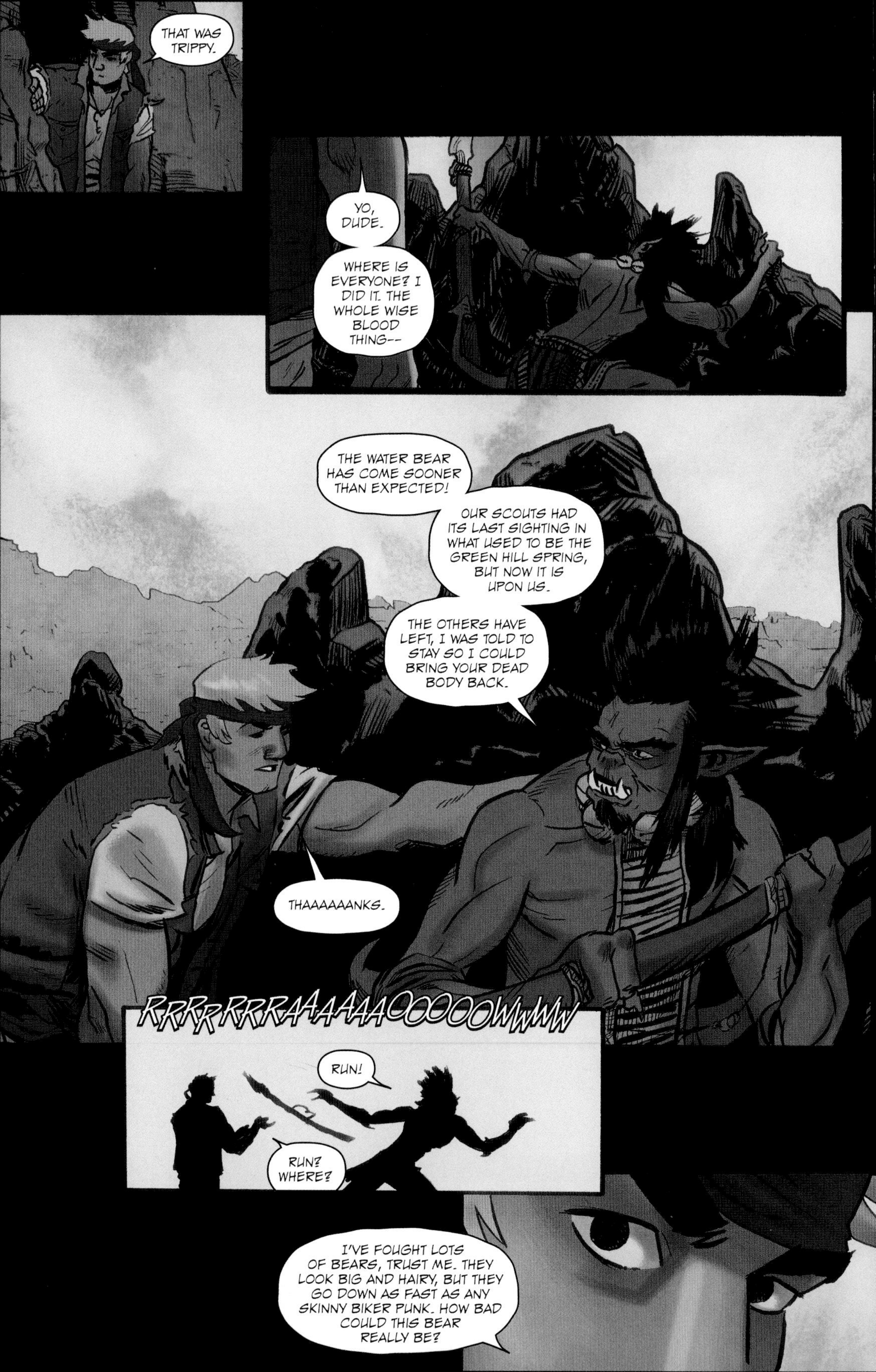
THAT WAS TRIPPY.
YO, DUDE.
WHERE IS EVERYONE? I DID IT. THE WHOLE WISE BLOOD THING--
THE WATER BEAR HAS COME SOONER THAN EXPECTED!
OUR SCOUTS HAD ITS LAST SIGHTING IN WHAT USED TO BE THE GREEN HILL SPRING, BUT NOW IT IS UPON US.
THE OTHERS HAVE LEFT, I WAS TOLD TO STAY SO I COULD BRING YOUR DEAD BODY BACK.
THAAAAAAANKS.
RRRRRRRRAAAAAAOOOOOOWWWW
RUN!
RUN? WHERE?
I'VE FOUGHT LOTS OF BEARS, TRUST ME. THEY LOOK BIG AND HAIRY, BUT THEY GO DOWN AS FAST AS ANY SKINNY BIKER PUNK. HOW BAD COULD THIS BEAR REALLY BE?

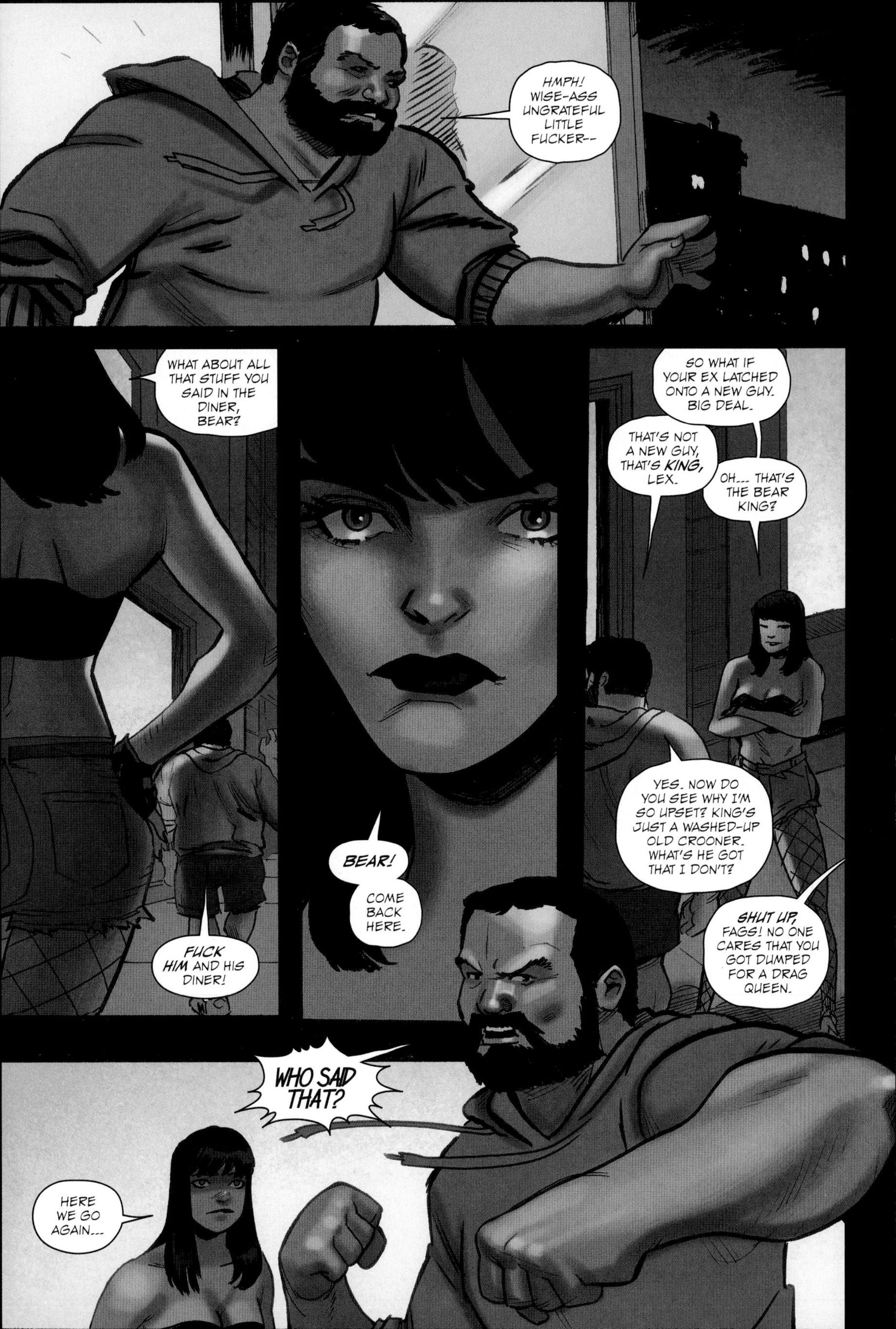
HMPH! WISE-ASS UNGRATEFUL LITTLE FUCKER--
WHAT ABOUT ALL THAT STUFF YOU SAID IN THE DINER, BEAR?
FUCK HIM AND HIS DINER!
BEAR!
COME BACK HERE.
SO WHAT IF YOUR EX LATCHED ONTO A NEW GUY. BIG DEAL.
THAT'S NOT A NEW GUY, THAT'S KING, LEX.
OH... THAT'S THE BEAR KING?
YES. NOW DO YOU SEE WHY I'M SO UPSET? KING'S JUST A WASHED-UP OLD CROONER. WHAT'S HE GOT THAT I DON'T?
SHUT UP, FAGS! NO ONE CARES THAT YOU GOT DUMPED FOR A DRAG QUEEN.
WHO SAID THAT?
HERE WE GO AGAIN...

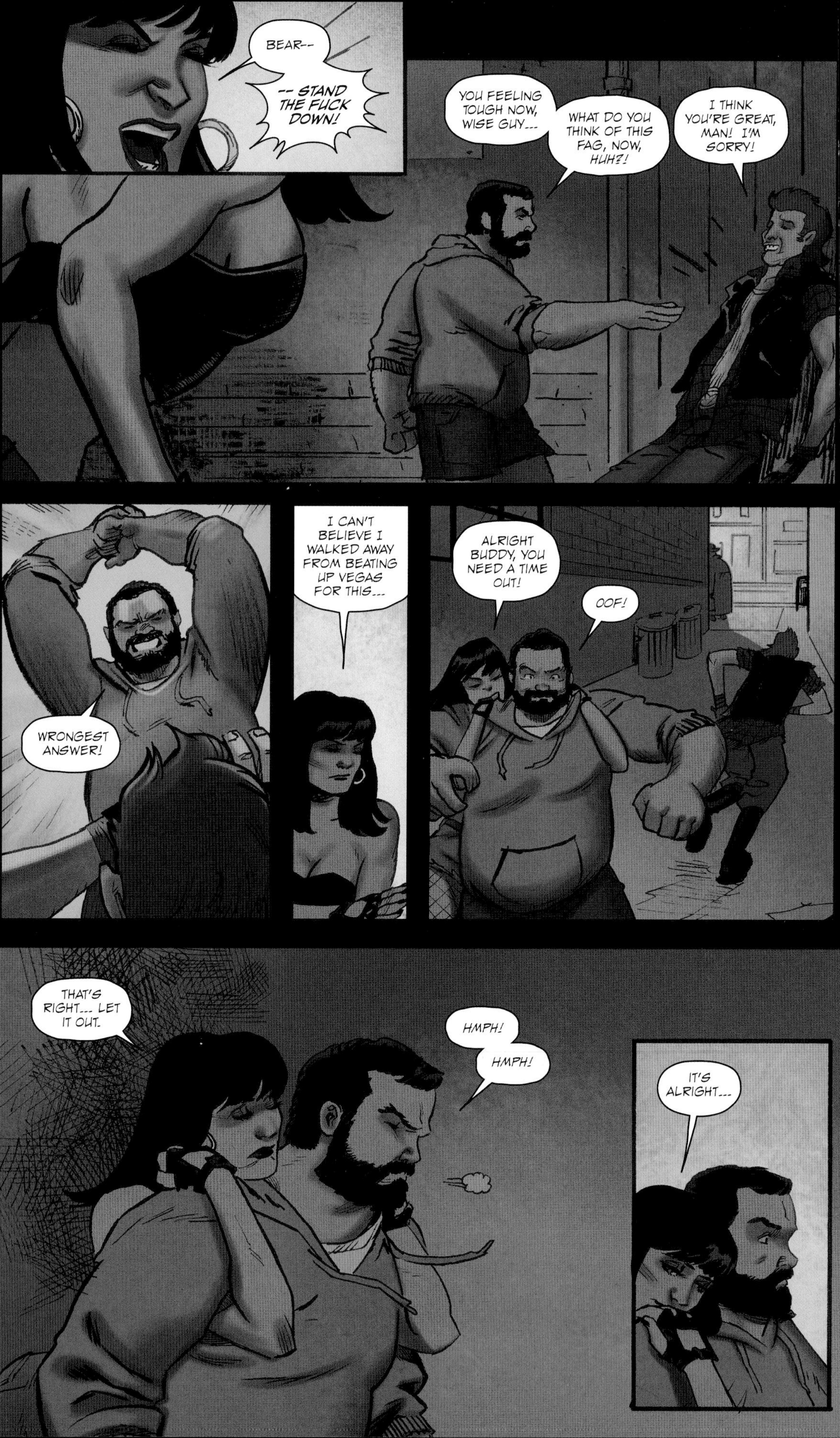
BEAR--
-- STAND THE FUCK DOWN!
YOU FEELING TOUGH NOW, WISE GUY...
WHAT DO YOU THINK OF THIS FAG, NOW, HUH?!
I THINK YOU'RE GREAT, MAN! I'M SORRY!
WRONGEST ANSWER!
I CAN'T BELIEVE I WALKED AWAY FROM BEATING UP VEGAS FOR THIS...
ALRIGHT BUDDY, YOU NEED A TIME OUT!
OOF!
THAT'S RIGHT... LET IT OUT.
HMPH!
HMPH!
IT'S ALRIGHT...

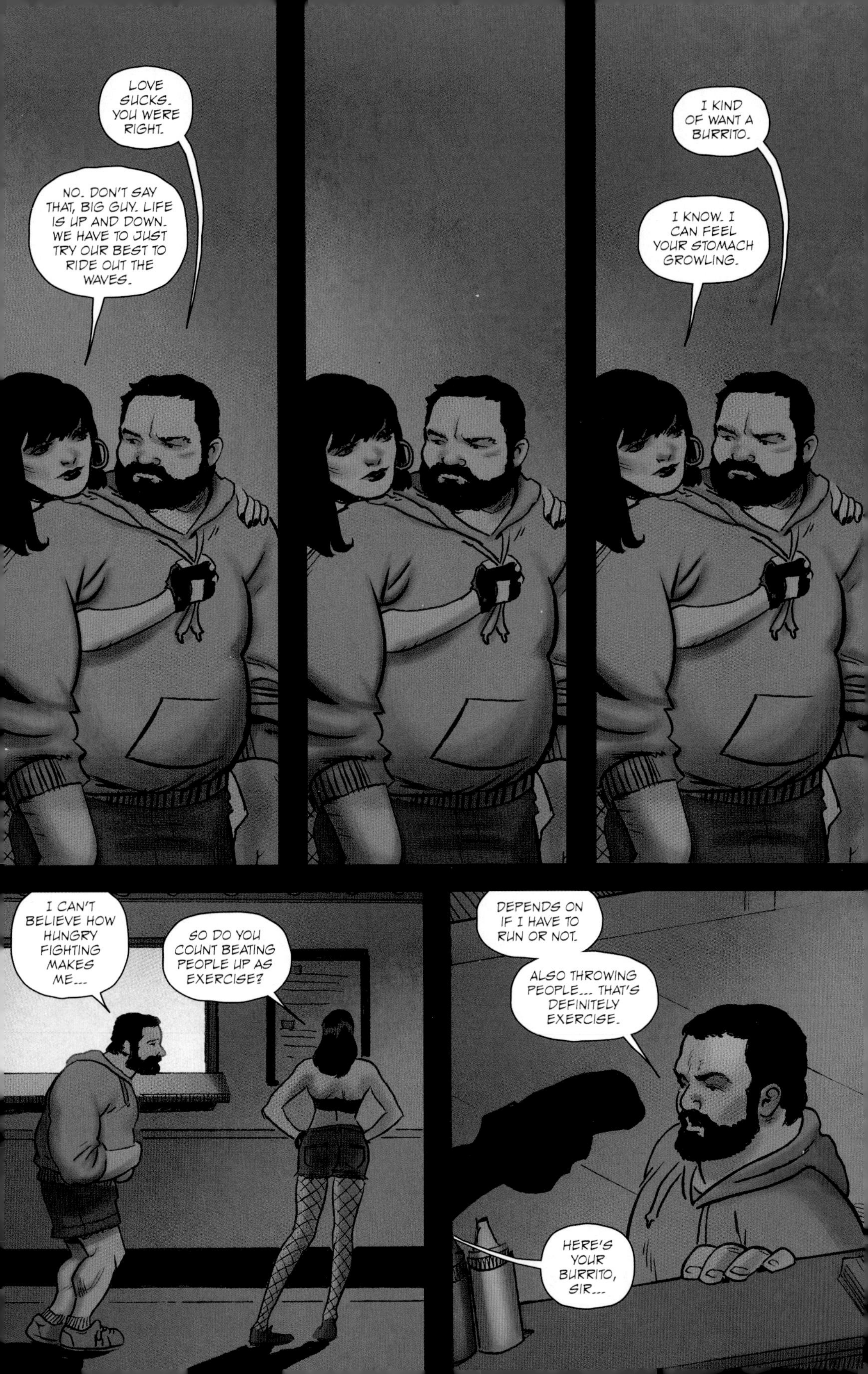
LOVE SUCKS. YOU WERE RIGHT.
NO. DON'T SAY THAT, BIG GUY. LIFE IS UP AND DOWN. WE HAVE TO JUST TRY OUR BEST TO RIDE OUT THE WAVES.
I KIND OF WANT A BURRITO.
I KNOW. I CAN FEEL YOUR STOMACH GROWLING.
I CAN'T BELIEVE HOW HUNGRY FIGHTING MAKES ME...
SO DO YOU COUNT BEATING PEOPLE UP AS EXERCISE?
DEPENDS ON IF I HAVE TO RUN OR NOT.
ALSO THROWING PEOPLE... THAT'S DEFINITELY EXERCISE.
HERE'S YOUR BURRITO, SIR...

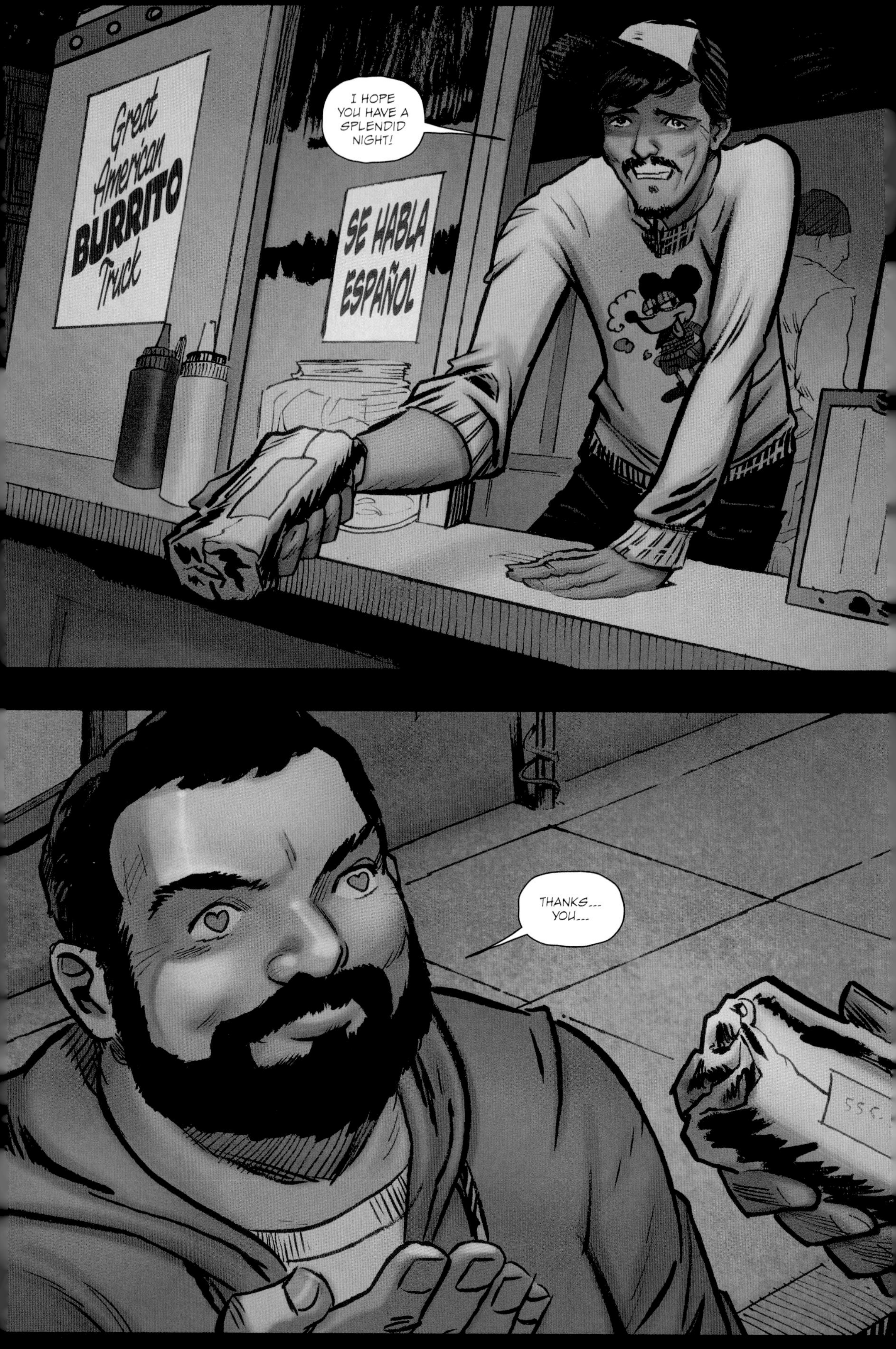
Great American BURRITO Truck
SE HABLA ESPAÑOL
I HOPE YOU HAVE A SPLENDID NIGHT!
THANKS... YOU...

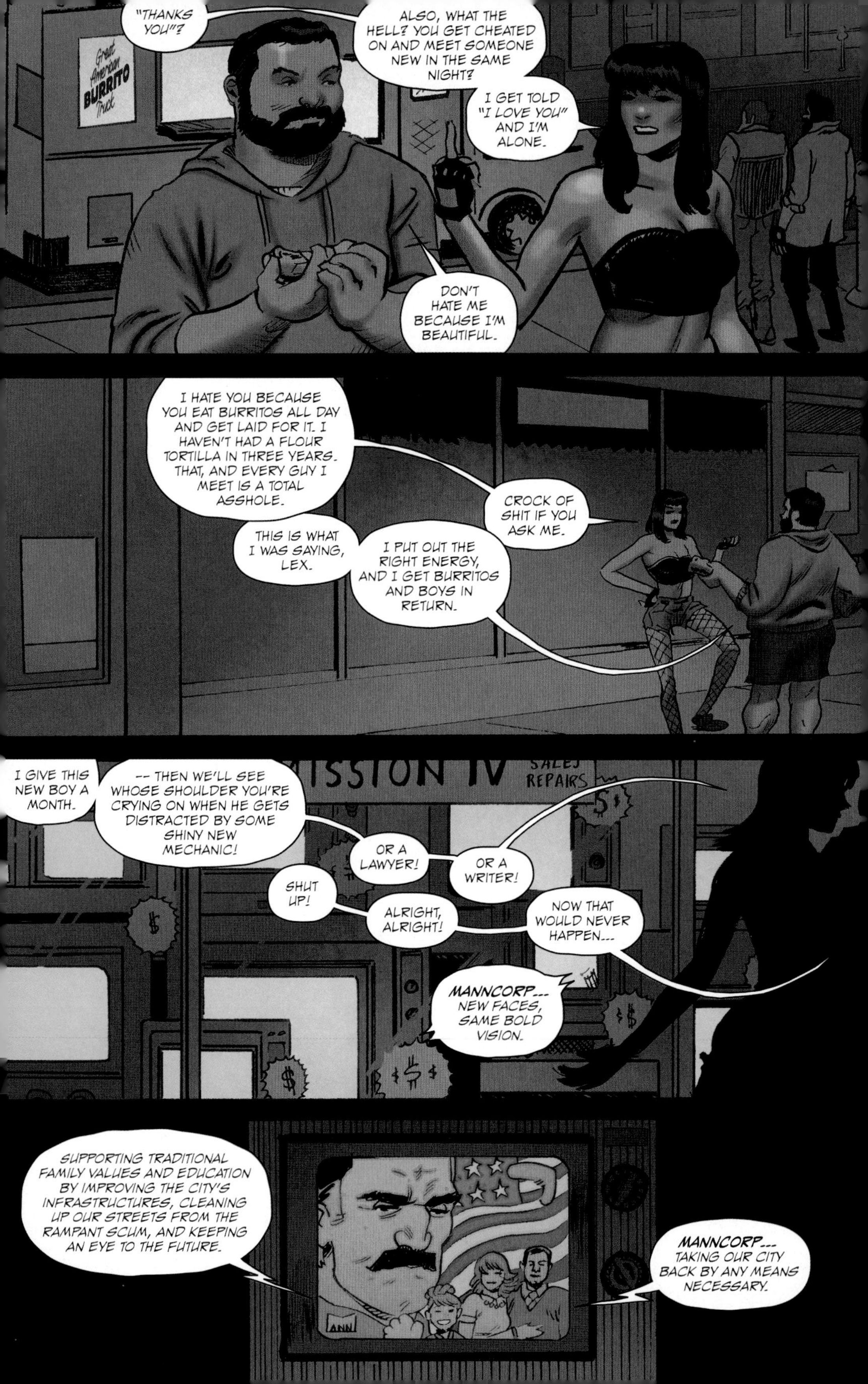
"THANKS YOU"?
ALSO, WHAT THE HELL? YOU GET CHEATED ON AND MEET SOMEONE NEW IN THE SAME NIGHT?
I GET TOLD "I LOVE YOU" AND I'M ALONE.
Great American BURRITO Truck
DON'T HATE ME BECAUSE I'M BEAUTIFUL.
I HATE YOU BECAUSE YOU EAT BURRITOS ALL DAY AND GET LAID FOR IT. I HAVEN'T HAD A FLOUR TORTILLA IN THREE YEARS. THAT, AND EVERY GUY I MEET IS A TOTAL ASSHOLE.
CROCK OF SHIT IF YOU ASK ME.
THIS IS WHAT I WAS SAYING, LEX.
I PUT OUT THE RIGHT ENERGY, AND I GET BURRITOS AND BOYS IN RETURN.
ISSION IV
SALES REPAIRS
I GIVE THIS NEW BOY A MONTH.
-- THEN WE'LL SEE WHOSE SHOULDER YOU'RE CRYING ON WHEN HE GETS DISTRACTED BY SOME SHINY NEW MECHANIC!
OR A LAWYER!
OR A WRITER!
SHUT UP!
ALRIGHT, ALRIGHT!
NOW THAT WOULD NEVER HAPPEN...
MANNCORP... NEW FACES, SAME BOLD VISION.
SUPPORTING TRADITIONAL FAMILY VALUES AND EDUCATION BY IMPROVING THE CITY'S INFRASTRUCTURES, CLEANING UP OUR STREETS FROM THE RAMPANT SCUM, AND KEEPING AN EYE TO THE FUTURE.
MANNCORP... TAKING OUR CITY BACK BY ANY MEANS NECESSARY.

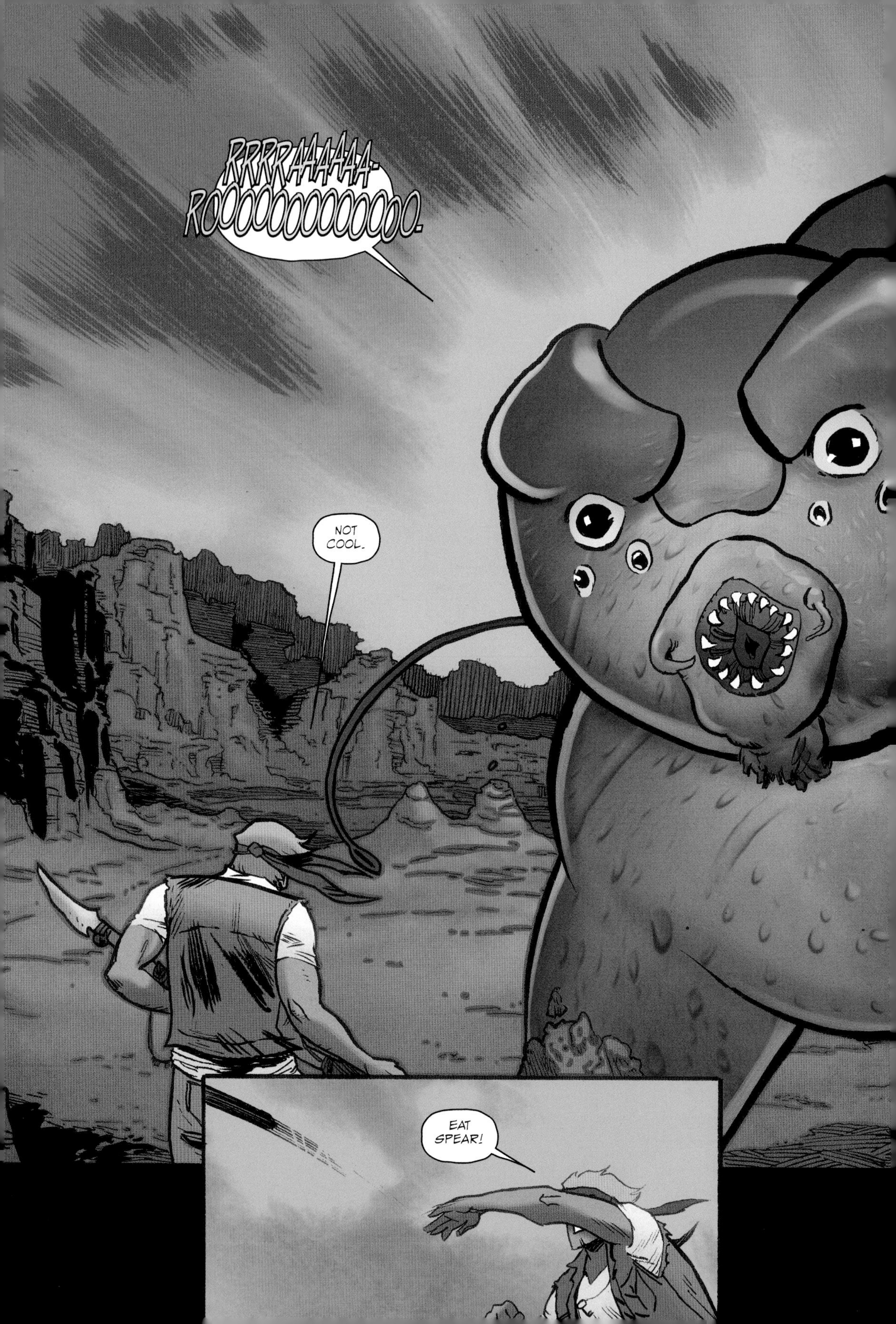
RRRRAAAAAAA-ROOOOOOOOOOOOOO.
NOT COOL.
EAT SPEAR!

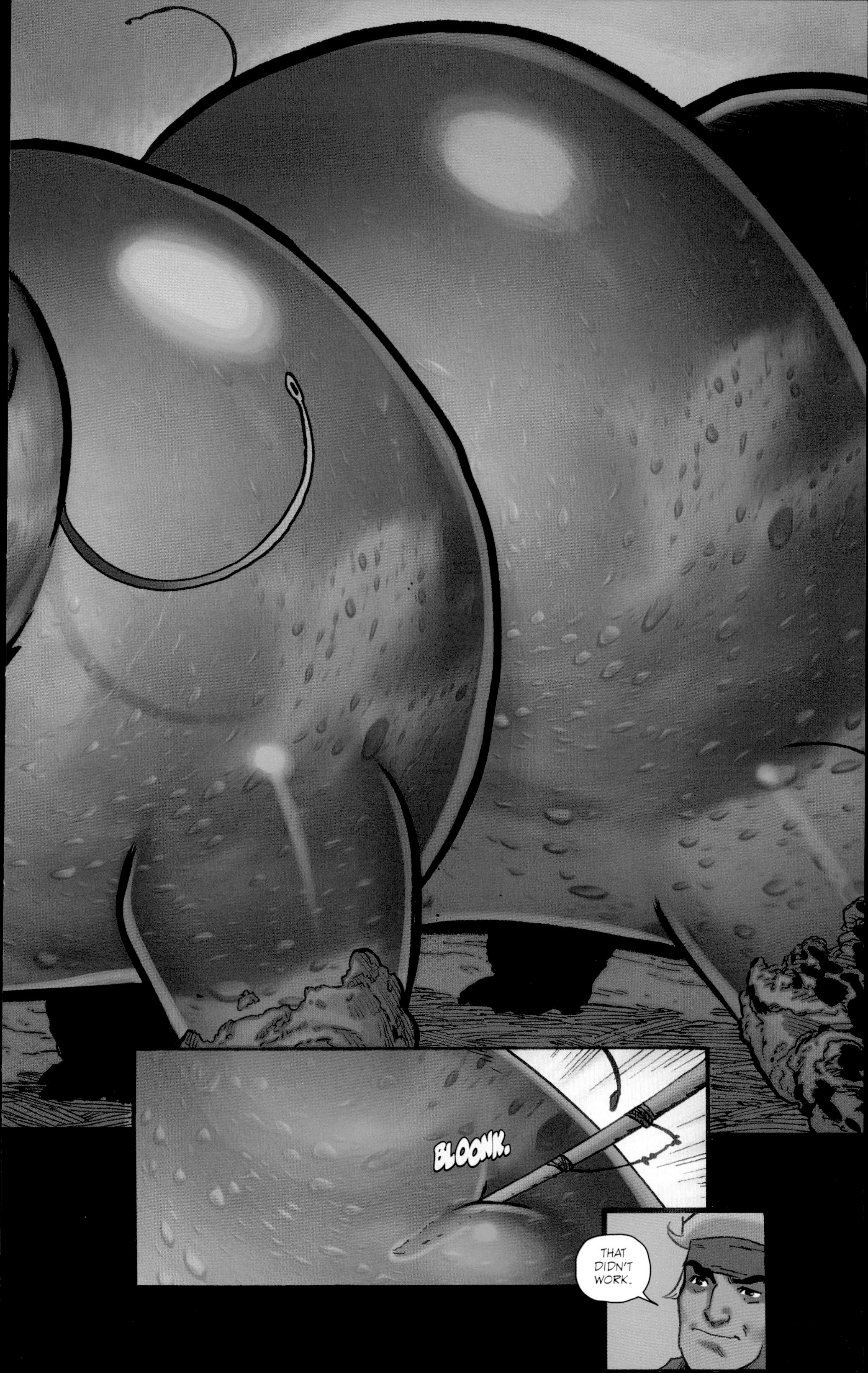
BLOONK.
THAT DIDN'T WORK.

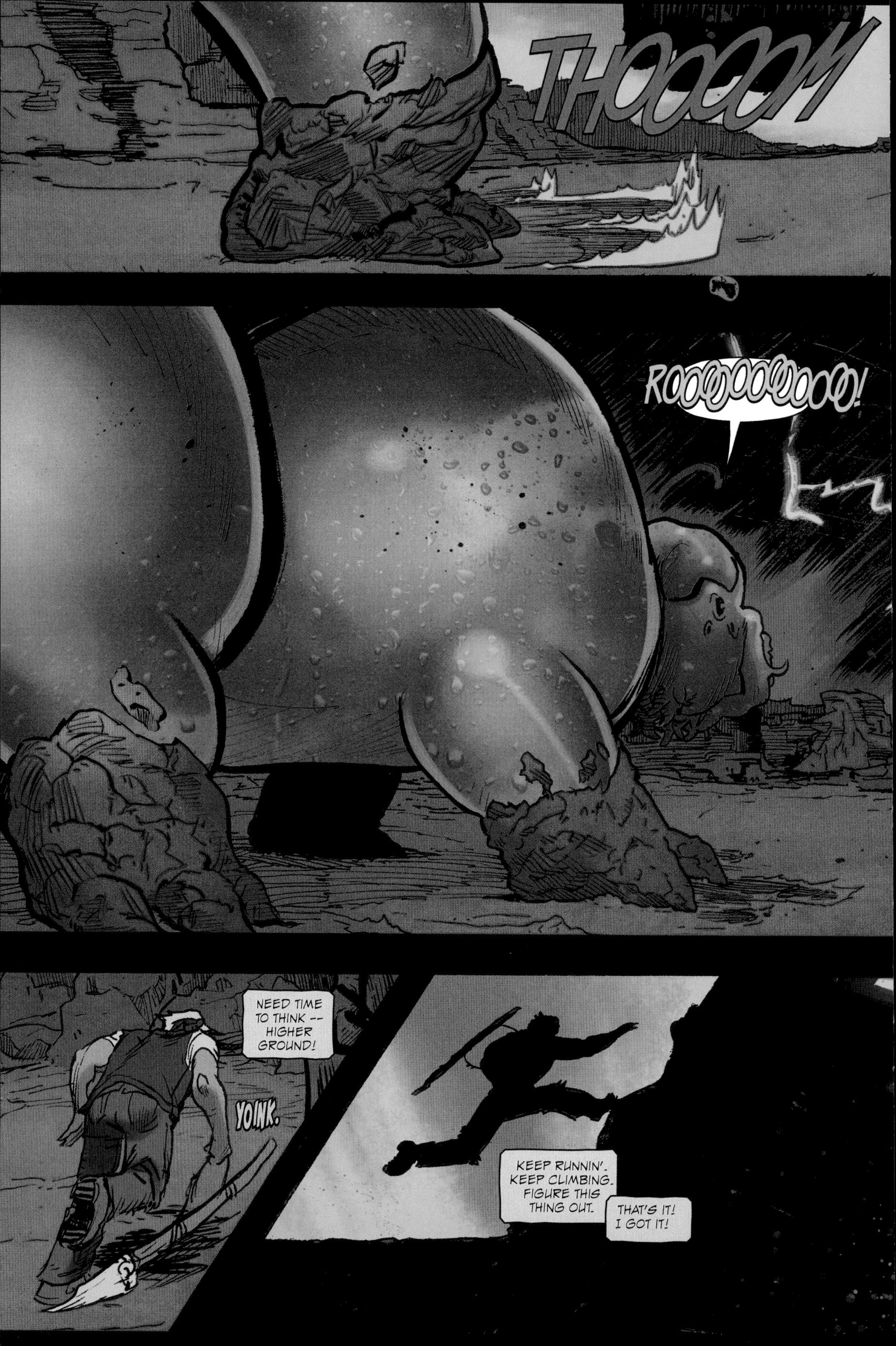
THOOOOM
ROOOOOOOOOOO!
NEED TIME TO THINK -- HIGHER GROUND!
YOINK.
KEEP RUNNIN'. KEEP CLIMBING. FIGURE THIS THING OUT.
THAT'S IT! I GOT IT!

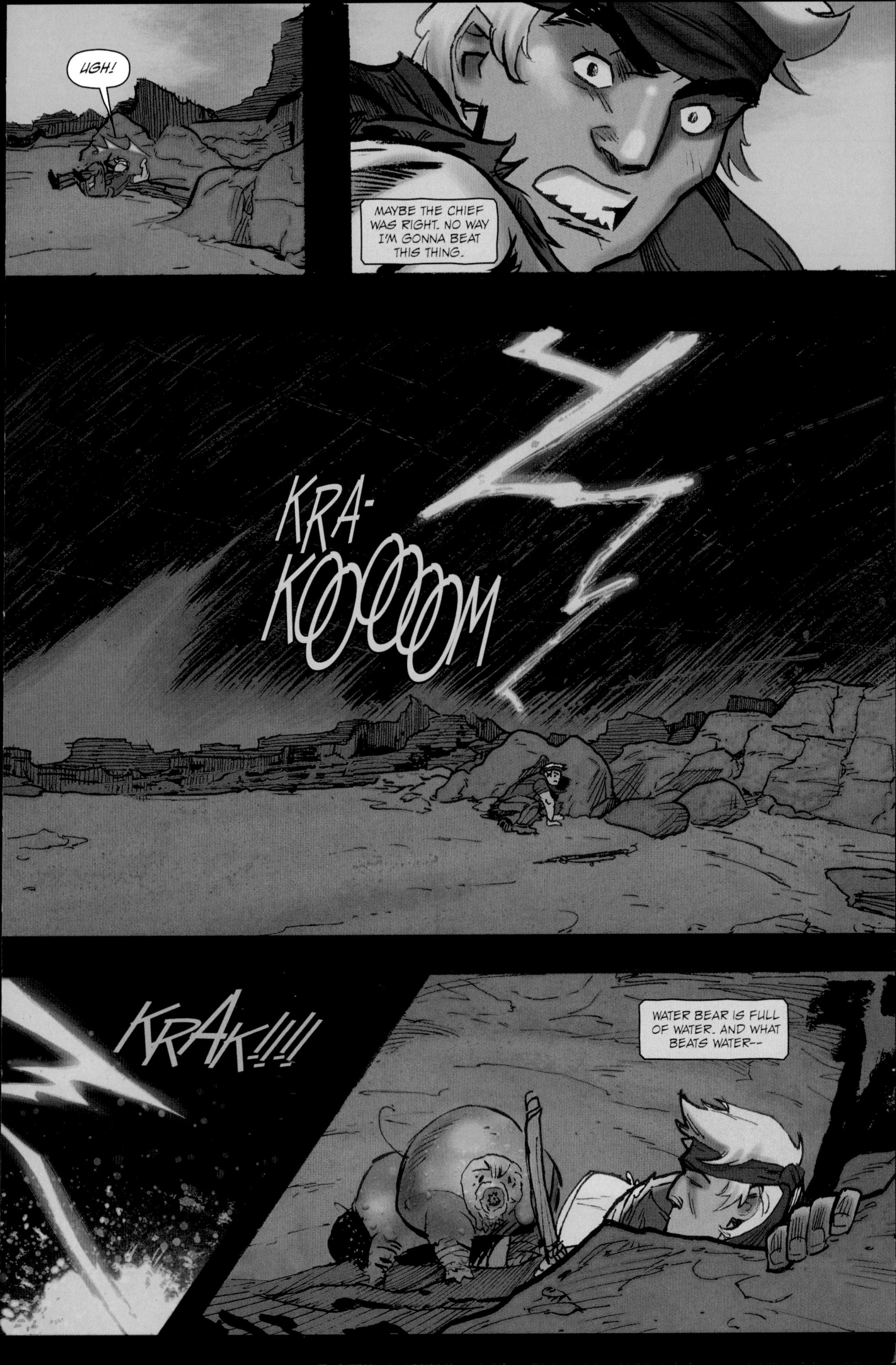
UGH!
MAYBE THE CHIEF WAS RIGHT. NO WAY I'M GONNA BEAT THIS THING.
KRA-KOOOOOM
KRAK!!!!
WATER BEAR IS FULL OF WATER. AND WHAT BEATS WATER--

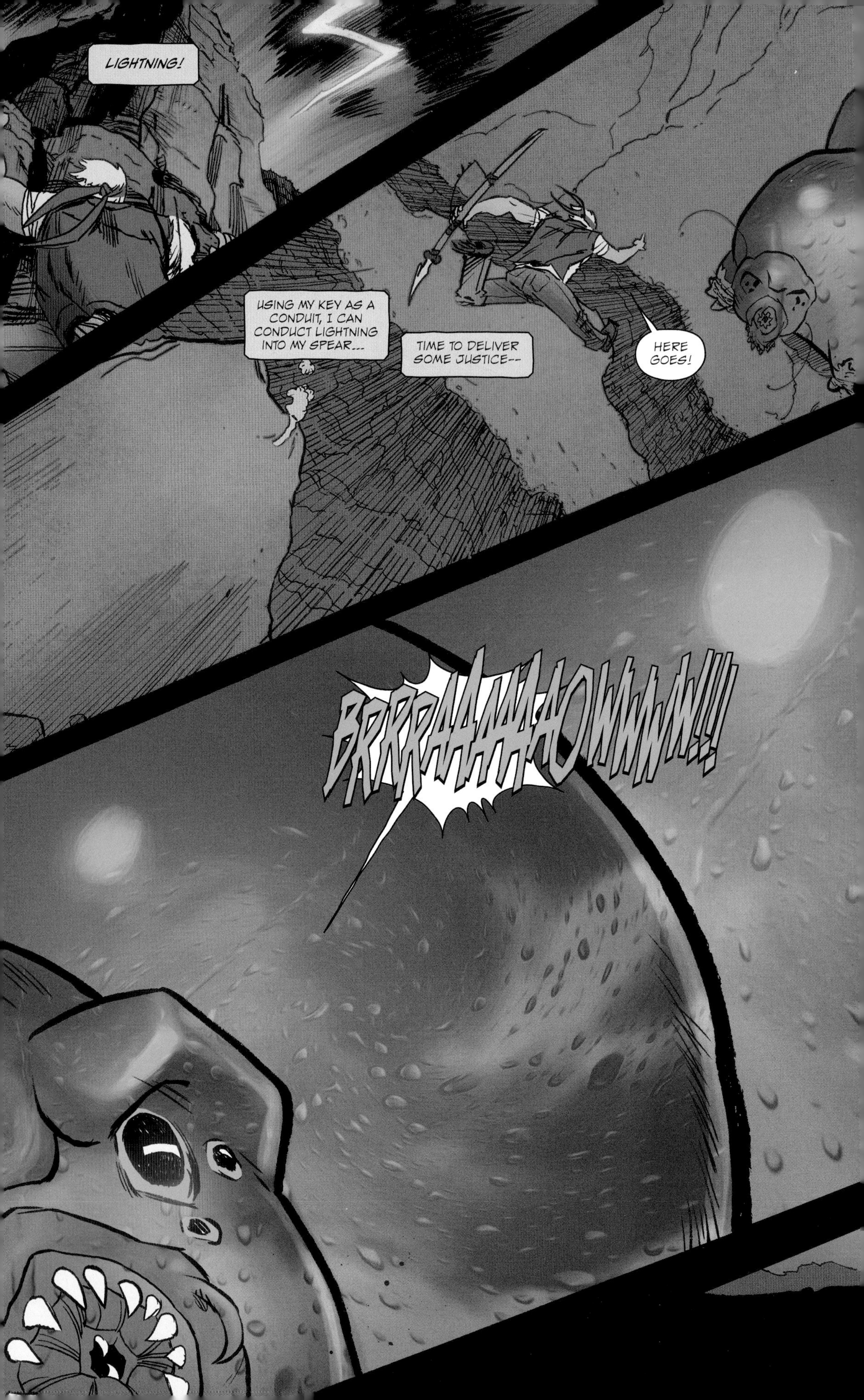
LIGHTNING!
USING MY KEY AS A CONDUIT, I CAN CONDUCT LIGHTNING INTO MY SPEAR---
TIME TO DELIVER SOME JUSTICE--
HERE GOES!
BRRRAAAAAAOWWWW!!!

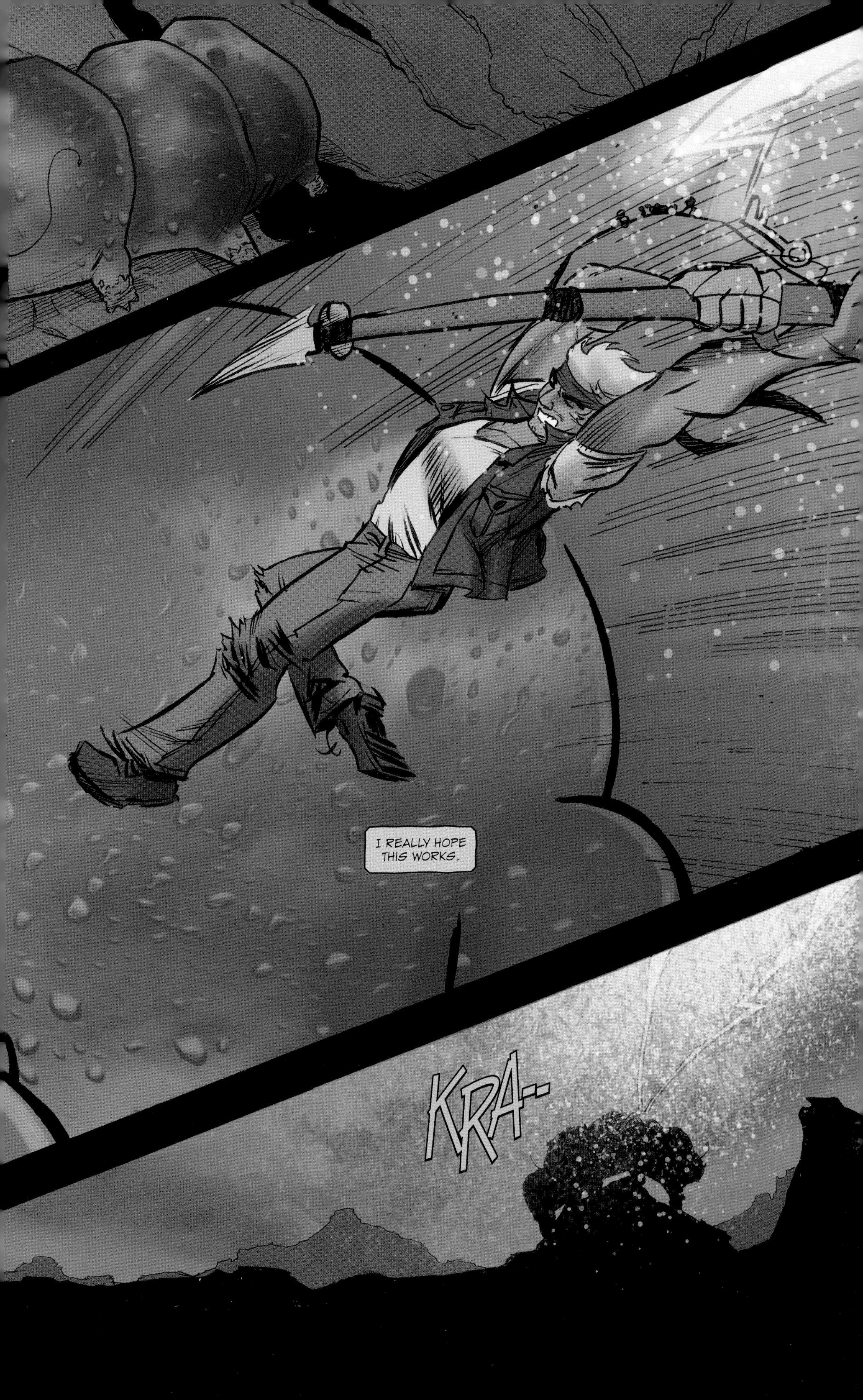
I REALLY HOPE THIS WORKS.
KRA--

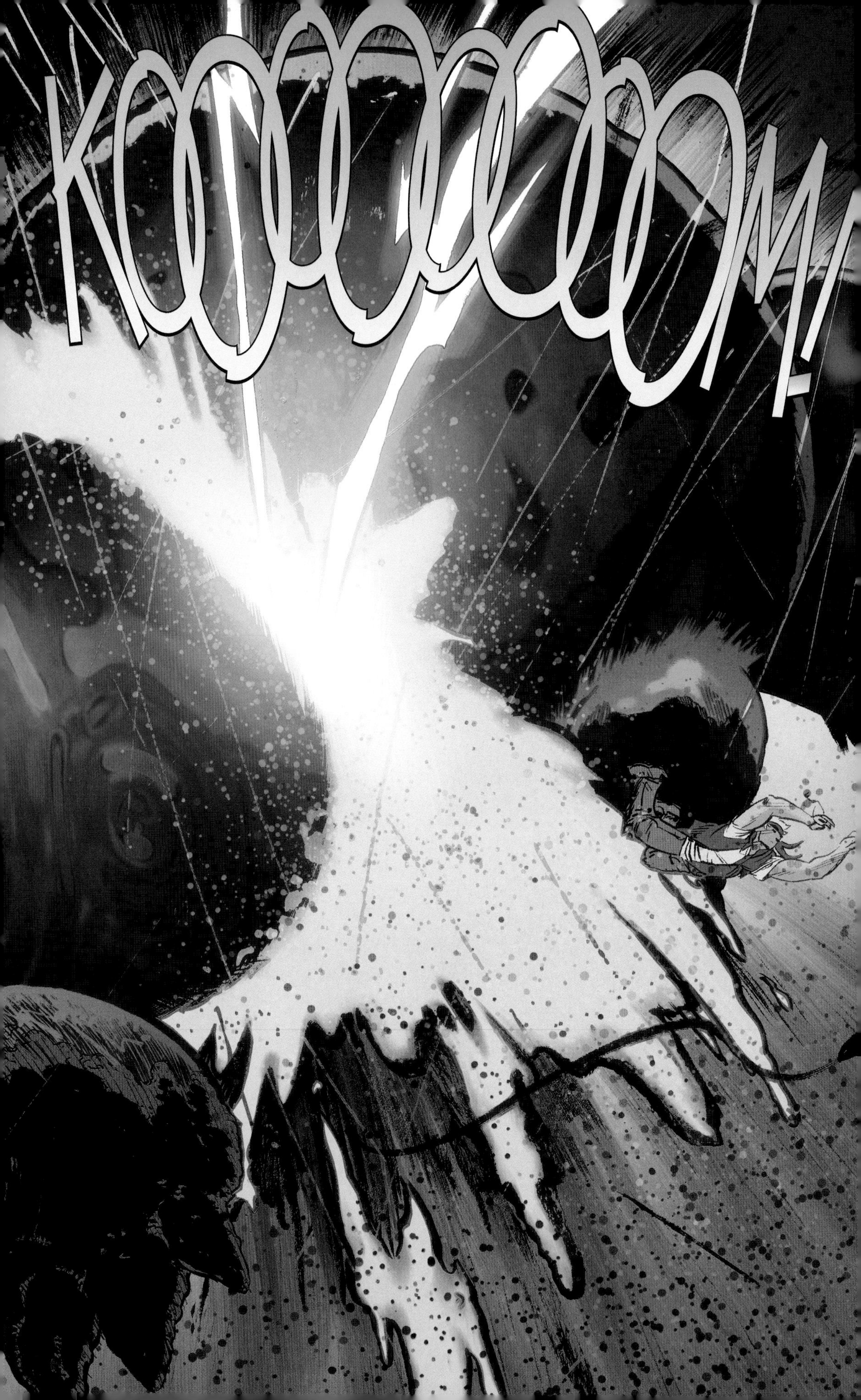
KOOOOOOOOM!

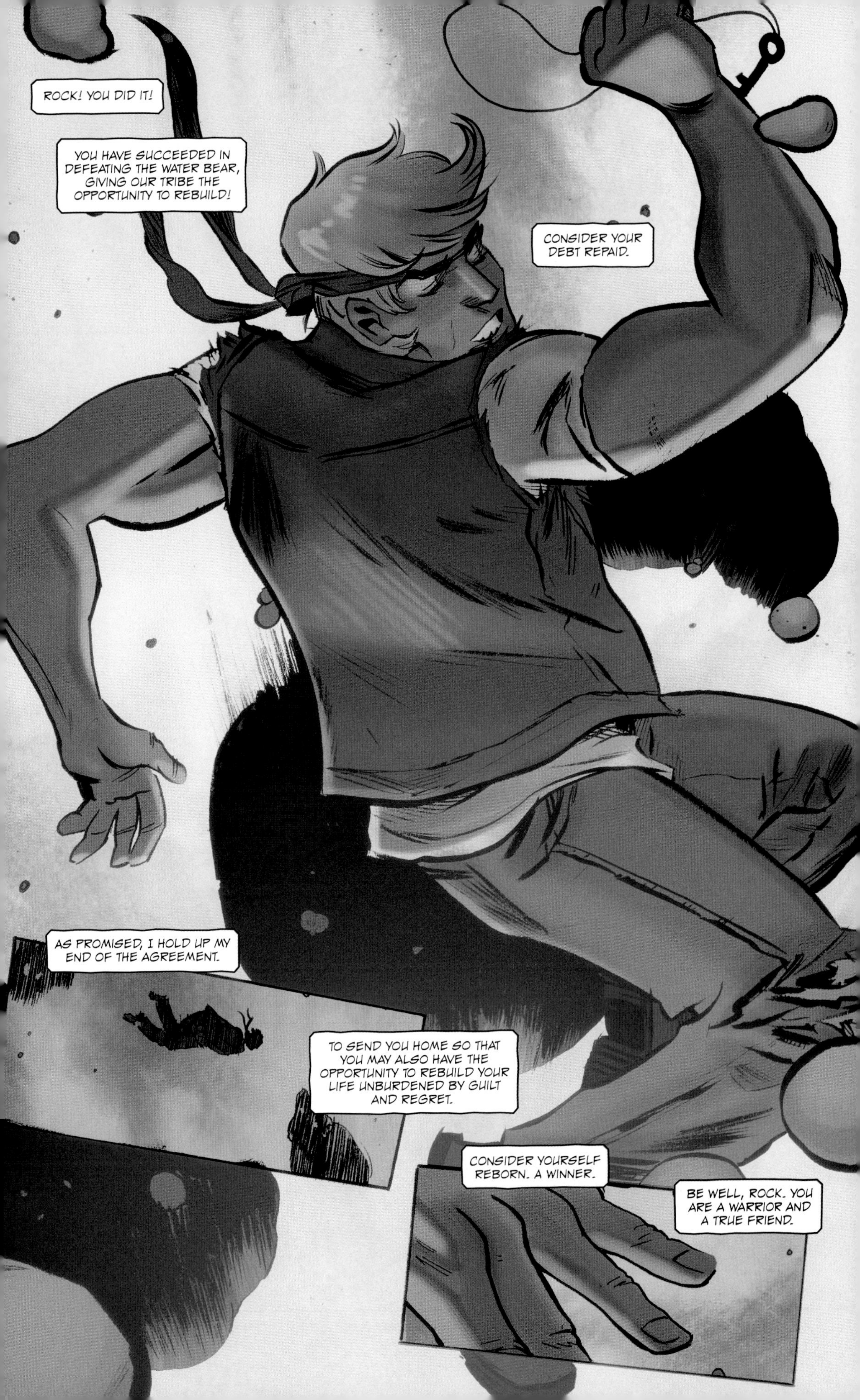
ROCK! YOU DID IT!
YOU HAVE SUCCEEDED IN DEFEATING THE WATER BEAR, GIVING OUR TRIBE THE OPPORTUNITY TO REBUILD!
CONSIDER YOUR DEBT REPAID.
AS PROMISED, I HOLD UP MY END OF THE AGREEMENT.
TO SEND YOU HOME SO THAT YOU MAY ALSO HAVE THE OPPORTUNITY TO REBUILD YOUR LIFE UNBURDENED BY GUILT AND REGRET.
CONSIDER YOURSELF REBORN. A WINNER.
BE WELL, ROCK. YOU ARE A WARRIOR AND A TRUE FRIEND.

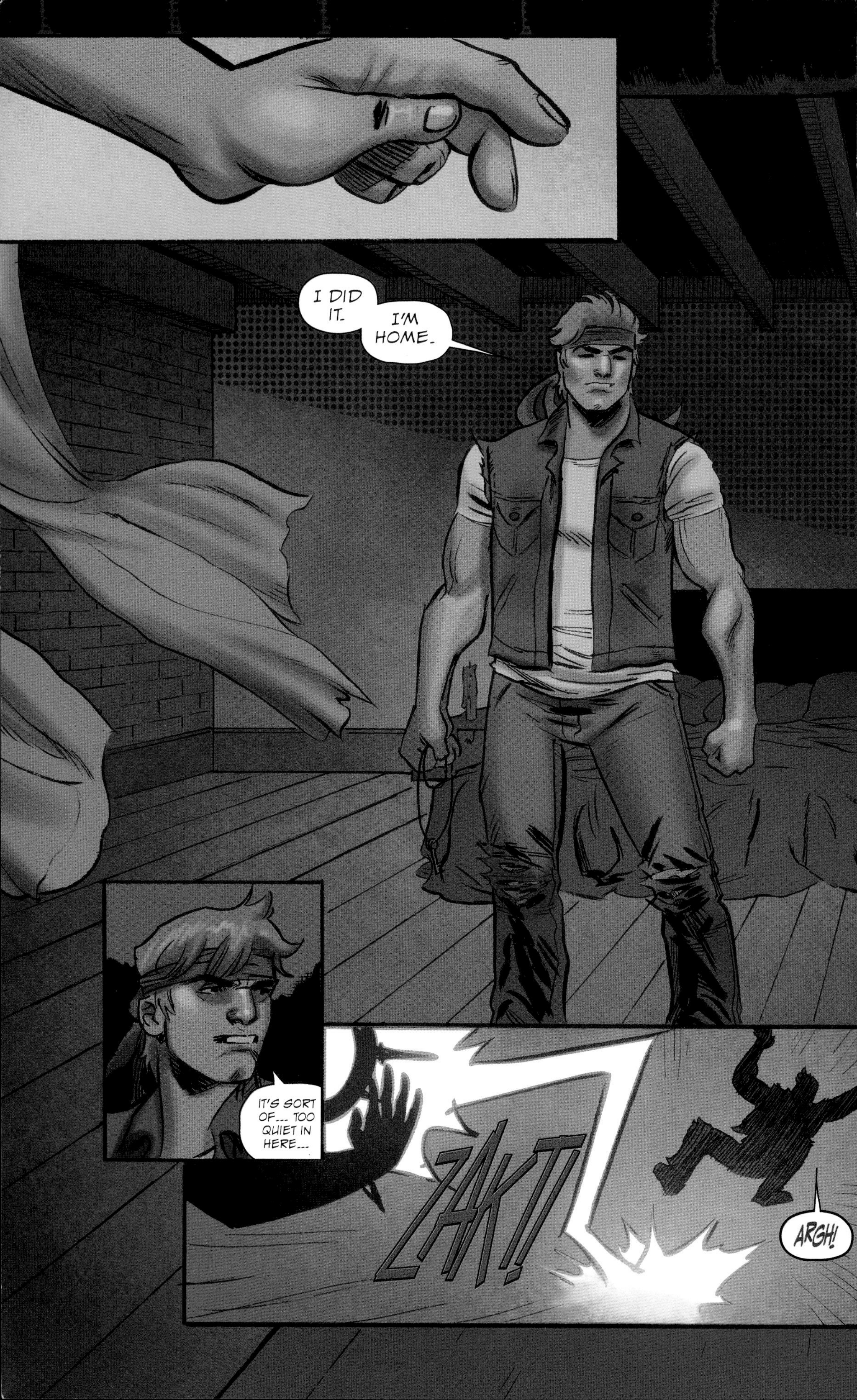
I DID IT.
I'M HOME.
IT'S SORT OF... TOO QUIET IN HERE...
ZAKT!
ARGH!

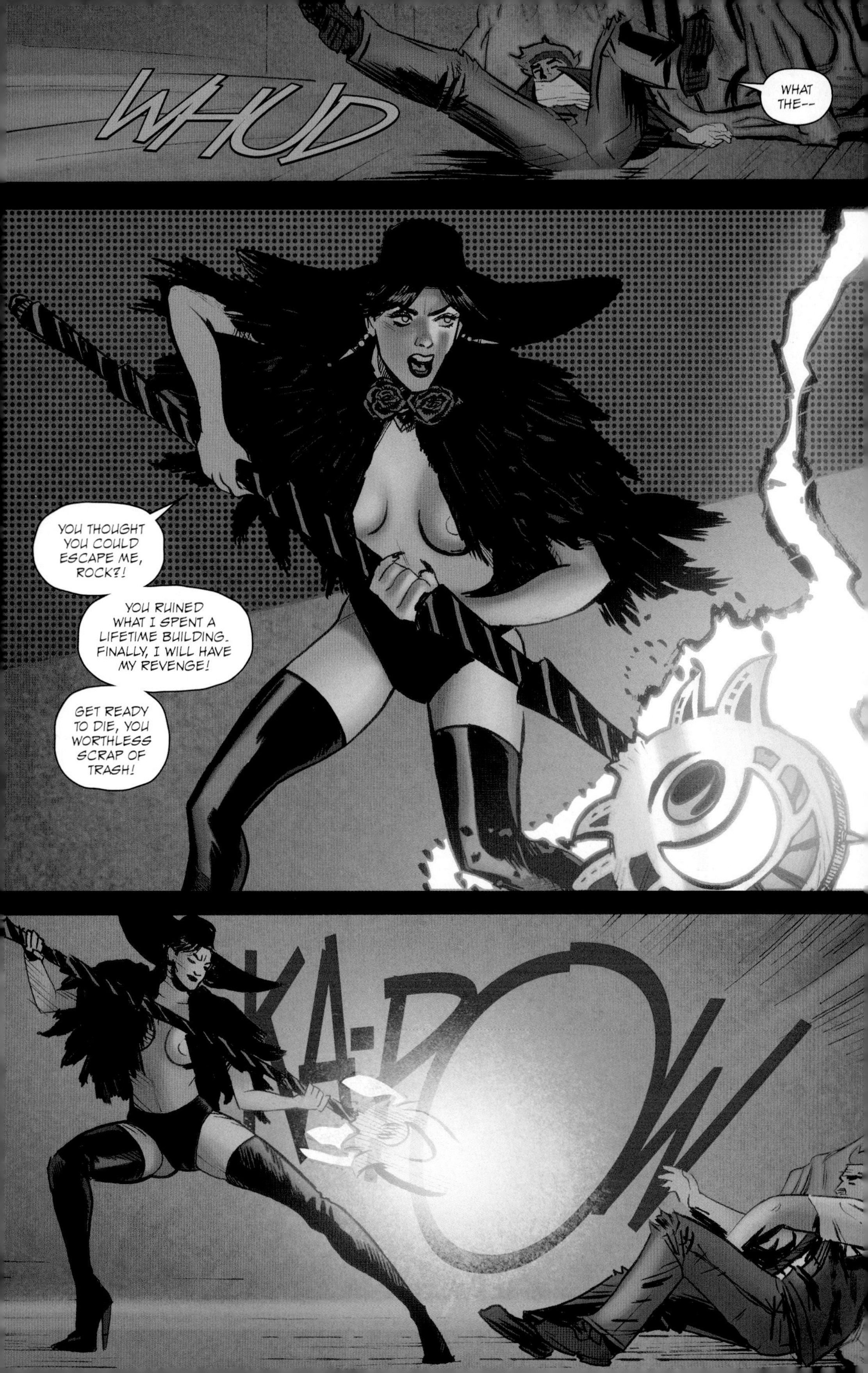
WHUD
WHAT THE--
YOU THOUGHT YOU COULD ESCAPE ME, ROCK?!
YOU RUINED WHAT I SPENT A LIFETIME BUILDING. FINALLY, I WILL HAVE MY REVENGE!
GET READY TO DIE, YOU WORTHLESS SCRAP OF TRASH!
KA-BOW

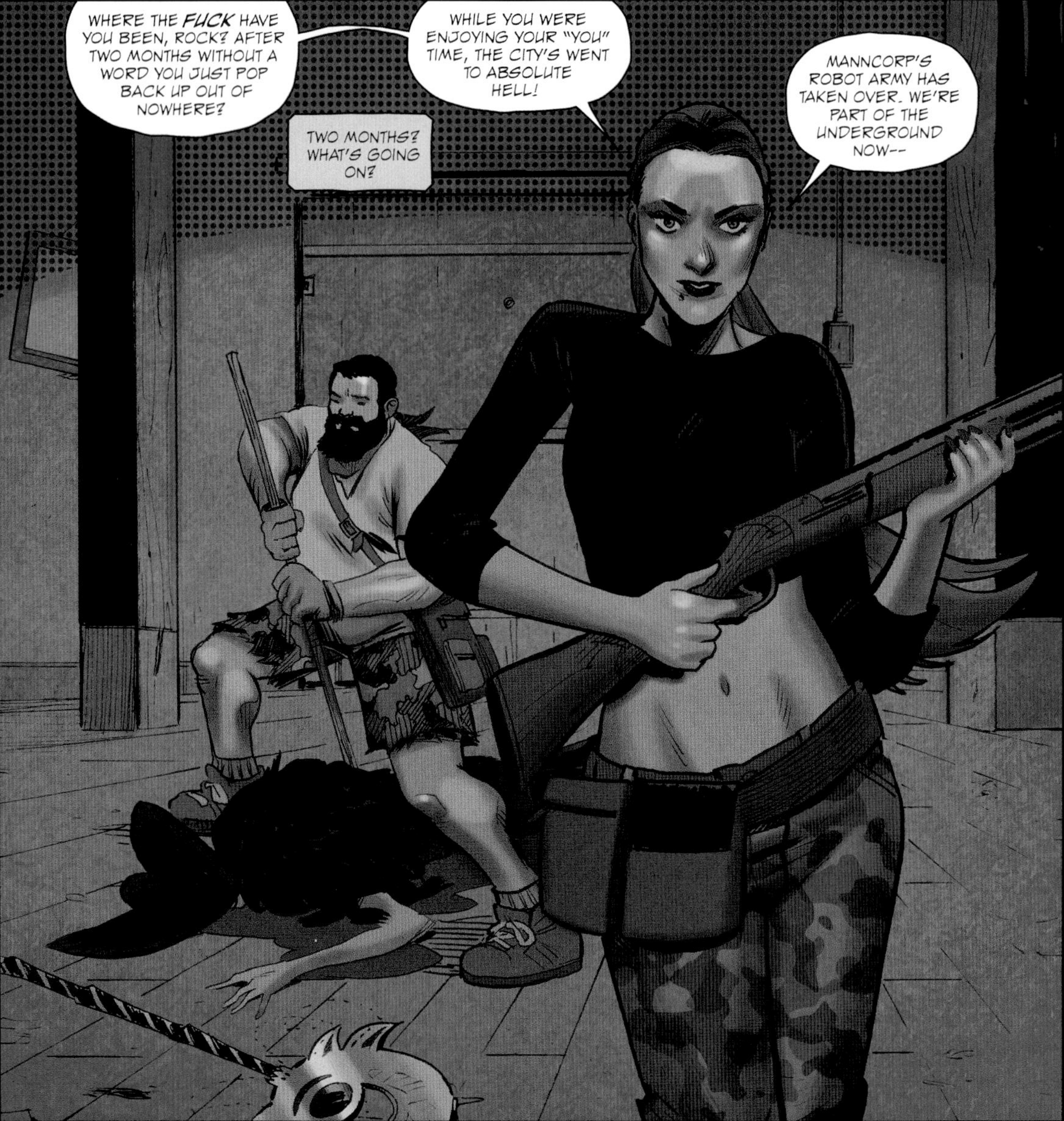
WHERE THE *FUCK* HAVE YOU BEEN, ROCK? AFTER TWO MONTHS WITHOUT A WORD YOU JUST POP BACK UP OUT OF NOWHERE?
WHILE YOU WERE ENJOYING YOUR "YOU" TIME, THE CITY'S WENT TO ABSOLUTE HELL!
TWO MONTHS? WHAT'S GOING ON?
MANNCORP'S ROBOT ARMY HAS TAKEN OVER. WE'RE PART OF THE UNDERGROUND NOW--

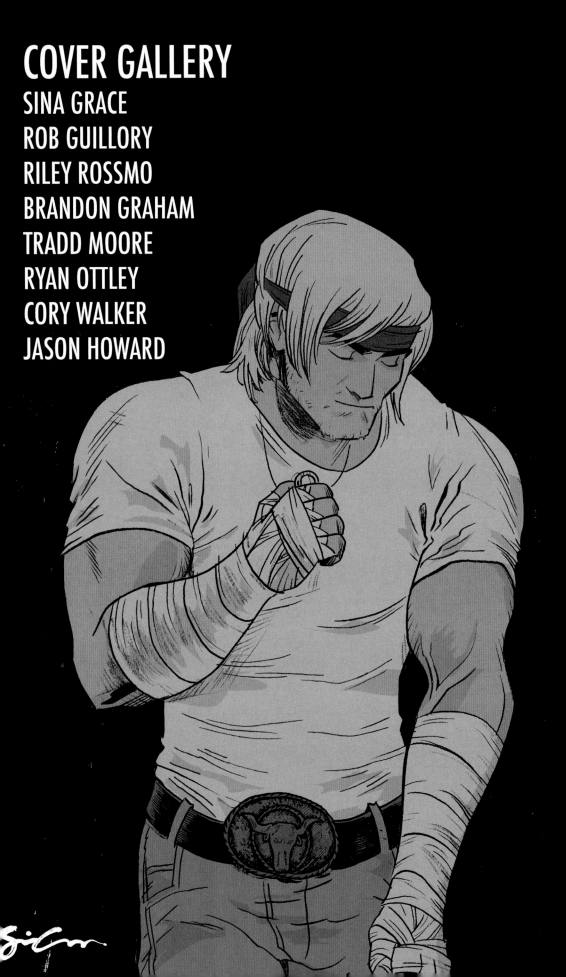

COVER GALLERY

SINA GRACE
ROB GUILLORY
RILEY ROSSMO
BRANDON GRAHAM
TRADD MOORE
RYAN OTTLEY
CORY WALKER
JASON HOWARD

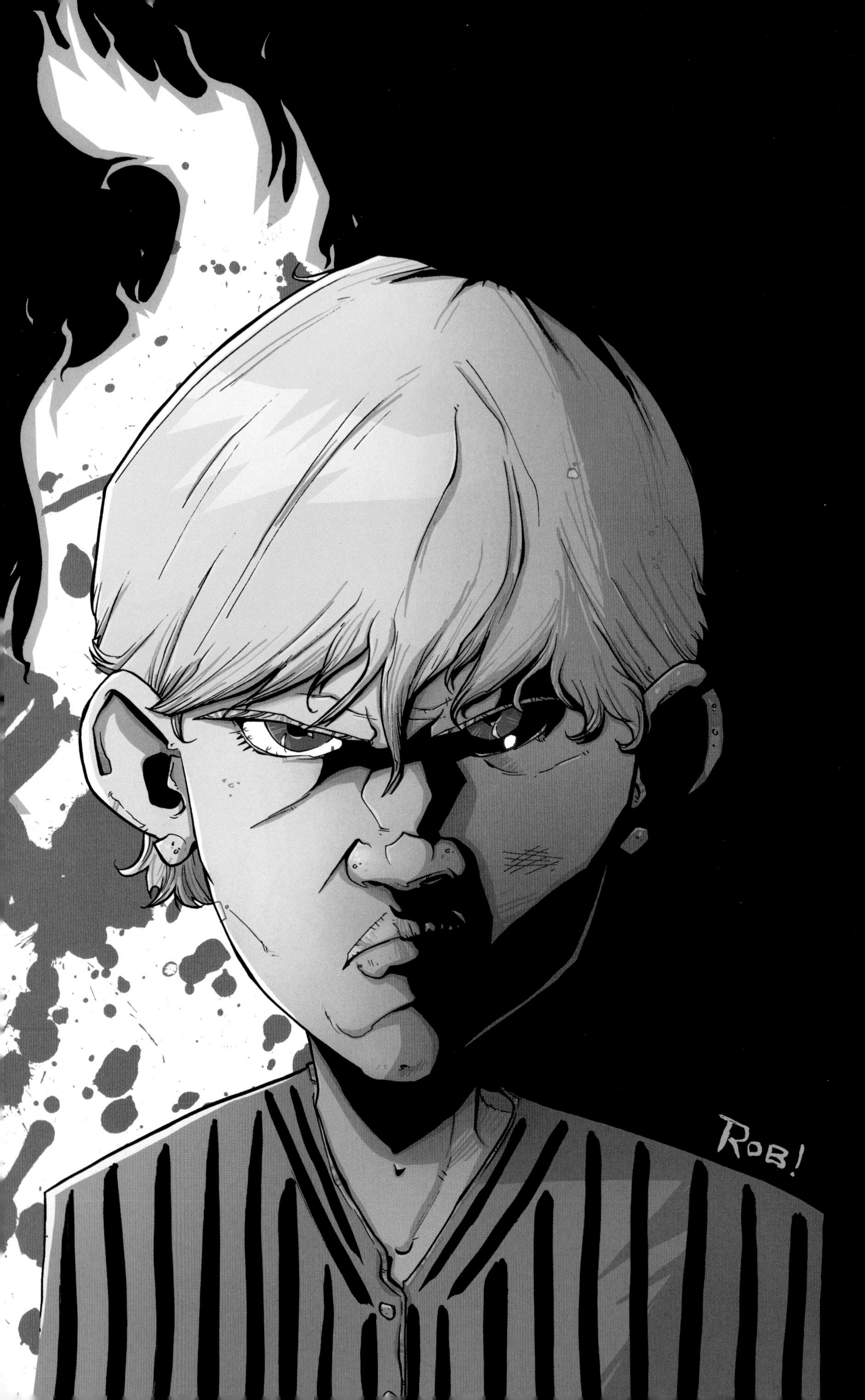
ROB!

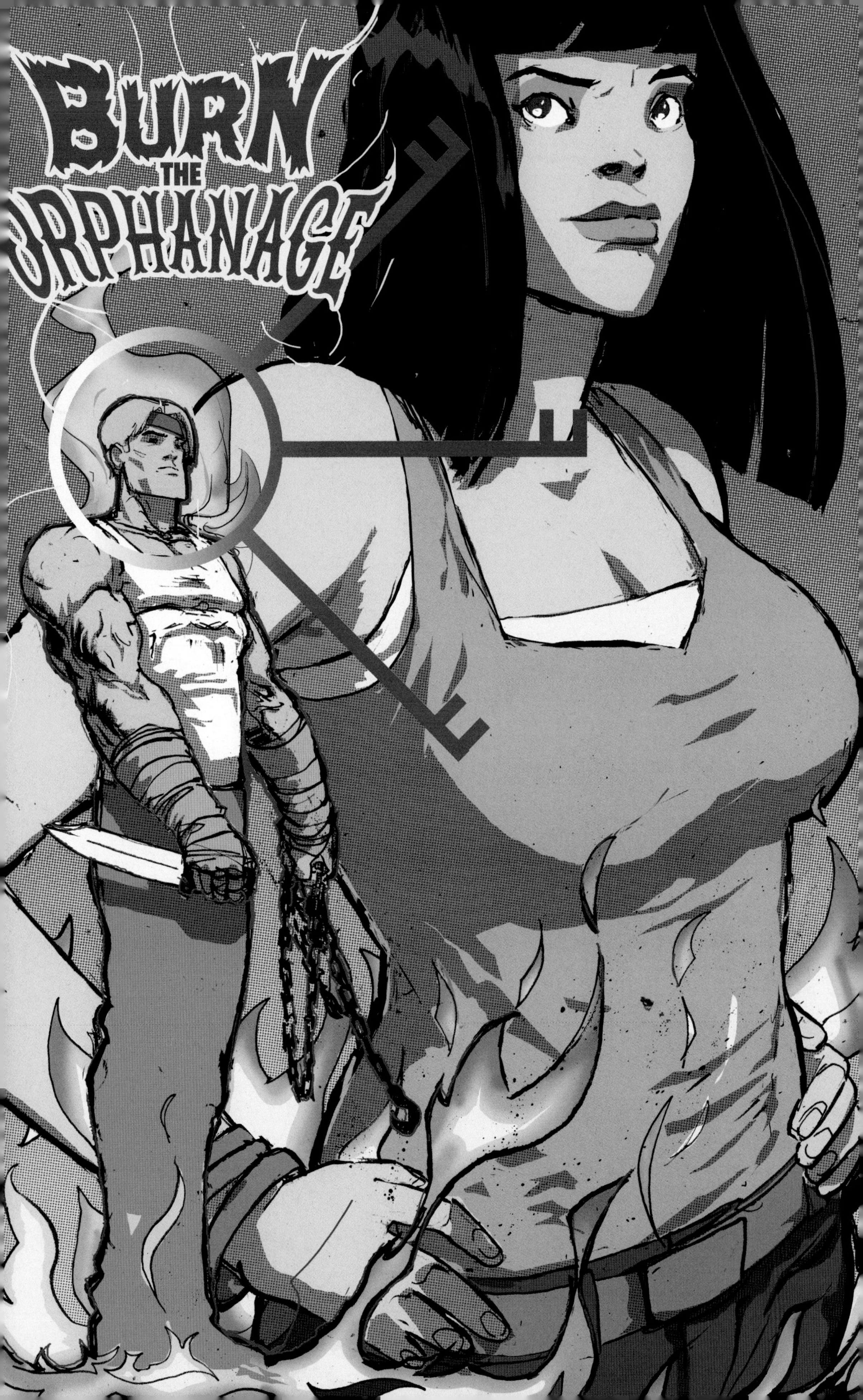
BURN
THE
ORPHANAGE

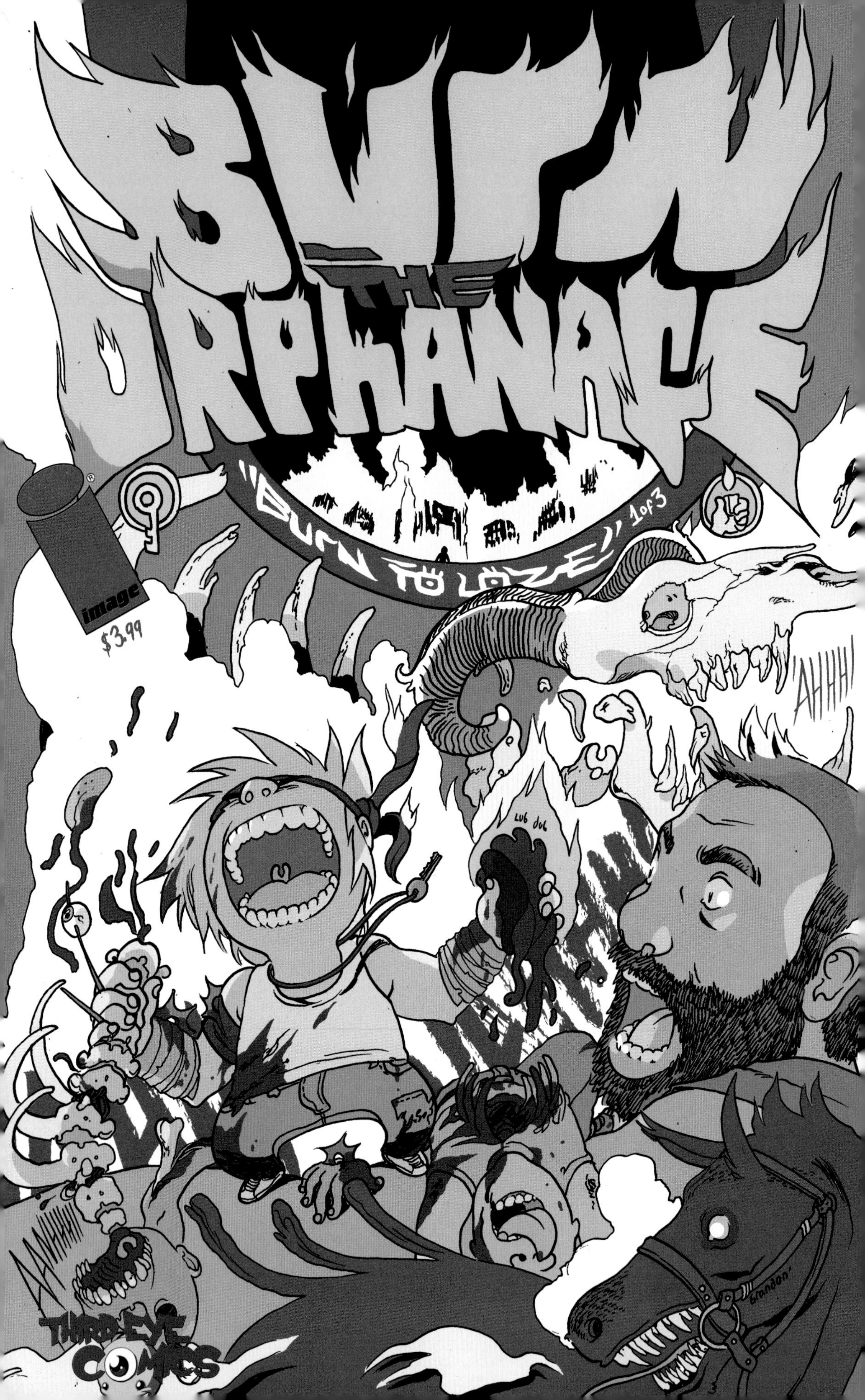
BURN THE ORPHANAGE
"BURN TO LOZE" 1 of 3
image
$3.99
AHHH
LUB DUB
THIRD EYE COMICS

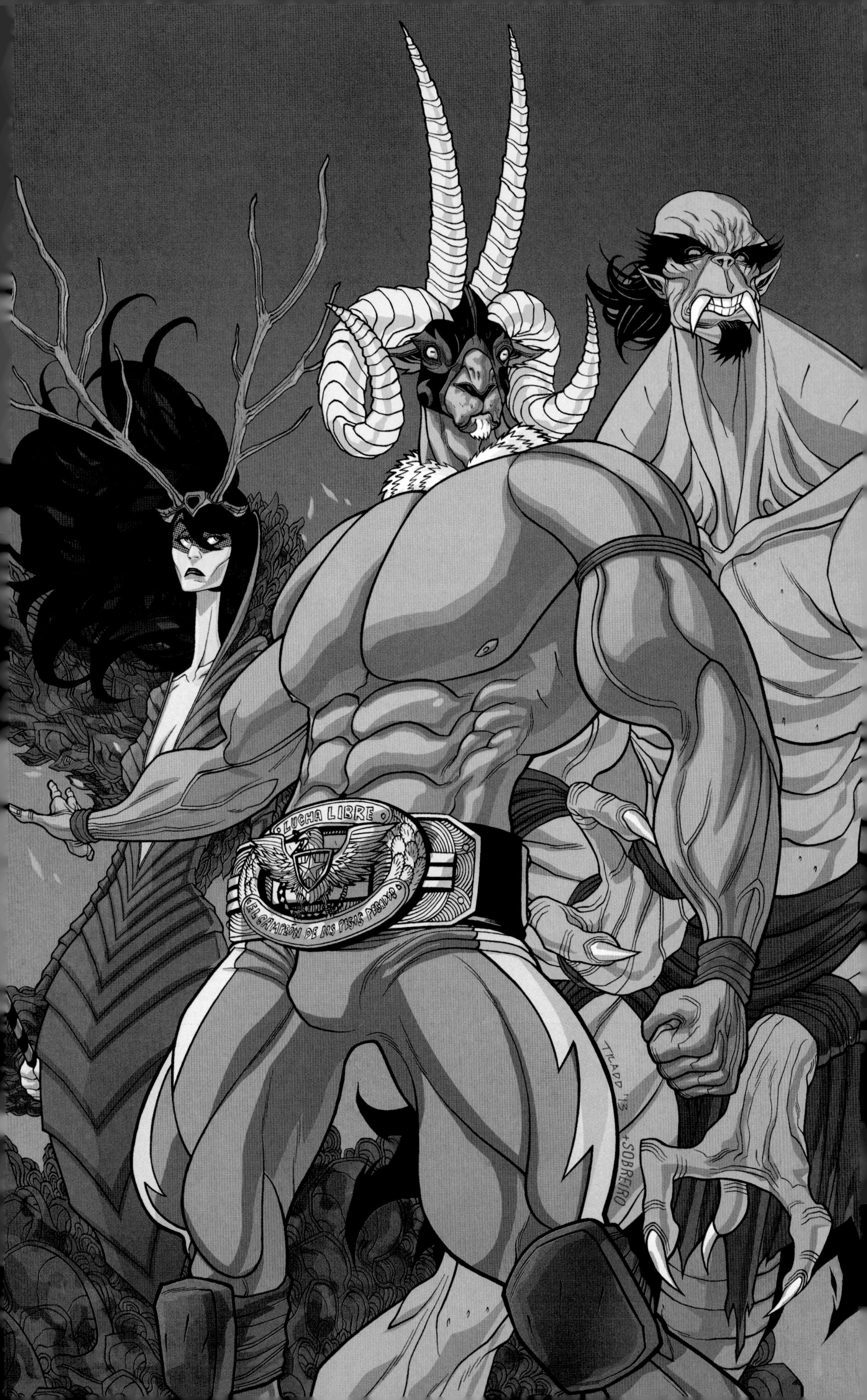
LUCHA LIBRE
EL CAMPEÓN DE LOS PESOS PESADOS
TICADO '13
+SOBREIRO

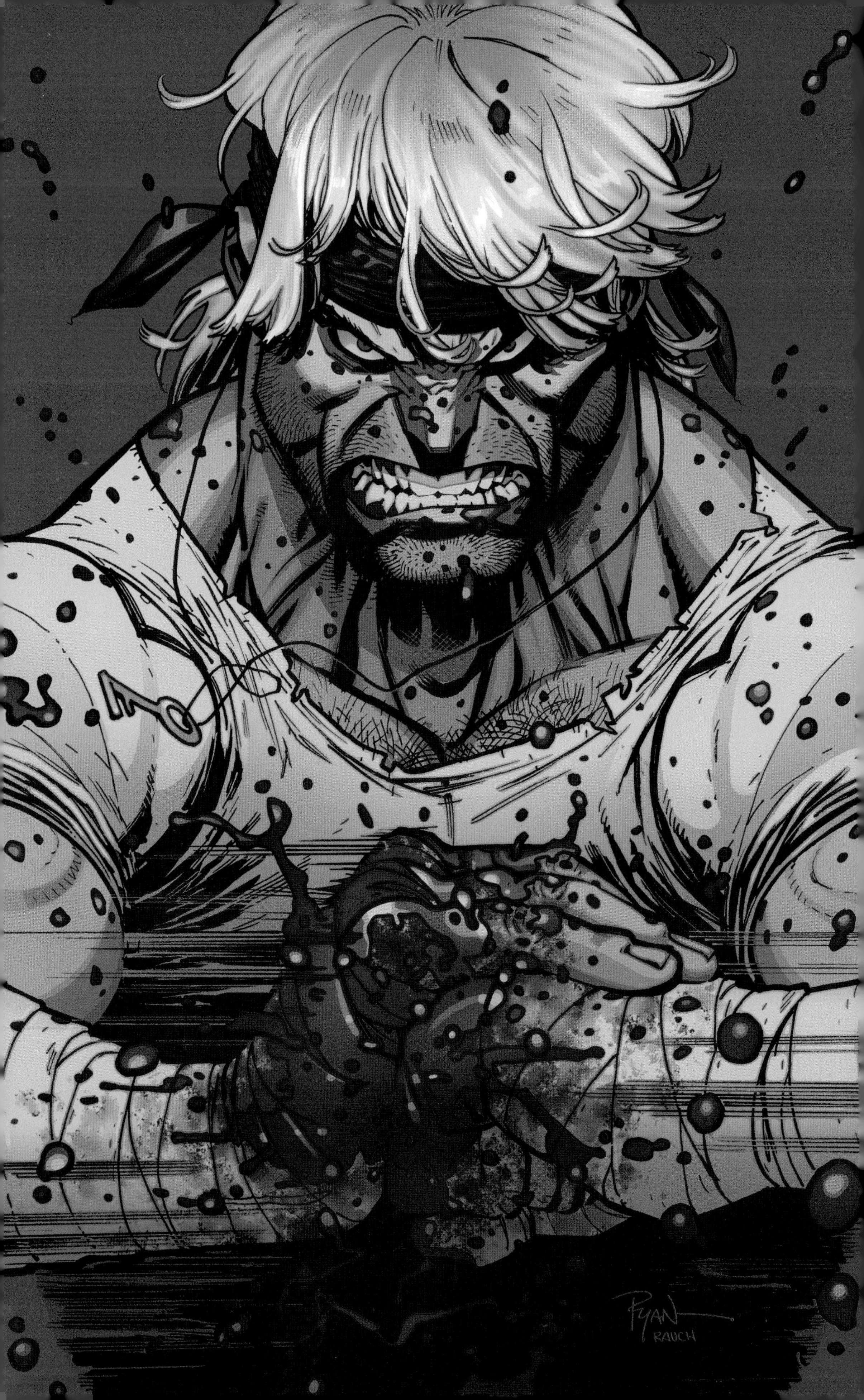
RYAN
RAUCH

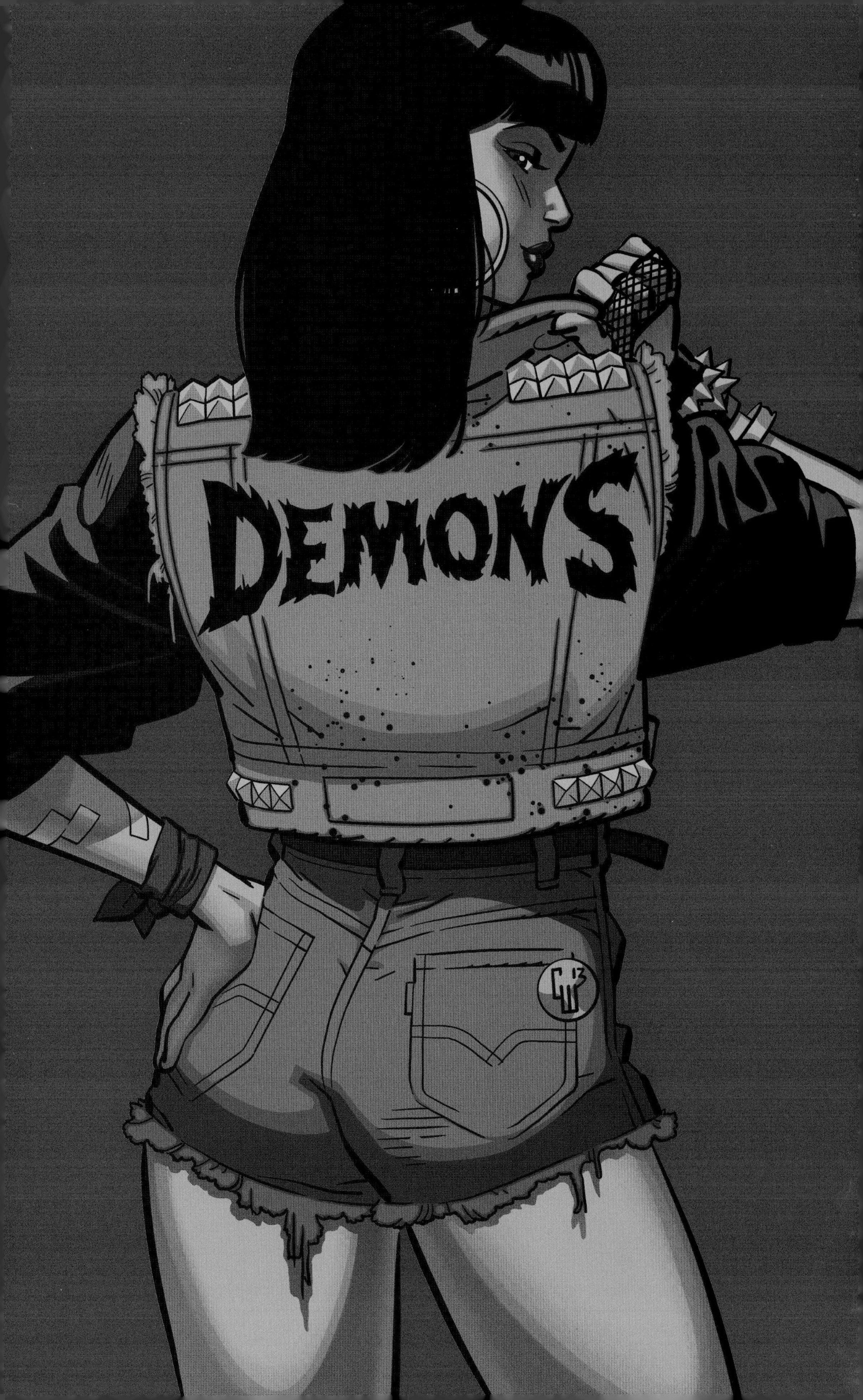
DEMONS

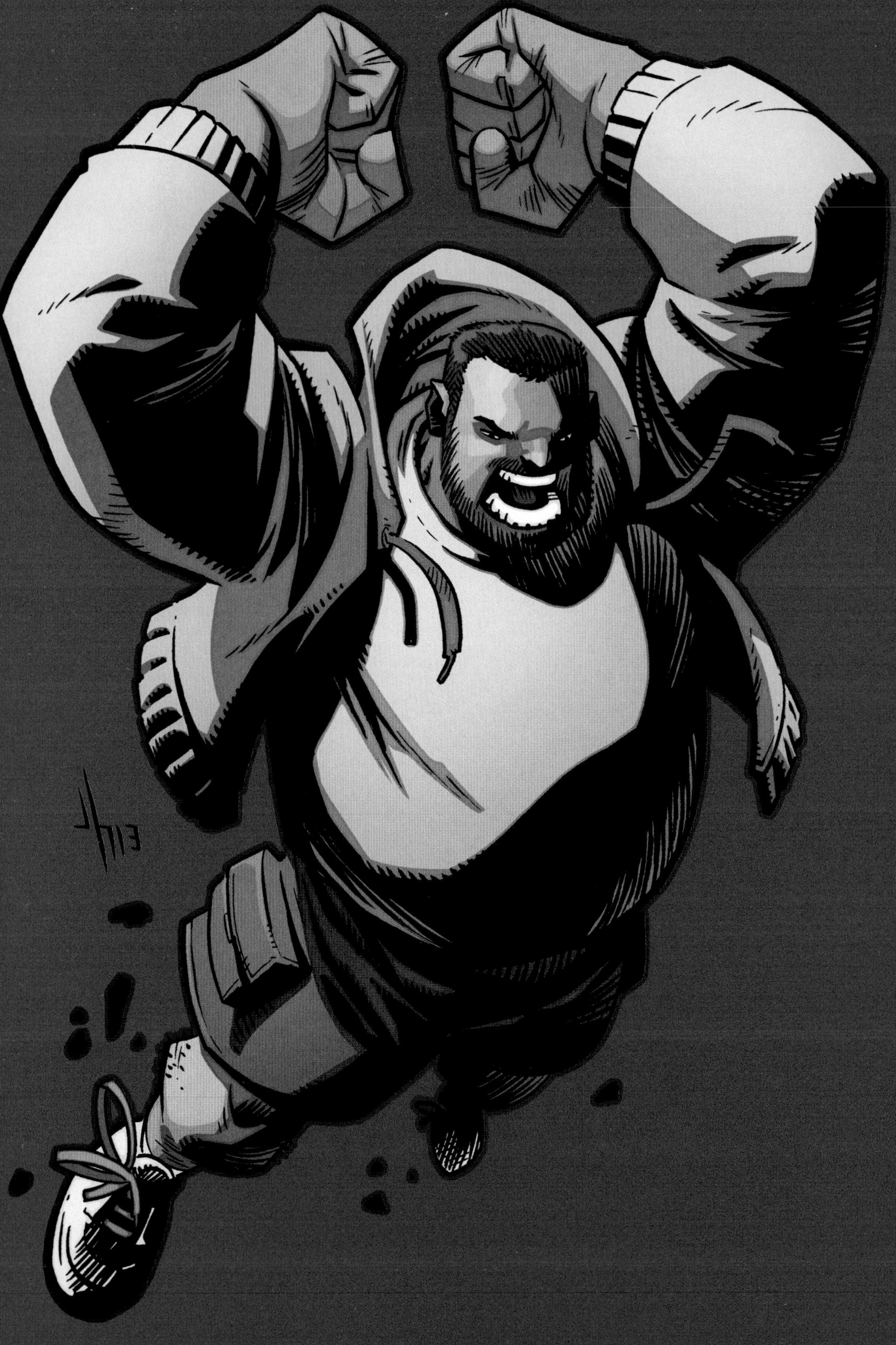